Schools Council
Research Studies

Evaluation
and the
Teacher's Role

OTHER BOOKS IN THIS SERIES

The Universities and the Sixth Form Curriculum
Entry and Performance at Oxford and Cambridge, 1966–71
Pattern and Variation in Curriculum Development Projects
The Examination Courses of First Year Sixth Formers
Mass Media and the Secondary School
Paths to University: Preparation, Assessment, Selection
Gifted Children in Primary Schools
Evaluation in Curriculum Development: Twelve Case Studies
Some Aspects of Welsh and English: a Survey in the Schools of Wales
Attitudes to Welsh and English in the Schools of Wales
Purpose, Power and Constraint in the Primary School Curriculum
A Level Syllabus Studies: History and Physics
Pre-school Education
Physical Education in Secondary Schools
The Quality of Listening
The Effects of Environmental Factors on Secondary Educational Attainment
    in Manchester: a Plowden Follow-up
Environmental Studies Project (5–13): an Evaluation
Nuffield Secondary Science: an Evaluation
Education of Travelling Children
Authority and Organization in the Secondary School
The Aims of Primary Education: a Study of Teachers' Opinions
A Science Teaching Observation Schedule
Science 5–13: a Formative Evaluation
The Development of Writing Abilities (11–18)
The Reliability of Examinations at 16+
O Level Examined: the Effect of Question Choice
Parents and Teachers
Curriculum Evaluation Today: Trends and Implications
Processes and Products of Science Teaching
Sixth Form Syllabuses and Examinations: a New Look
CSE and GCE Grading Standards: the 1973 Comparability Study
Children and their Books
The Moral Situation of Children
From Council to Classroom: an Evaluation of the Diffusion of the Humanities
    Curriculum Project
Conceptual Powers of Children: an Approach through Mathematics and
    Science
Ability and Examinations at 16+

Schools Council
Research Studies

Evaluation and the Teacher's Role

Edited by Wynne Harlen

Papers from members of the Schools Council
project evaluators' group on the role of
evaluation in innovation within the school

Macmillan Education

First published 1978

ISBN 0 333 24684 5 Boards
ISBN 0 333 24685 3 Limp

Published by
MACMILLAN EDUCATION LTD
Houndmills Basingstoke Hampshire RG21 2XS
and London
Associated companies in Delhi Dublin
Hong Kong Johannesburg Lagos Melbourne
New York Singapore and Tokyo

Text set in Great Britain at The Pitman Press, Bath.
Printed in Hong Kong.

British Library Cataloguing in Publication Data

Evaluation and the teacher's role. — (Schools
Council. Research studies; 0306-0292).
1. Educational surveys — England
2. Teachers — England
I. Harlen, Wynne   II. Series
371.2   LB2823
ISBN 0-333-24684-5
    0-333-24685-3 Pbk

Contents

Tables and figures   viii

Introduction   ix
Intentions   ix
Uses of the book   x
The form of the book   xi
Outline of the chapters   xii

1   Evaluation and individual pupils   1
Wynne Harlen
The purposes of evaluating individual pupils   4
What information is relevant for an evaluation?   7
Gathering information: general considerations   11
Some techniques and instruments for evaluation of individual
     pupils   15
Conclusion   26
Further considerations   27

2   Recording the progress of individuals   29
John Hayter and Ray Jackson
Introduction   29
Teachers' attitudes towards records   30
Problems of keeping and using records   36
The purpose and value of record keeping   40
Examples of recording systems   42
The way forward   45

3   Classroom accountability and the self-monitoring teacher   47
John Elliott
Accountability and self-evaluation   47

Towards a methodology of self-evaluation   57
Self-monitoring techniques   77

4   Organization for learning   91
David Hamilton and Joan Hickmott
Evaluation and organizational forms   93
Aims and general strategies for the evaluation of
    organizational settings   94
Four examples   95
Concluding remarks   100

5   Making curriculum decisions   102
Keith Cooper
The influence of value judgements on curriculum decisions   103
The information base for curriculum decisions   104
Constraints on curriculum decisions   107
Further considerations   111

6   The evaluation of the school as a whole   113
Ray Jackson and John Hayter
The meaning for 'whole school' and 'evaluation' in this
    context   114
Decision areas requiring evaluative information   116
Evaluation for whom and by whom?   116
Some previous attempts at school evaluation   120
Case histories of two evaluation studies   123
School sponsored evaluation   126
Sample of a school profile   129
Evaluation by means of a school profile: some possible
    items for investigation   132

7   Summing up the issues raised   140
Wynne Harlen
The nature of evaluation   141
What use is evaluation?   143
Values and evaluation   145
Accountability and evaluation   146
Communication and evaluation   148
Conclusion   150

	Appendices — illustrative material	153
I	Primary school records (New Ash Green County Primary School, 1974)	155
II	Progress in Learning Science record sheet	159
III	Record of Personal Achievement (Swindon) — sample pages	163
IV	A teacher's record of the integrated day	167
V	School Board inspection (Norwich, 1870s)	167
VI	Examination and inspection of schools generally (1882)	171
VII	Projects mentioned in this text	175
	Index	179

Tables and figures

Tables

2.1	Attitudes of secondary school teachers towards records	30
2.2	Records kept in secondary schools	34
2.3	Pupil's work card	42
6.1	Decision areas for evaluative evidence	117
6.2	Link between decision makers and decision areas	118
6.3	Indicators of effective activity in the school	125
6.4	Profile of school services	128

Figures

1	Decision making without feedback	9
2	Decision making with feedback	10
3	Progress record	21

Introduction

INTENTIONS

One consequence of the rapid growth in the study and application of evaluation has been an acknowledgement that wherever decisions are being made there is a role for evaluation to play. At one time, when curriculum development was preoccupied by the task of renewing resources for teaching, the decisions which were the focus of evaluation activities chiefly concerned the effect of changes in materials and methods. The information was gathered largely for the benefit of the developers and disseminators of curriculum changes, whose interests and audience were schools in general rather than any one particular school. The decisions made by teachers within a school, either in the context of attempting to implement change or in the normal course of teaching, have until quite recently been ignored by evaluators' activities. Innovations which take place inside a school, whether initiated from within or outside the school, are obviously at the heart of development in education, and teachers should be able to find help in preparing for changes and monitoring their effect. It is the purpose of this book to discuss how evaluation can assist in taking decisions about the organization, methods and content of work in schools.

Decisions within a school vary in their sphere of influence — that is the number of people affected by a decision, and in the level at which they are taken — the number of people normally involved in taking them. The chapters in this book between them cover decisions where the sphere of influence is as small as an individual pupil and as large as the whole school, and from levels of decisions made by one teacher without affecting others to those which involve negotiation between heads, teachers and persons outside the school. Beginning with two chapters which concern evaluation by a teacher with respect to individual pupils, the focus changes in the third chapter to methods which a teacher can use for self-evaluation; later chapters consider questions of change in organization and the curriculum which involve decisions at departmental, or in some cases, school level and, finally, the evaluation of the school as a whole.

Evaluation with respect to the individual pupil, teacher, class and school is equally relevant to primary, middle and secondary schools and the authors of the various chapters have tried to cater for the variations and similarities in interests and problems of teachers in different types of school. The overall purpose has been to attempt to describe the role of evaluation and to illustrate through examples how it can affect those within the school. The strategies and methods of evaluation which are suggested have been chosen, wherever possible, to be ones which can be used by teachers or others who have no training or experience in evaluation. The book is not a do-it-yourself manual for evaluation, however, and it will be necessary to follow up some of the references given in order to find out more about a particular technique. Its aim is to show what evaluation can do in the context of school-based decisions and to pass on to teachers the approaches to evaluation problems which others have found useful.

USES OF THE BOOK

This is not a book for fireside browsing or reading in bed; in fact it is unlikely that many will read it from cover to cover. However, this is not seen as a negative feature, for, as one of the best read of the authors commented, 'Some of my most useful books are ones I've never read!' Nor did he mean that they were useful only as doorstops, but rather for concentrated study of selected parts, not for reading as one reads a novel.

The discussion provoked by various sections of this book will, it is hoped, lead to teachers being able to identify their evaluation problems more clearly and to work towards the solutions most appropriate in particular cases. Thus one of the main uses of the book is to provide material for study by groups of teachers. School staff conferences may well be concerned with problems of evaluation and could find one or more sections from the book useful as focusing documents. Similarly, this book has a use in meetings of teachers from different schools at teachers' centres where innovations in method or organization or curriculum content are being introduced or proposed. It should be particularly helpful to groups undertaking local curriculum development projects. With these functions in mind, several chapters end with a series of questions for discussion which could either be a basis for further study or starting points for taking up some of the issues raised in relation to particular problems or situations.

It is not only practising school teachers, however, who are concerned with evaluation within the school; the work of LEA advisory and support staff, college lecturers and all who take part in pre- or in-service training touches at some point upon the decisions which are made within a school. We think that this book may be useful to advisers or lecturers in planning in-service courses which take account of evaluation activities within a school, and may provide a framework of points for study in such courses. We hope it will also be helpful as a part of pre-service training courses to draw attention to important decisions made within a school and the part of the teacher's role which is concerned with evaluation.

In order to facilitate use of this book as a resource, and so that individual readers or groups can identify the sections which are of most relevance to them, the main part of this introduction consists of an outline of the various chapters and of the issues which run as cross currents through the book. Chapter 7 takes up these issues in a way which attempts to leave them open for further discussion rather than to resolve them. First, however, a few words about the form of the book and how it came to be written.

THE FORM OF THE BOOK

The idea of producing this book grew out of the work of the Schools Council Evaluators' Group. This group was started in 1968 and consists of representatives from curriculum development projects who have a particular interest in or responsibility for evaluation. Though the membership of the group changes there has been sufficient continuity from year to year to build up experience which may be useful to others. One way of passing on this experience and of informing a wider audience about evaluation activities has been through the production of books in the Schools Council Research Studies series. The two so far published have been *Evaluation in Curriculum Development: Twelve Case Studies* (1973) and *Curriculum Evaluation Today: Trends and Implications* (1976). These both relate to the role of evaluation in curriculum development projects more than to matters about which teachers have to make decisions. However, it was realized that the part which teachers' decisions play in curriculum development, after the projects have finished their development work, is central to the process of innovation, and it was felt important to give attention in this next book to the evaluation which is part of the work within a school.

The main evaluators' group formed a small working group of those interested in evaluation by teachers to discuss the general outline of a possible publication and to suggest authors from among those working in the field. Some of the people invited to contribute were not at the time involved in projects sponsored by the Schools Council, and since the start of the work some have moved to other posts. Nevertheless, the seven authors who, in

1974, originally undertook to contribute chapters met regularly at the Schools Council with members of the Council staff to discuss successive drafts of the chapters. Groups of teachers have also studied several chapters at first or second draft stage and have given comments which have been valuable in revising these earlier drafts. Final drafts of chapters were prepared and submitted to Schools Council committees in summer 1976.

Each chapter has been written by one author or by two in collaboration. Although each contribution has been studied and discussed by the working group and changes have been made in response to comments and criticisms, nonetheless the chapters retain the structure and style of the particular author(s). No attempt has been made in editing to achieve uniformity in writing style since to do so would inevitably destroy the form and impact of the communication which the author created. Some authors have felt it important to make clear that their contribution is a personal statement and have therefore written in the first person, whilst others preferred to write in the third person, and some have used the anonymous 'we'. In a book which is probably not going to be read as a continuous whole we, the authors, felt that changes in style would not be likely to disturb the reader to any extent and we hope that it will not do so.

OUTLINE OF THE CHAPTERS

Chapter 1   Evaluation and individual pupils

This chapter discusses evaluation in the context of making daily classroom decisions about pupils' learning experiences. In the introductory sections the meaning of gathering and using information in this context in practice is illustrated through short examples. Several reasons for the importance of this kind of evaluation are discussed; the main ones being that the information about pupils can be used in an attempt to match experiences to development of individuals, as a basis for cumulative records which reveal in what respects progress is or is not being made by a pupil, to enable a teacher to reflect upon how effectively she provides opportunities for different kinds of development, and also to pass on to others who have to make decisions about the pupils' learning environment.

The question of what information to gather about a pupil for these various purposes is discussed, emphasizing the value of a profile of various relevant abilities, attitudes and other personal characteristics as compared with a global assessment. Deciding what information is relevant naturally has implications for how it can be gathered. Approaches to collecting information are considered first in general terms, where the pros and cons of various kinds of test for these purposes are discussed, and later in terms of techniques and instruments which can be used. Examples are given of diagnostic tools which have been produced for use with individuals, group methods in which pupils report their opinions and self-perceptions as well as what they have learned, group and individual tests of conceptual development, and checklists and other techniques for helping teachers to gather information by focused observation.

Chapter 2   Recording the progress of individuals

A theme running through this chapter is that the importance of an efficient and effective system of record keeping is increasing in the light of recent trends in such things as the move towards more individualized methods, greater mobility of the school population and the frequency of staff changes within a school. It is no longer satisfactory for teachers to carry in their heads the information they need, but neither is it worthwhile writing records which are not used. The problems which arise as to what kinds of records might be made, for what purposes, and by whom are the ones addressed in the chapter.

The starting points are two surveys of teachers' comments about, and attitudes towards, record keeping. One was carried out among secondary school teachers and a smaller but more detailed one involved primary school teachers. Examples of record systems developed in schools are cited in the chapter and given in some extracts at the end of the book (see Appendices I–IV).

A section on records in the secondary school includes a summary table which lists a variety of items which may be recorded, giving for each the nature of the record, its custodian, its user and additional comments. It suggests as criteria which a school might apply in evaluating its record system whether the records are kept efficiently and whether they are used effectively.

A discussion of problems of keeping and using records, relevant equally to primary and secondary teachers, considers both reports to parents and records which remain within the school. The issues raised include those of bias and confidentiality, and the conclusion reached is that, despite the problems of interpreting and storing information safely, the dangers of not having it outweigh the risks of its inappropriate use.

It is suggested that the task of devising or revising a system of class records should begin with defining the purposes it is intended to serve. Several purposes are suggested and three taken in more depth and illustrated by examples:

1 enabling a pupil to record his own progress,
2 enabling a teacher to plan appropriate learning experiences,
3 helping the teacher to plan a balance of various activities within an integrated timetable.

Chapter 3   Classroom accountability and the self-monitoring teacher

The chapter begins with a discussion of the concept of classroom accountability. One popular model of accountability judges the effectiveness of teachers on the basis of the achievement of their pupils in relation to pre-specified objectives. This is rejected by the author on four main counts: because it is based on a false assumption that teachers can be held accountable to only one section of society, the one which determines the objectives; because pupils' achievement is not related to teachers' effectiveness in a straightforward cause-effect manner; because the complexity of influences and circumstances in the classroom makes it unjust to hold a teacher responsible for outcomes in pupils, and because it denies teachers any part in evaluating their own intentions and actions. In place of this model the author prefers one which he describes as a democratic model which implies that teachers have a part in deciding what is worth teaching, taking into account what seems worthwhile for a variety of sections of society, and in which judgements are not made on teachers until they have been answered or accepted by teachers themselves.

The discussion of accountability has brought the notion of self-evaluation by teachers into a central position and this becomes the theme for the rest of the chapter. The theory which is described draws upon and is illustrated by examples from the work of the Ford Teaching Project, of which the chapter's author was director. In this action-research project teachers were helped to clarify the consequences for their own actions of embracing aims such as 'enabling pupils' independent reasoning'. Classroom observers then helped them become conscious of any gaps between the kinds of behaviour which they agreed were consistent with their aims and the actual behaviours they displayed. Pupils' accounts of how they interpreted certain actions and words of the teacher were compared with the account of the teacher's intentions and the records of the observer in a three way cross-checking which was named 'triangulation'. The role of the observer in helping a teacher look at his performance more objectively was eventually taken over from the researchers by teachers themselves, one acting as the observer for another. Judgements about a teacher's performance were sought from two sources – pupils and teachers in the project, which were acknowledged as not really being sufficient for a fully democratic model of accountability, but with this limitation the author claims that the project establishes a system within which accountability can be a positive rather than a negative force.

Chapter 4   Organization for learning

This chapter takes as its starting point four examples of changes of the kind which schools face in adapting to reorganization, curriculum innovations or new approaches to the use of staff and buildings. Such changes are not, however, simply changes in organization but a way of putting into practice a set of aims, and they cannot be evaluated without considering the events which led up to them or the changes in educational processes which they are intended to facilitate.

The increasing importance for curriculum evaluation of patterns of organization is linked to the shift of emphasis of curriculum development away from materials renewal or production towards the training of teachers and changes in organization which are required if new ideas rather than only new activities are to be implemented. Several general strategies for evaluation of organization are suggested, though it is pointed out that the ones which are appropriate in a particular case will depend upon who is to receive and use the information.

In order to relate the general strategies to specific examples the authors return to the four types of change which form the introduction to the chapter. The four are curriculum integration — any of a cluster of changes which attempt to redraw boundaries of areas within the curriculum — mixed-ability grouping, team teaching and open-plan organization. Different kinds of questions which evaluation might address are suggested for each of these. For example, in the case of curriculum integration, it may be important to find out what exactly is being integrated, what does integration mean to those who have to implement it, who plans and controls the integration, why it was suggested, on whose initiative, how it affects the pupils, and so on. Answers to such questions may be important in an attempt to find out how an organizational change is working and in making further decisions about it.

Chapter 4 gives some guidelines to the kinds of questions which can be asked about organizational changes, but the authors are careful to point out that an evaluation is more than the process of gathering information and that without detailed knowledge of a particular situation and its attendant value-system it is impossible to say what information will be relevant. The evaluation must respond to the changing image of the process which is revealed as the investigation proceeds.

Chapter 5   Making curriculum decisions

The author discusses how decisions made about the curriculum are affected by various factors which are always present but not always consciously acknowledged. Three of the main factors are discussed: the values held by those who take decisions, the information available to them and the constraints provided by the human and material context in which decisions are taken. These are elements which affect curriculum decisions at all levels from school policy to individual pupil, and the author discusses them 'in the hope that a prior awareness of factors which may not be apparent at the time will help in making the decisions'.

On the subject of the influence upon a decision of the values of those involved it is suggested this influence is present and unavoidable whether the decision is about the choice of a textbook, teaching strategy or a major re-organization of the school. Although the implications of recognizing that this is so have not been worked out, it is suggested that open discussion of value positions offers a better way forward than deprecation of the fact that current decisions are value based.

Decisions about the curriculum are made on the basis of varying amounts of relevant information. Teachers rarely have time to gather or have access to all the information which could be relevant to a particular decision, but 'it is usually possible to find out more than we already know'. Some sources of written information particularly relevant to curriculum decisions are suggested: this might help to supplement information in ways described in other chapters.

Of the constraints which operate in the context of taking decisions about the curriculum, the time available to teachers both in the classroom and out of school is thought to be the most acutely felt. What time is available has to be allocated according to priorities, and this applies too in the case of a second major constraint: the materials, money and other resources available. Decisions which affect others in the school will also involve some negotiation, some give and take, and will thus be influenced by the opinions, values and demands of others.

Chapter 6   The evaluation of the school as a whole

A school can be evaluated by many different people for many purposes and on the basis of a wide variety of types of information. The subject cannot be treated overall in a simple chapter and what is attempted is a brief overview of the several distinct areas of decision which require evaluative information about a school, followed by a review of methods, both past and present, which have been used. These include the work of inspectors, researchers and others external to the school, methods which teachers can use to evaluate their own school, and approaches in which external and internal influences combine.

A discussion of the various audiences for and purposes of evaluating a school as a whole unit or evaluating a department or particular provision with-in the school underlines the importance of fitting methods of evaluation to a particular purpose. With so many variables operating there is no attempt to generalize as to how a school can be evaluated; instead different approaches are illustrated through two examples: one where an outside consultant participated in the evaluation, the other where the evaluation was carried out by the school staff.

The remainder of the chapter discusses what a school can do for itself. One approach, that of drawing up a school profile, is suggested as a summary of various kinds of information which, when brought together, help to reveal areas where action should be taken to improve a school's effectiveness. A suggested detailed list of items which could be included in the profile is provided at the end of the chapter.

Chapter 7   Summing up the issues raised

The issues brought out in this chapter are ones which are likely to be among those occurring during the reading of earlier parts of the book.

What is the nature of evaluation? Can a single definition draw together the various meanings given to it in the different contexts considered in the book? What distinctions can be drawn between evaluation and assessment? Between evaluation and research?

To what extent ought teachers to be responsible for evaluating various aspects of their work and their schools? To what extent can they take this responsibility? What forms of help from 'outsiders' enable the 'insiders' in the schools to take responsibility for evaluation activities?

Who benefits from evaluation? Is there sufficient relevant information available in some cases for evaluation to be of benefit to anybody? What is 'relevant' information?

How important is it that evaluation information is influenced by the value systems and biases of those who gather it? How can decisions be taken on the basis of subjective evidence? To what extent is evaluation a 'political activity'?

Does evaluation by teachers remove the need for teachers to be evaluated by others? What criteria should teachers adopt in their own evaluation of their work? Who decides the goals towards which they work and against which their effectiveness is judged? Can a system of accountability be operated which does not restrict teachers' freedom of action? Does this depend on self-evaluation by teachers?

In what ways can the communication of information useful for evaluation be improved? Who should have access to different kinds of information? How can data which are largely subjective be recorded and at the same time protected from misuse?

Is there a firm foundation for claiming that teachers are in the best position to examine how decisions are made and to collect information to improve this process? In what ways can teachers be helped, and help each other, to evaluate their work more effectively?

Wynne Harlen (Reading University, 1977)

1 Evaluation and individual pupils

Wynne Harlen

Decisions which affect the learning opportunities of individual children are made and have to be made as part of the everyday job of teaching. In making these decisions teachers use information about their pupils and in so doing are practising the kind of evaluation which is the subject of this chapter, evaluation which is an ongoing part of the teaching – learning process as distinct from evaluation which is summative or carried out for the purpose of grading or selection. The discussion here attempts to examine the kinds of information about pupils which are most relevant for day-to-day and moment-to-moment decisions, to discuss how and why the various kinds of information are used and to give examples of methods recently developed for gathering them.

Perhaps the most important distinguishing feature of this ongoing, formative, evaluation is that it is a starting point for action and not an end point, as in the case of several other kinds of evaluation. It is a process of finding out and reflecting upon where children have been, what stages in their learning they have reached, as a basis for deciding where and how they might be helped to go further. Conventional tests and examinations have a role in this process but only as an occasional statement of the state of the budget rather than as part of the business of keeping the daily accounts. Putting this more formally gives a working definition of evaluation with respect to individual pupils as '*the process of obtaining information about all relevant aspects of a pupil's experience and attributes for making decisions about the learning environment which encourage the pupil's progress and increase the teacher's effectiveness*'.

In practice, the information is being picked up in daily events such as these:

> *Sarah, a seven year old, was making jam tarts and while she was rolling out the pastry her teacher took the opportunity to find out what Sarah thought was happening to the total amount of pastry as it was spread out more and more. Did she think there was any more pastry after she had finished rolling than before? 'No, it's the same, it just gets thinner.'*

1

What about when the tarts were cut out and the pastry was in pieces?
'Well it's still the same pastry as before because we haven't made any
more or taken bits away.' After cooking they talked about the difference
in the size of the tarts, which had risen. Sarah explained that this was
'because the pieces have moved apart in the cooking; it's not really any
more.' Would anything have changed in the cooking? 'Yes, I think they
must be heavier, because they're bigger.'

From this conversation, all part of working together at the cooking table,
the teacher found out that Sarah was not confused about the effect of changes
in distribution on the total quantity of substance, but her ideas of weight
were still not dissociated from size. In fact, the teacher reflected, most of
Sarah's experience would have led her to conclude that bigger things are
always heavier than smaller ones. The next time Sarah was balancing things on
the scales the teacher made sure the collection included many small heavy
things and large lighter ones. To draw Sarah's attention to the weight as
opposed to size the teacher asked her to hold the objects and try to judge
which would be heavier before putting them in the pans.

A secondary science teacher was using the Nuffield Combined Science
programme with first year pupils. They were investigating the rate of
cooling of soup in insulated containers, as part of the introduction to
the use of thermometers. Whilst passing from group to group to see if
they were able to read the thermometers the teacher asked the pupils
what they thought was special about the containers. What kept the soup
warm? All thought that it was something to do with the lid, for they
evidently only thought of heat moving upwards and paid no attention
to the sides. Instead of continuing with the next experiment in the
programme he asked them to devise ways of showing that the lid was
the effective part. Some thought the sides might be important too, so
they carried out various experiments with different combinations of lids
and sides. When non-insulating containers were used, they could feel the
heat; they began to appreciate that it could travel in all directions and
their original experiment made more sense to them.

Apart from the immediate action which the teacher took in this instance
he was also alerted to the difficulty children have in envisaging conduction of
heat through materials. This information he kept in mind later when the
subject of transfer of heat was being studied in more depth. He took care to
find out the children's existing ideas and experience and to build upon these
instead of assuming that experiments suggested in the programme would
necessarily be understood.

Benny is a ten-year-old whose manner suggests confidence and maturity. He converses easily with adults and children alike. He has a lively curiosity which has led him to grasp such things as the working of an internal combustion engine, showing a considerable grasp of concepts about forces and energy. He is not narrow in his interests, he plays a guitar, enjoys music and even composed a carol which was performed by himself and some friends to the rest of the class at Christmas. He lives in the country and has considerable knowledge about, and sensitivity towards living things in his environment. But he has only just begun to read with any fluency, and his writing is poor both in content and appearance. For several years it seemed that he just did not see any point in writing and he obtained all his information from talking to people and from television rather than books.

Benny's teachers in the primary school have been aware of his weakness in reading and writing skills and have made use of his interests in animals and in farm machinery, for instance, to encourage his effort in this area. At the same time they have been aware of his well advanced abilities and concepts and at no time have thought of him as 'below average' or 'backward'; his weakness in communication skills has not been seen as a reason for denying him opportunities for progress in other aspects of his development. He is fortunate; many children similar to Benny might be written off as 'dull' or 'less able' because the only information considered to be of importance to their education is the ability to read and write. The wider profile not only helped Benny's teachers to build upon his strengths, but also prevented the weakness in one area leading to his being labelled in a way which could have affected the attitude of others towards him and his own attitude to school.

The examples just given might seem to concern rather small decisions but it is the cumulative effect of such small decisions which determine the learning experiences of our pupils. Honest reflection by teachers and classroom observation reveals that these decisions are not always thought out; at times they are more like instinctive reflex actions. Inevitably some decisions have to be made in this fashion but it is likely that even these off-the-cuff decisions will benefit from a close study of the process and the information needed for decision making.

Teachers always do find out about individual pupils' performances — by marking books, setting tests, question and answer sessions, etc. — but vary in the degree to which this knowledge is used in making classroom decisions. In some instances the teacher prefers to teach a class as a whole, treating the pupils more or less alike, in which case one set of decisions covers all the pupils. Here the teacher probably restricts information gathered about individuals to achievement testing, marking their books and end of term examinations. She may use this information to correct inaccuracy in certain pupils but, by and large, continues to give the same lessons to all. In other cases teachers are making greater allowances for varieties in the interests, abilities and backgrounds of their pupils and it is in these situations that evaluation of individuals becomes part of teaching.

THE PURPOSES OF EVALUATING INDIVIDUAL PUPILS

Though it may seem that the informal primary school provides the best setting for catering for variations between individuals, such a conclusion undervalues the successful efforts to make similar provision in secondary schools. Mixed-ability grouping, by its title and nature, acknowledges the variety which is represented in secondary classes. Teachers who might previously have used only whole-class teaching methods (despite the variations between pupils which exist in streamed classes anyway) have adapted their methods so that pupils work individually or in small groups and there is opportunity to match activities to the varied interests and abilities of the pupils. Of course secondary teachers generally have less chance to get to know their pupils than primary teachers, and they teach many times more pupils, so the techniques for gathering information in the primary and secondary settings may vary. Nevertheless, the purposes and the overall process of evaluation are the same despite the different situations. Whether the teacher is a subject specialist or class teacher evaluation is part of her work when, for instance, she uses information about pupils' previous learning and level of development to set realistic goals, she takes into account their existing interests and attempts to extend them, she provides conditions in which the pace and mode of learning can be varied to suit individuals.

Besides the guidance of short-term decisions there are other reasons for gathering information about individuals which should be included here. A cumulative record of information gathered either formally or informally provides data in which a pupil's progress over a period of time can be observed. There are often problems of interpreting such records unless the criteria applied on each occasion are kept the same or are clearly stated on the record. The usual record of marks accumulated over a year's work does not generally show trends very clearly, especially if assessments for different kinds of work, tests, homework, projects are all listed together. Keeping separate records of different kinds of work helps to some extent in making cumulative data more useful, but, if a major purpose of the assessment is to record progress, similar criteria should be applied at each assessment, such as in the method of recording progress mentioned later (pp. 20–21).

Cumulative records contribute to evaluation only if they are used and there are two main ways in which they can be used. If a pupil has not been making progress when the teacher has expected progress, she might take a closer look at various aspects both of her own teaching and of the pupil. The order in which these are suggested is deliberate and might well be debated. Traditionally, the assumption has been that the pupil is at fault if he doesn't learn, but there is a growing willingness to look for the fault elsewhere. Especially among teachers who are open to constant evaluation of their work, the idea that 'I said it, so he heard it' is no longer accepted. Perhaps I did say it, and he could have heard it, but he wasn't able to make sense of it. The first response to lack of progress in pupils is now likely to be an examination of whether the pupils had the opportunity, seen from their point of view, to make any progress of the kind expected. The pupil's view and the teacher's view of the same event may be very different, and it takes a special effort on the part of the teacher to find out if the pupil really has had the learning opportunities which were assumed. The subject of self-evaluation by teachers is taken up in Chapter 3, so at this point it is only necessary to mention that keeping cumulative records and using them has value as a basis for reflection on the provision being made for individual pupils.

It may well be that the pupil has had satisfactory experiences in the area concerned and so it is necessary to look more closely at the profile of the child. Records may help in deciding whether the lack of progress is in several areas of the child's development or is restricted to one. For instance, poor ability to communicate verbally might have various causes, one of which could be lack of anything interesting to communicate, which in turn may be the result of stifled curiosity. If records show that questioning and curiosity are also affected, this might be an indication that the child needs help to feel free to ask questions, to relate to his surroundings, to feel more secure. But if lack of the questioning and curiosity are not associated with the lack of progress in communication, then other possible causes would be sought.

A further reason for gathering information about individual children is so that other teachers can be helped by it when they are dealing with pupils. It is not possible for teachers to wait until they know their pupils before making any decisions about materials and experiences; these have to be planned in advance whether the pupils are known or not. However, detailed records could play a large part in this, if passed from one teacher to another, especially if common criteria for describing the characteristics of pupils were agreed and adhered to by those giving and receiving the information. Objections to passing on records (discussed more fully in Chapter 2) commonly refer to 'biasing' a new teacher about individual pupils, but if the information is a record of assessments which are as objective as possible the disadvantages to the pupil of communicating it are far outweighed by the advantages of guiding the new teacher in making provision for experiences in which he can succeed.

Summarizing the reasons so far mentioned we can put them under four main headings:

— to gather information about a wide range of pupil characteristics as feed-back for making decisions about the learning environment, especially in the context of matching experiences to individual pupils;

— to accumulate records which enables progress, or lack of it, to be observed and corrective action taken;

— to provide information which enables a teacher to reflect on the effectiveness of her own actions in regard to individual pupils;

— to inform other teachers who may have to make decisions about the pupils.

This list, selected for its relevance to evaluation of individuals as defined on page 1, leaves out many reasons frequently given for making assessments, which should be mentioned for the sake of giving a complete picture. In a comprehensive list of reasons for assessment given by R. N. Deale (1975) the following are included in addition to the ones we have already discussed:

— to allocate pupils to streams or sets

— to compare progress of pupils under different teachers

— to compare new teaching materials with old

— to give an incentive to learning and an aid to remembering

— to inform parents about progress

— to inform employers or higher education institutions about attainment

— to decide about entering pupils for external examination.

These reasons suggest different uses for information about individual pupils, more relevant in some cases and in some schools than others. The decisions they involve are less concerned with 'improving the pupil's learning and the teacher's effectiveness' than the kinds of decision we have chosen to discuss in more detail. The complete list, including some very final decisions for an individual child, serves as a reminder that there can be dangers in assessment. Whenever pupils' work is marked, tested or even just recorded, there is a danger that the result will adversely affect the teacher's subsequent judgements. Teachers may allow their knowledge of a child's ability in one area to affect their judgement of his performance in another, for example, letting the neatness of drawing influence assessment in a science test or the politeness of a child improve the report of his academic work. This has been labelled the 'halo' effect and refers to distortion of teachers' judgements. In addition the teacher's knowledge of the child's ability has been claimed by several investigators, notably Rosenthal and Jacobson (1968) in *Pygmalion in the Classroom*, to affect the achievement of the pupils. Criticisms of the methodology employed in these studies suggest that the order of the effects should be treated with caution, but there seems reason to believe there is some real effect. The mechanism by which the pupil who is expected by the teacher to be bright actually makes more progress than a pupil who has lower expectations in the teacher's eyes is not by any means clear. The explanation which seems most favoured by Rosenthal and Jacobson is not in terms of time spent with 'high expectation' children but rather in terms of the quality of interaction between teacher and child. The teacher may attend more closely to those children she 'knows' to be bright, she may watch more carefully and may reinforce correct behaviour more quickly, and when he is wrong she may give him more time to correct himself, since she expects him to be right. But, whatever the reason, the important fact is that the knowledge of a child's assessment can lead to a self-fulfilling prophecy, the 'bright' children becoming brighter and the 'dull' more dull.

To suggest rejecting assessment altogether on account of the effect upon teachers' treatment of children would not only be to throw away all the positive aspects of assessment, but would also be asking for the impossible. Teachers are all the time assessing pupils, even if it is only acknowledged with a nod of the head or a tick on their work. The better course might be to avoid the labelling which accompanies assessment. The practice of summarizing a whole number of different abilities for no good reason in an overall score is common in situations where a more useful description of a child would be provided from a profile. The profile would reveal a child's strengths and weaknesses and enable a teacher to help him more readily; at the same time it makes redundant the overall score which is the cause of the labelling. Examples of profiles can be found in later sections (p. 21 and Appendix II).

WHAT INFORMATION IS RELEVANT FOR EVALUATION?

On many school reports at the present time, as on most in the past, there still appears a section which gives a summary assessment which is filled in with a single word 'excellent', 'good', 'average', etc. or with a grade or with a number. Its purpose is to signify to the pupil and to others the overall judgement of achievement during a certain time. To a teacher or anyone else trying to help the pupil this single assessment would be of little value, for a child is not equally 'good' or 'average' in all aspects of his learning, and a B overall probably masks an A in something and a C in something else. Someone wanting information to help the child would need information of much greater detail, not just one, or a handful, of numbers or letters which merge different kinds of data. In evaluation the concern is to have information which can be used as feedback for assisting learning and teaching, and rarely will overall judgements suffice for this purpose.

The information needed about a child in order to guide his work in a particular activity is determined by the specific abilities, concepts and attitudes which are the prerequisites and the goals of that activity. Does his previous learning and development enable him to master the new ideas which the activity involves or would he be likely to learn more by starting at a different point? In order to decide in a particular case, quite detailed knowledge of the child is required; knowing that his verbal reading quotient (VRQ) is 109 will not help in the choice of whether it is better for him to do A before B or to start with B. The relevant information in any particular case will include not only the child's previous achievement but also his social and emotional development, the ways of learning he has experienced and characteristics such as his rate of learning, his perseverance and his motivation.

When we are considering what is relevant, it is necessary to answer the question 'relevant to what?' In our case it is relevance to the context in which the information is to be used. The word 'feedback' has already been employed in describing the process of gathering and using evaluation information, and a feedback loop provides a good representation of the relationships between the information gathered about the pupil, changes in the learning environment made on the basis of the information and the goals which are the aim of the learning. To highlight the effect of the feedback, we consider first the situation in which decisions are made by a teacher without it. The term 'learning environment' is used here to indicate not only the activities and experiences which pupils encounter but the total situation in which they learn, since such things as the atmosphere of friendliness or fear, freedom of choice, encouragement or neglect may affect learning as much as the demands of an activity.

The main elements involved are the *teacher*, other parts of the *learning environment*, the *pupils*, the *goals* towards which the teacher and pupils are working, and a set of *external constraints* which may limit the teacher's decisions and directly influence the learning environment. In the situation where there is no feedback, the teacher makes decisions about the learning environment (including her own part in it) in the light of the goals she has in mind, both for individuals and for the whole class, and subject to the external constraints. The decision making may refer to the selection of a programme or course or a section within these, the materials to be provided, the modes of learning to be made available, the interaction allowed between pupil and pupil, the kind of support or restraint the teacher will provide, and many more similar factors.

The learning environment with which pupils interact is thus created as a

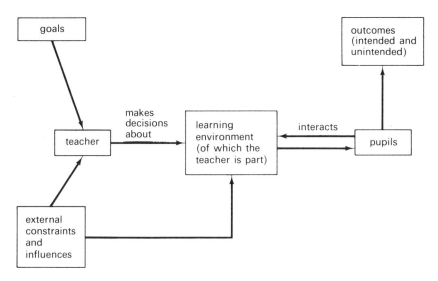

Fig. 1   Decision making without feedback

result of teachers' decisions and external constraints, in varying proportions. Once set up it is not, of course, a static entity; it is changed by the presence and action of the pupils at the same time as it changes the pupils. The changes in the pupils can be described as the *outcomes* achieved, which are not necessarily the same as the *goals*. Some achievement will be towards the goals, but inevitably some will be towards unintended, and probably undesired, outcomes.

The situation so far discussed provides information from pupils to teacher only through the achievement of goals, perhaps through formal or informal tests. Such information is necessarily restricted to certain easily measured goals and is summative in nature; that is, it comes at the end of a period of learning, not at the beginning, to serve as a basis for action. Where the learning environment is adapted to the pupils, then the decisions about it are informed by feedback about the pupils, about their interaction with the environment, and about the outcomes. But the pupils are not all the same, and we can no longer envisage one set of decisions and one learning environment for all of them. The decision-making model in which feedback is used therefore differs from Fig. 1, not only because of the addition of feedback loops, but also in the replacement of the word *pupils* by *pupil*. We now have to consider the model in Fig. 2 as one element in a model of decision making for a whole class. The complete model would have as many of these elements in it as there are pupils. What this means in practice is not a separate learning environment for each, but only that certain features of the environment are particularly suited to the individual child. The difference may only be in the teacher's expectations of the child, or in the part he plays in a group activity, or in the level at which he tackles a problem, or in the responsibility he is given.

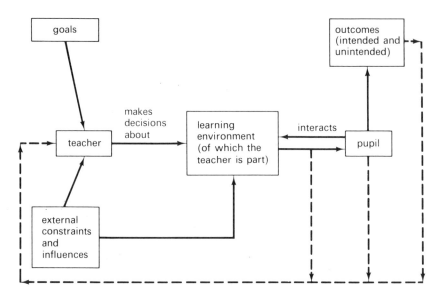

Fig. 2 Decision making with feedback

In Fig. 2, which represents an idealized model of decision making, the teacher's decisions are informed by the feedback as well as by consideration of the goals and external constraints. Through gathering information about the pupil's *interaction* with the learning environment, she finds out about such things as processes, modes of learning, interests, motor skill development; directly from the pupil, through dialogue, questioning and listening, the teacher finds out about how problems appear from the pupil's point of view, the kind of reasoning which is being applied, what sense is made of new experiences, and so on. Feedback from the constant monitoring of outcomes, from attempting to interpret both oral and written reports in terms of the development of various ideas, may prevent many of the more undesirable unintended outcomes from appearing. We cannot be so optimistic as to suggest that there will only be desirable outcomes, but at least the more damaging ones which arise from mismatching, boredom or frustration are hopefully diminished.

A note of caution is necessary in relation to the model proposed. As we have acknowledged it is an idealized model and not an empirical one intended to represent what actually happens in practice. In reality the decision-making process is very much more complex and a cycle of feedback may frequently be impossible to discern. Teachers sometimes have to decide what to do as an immediate reaction to their circumstances rather than as a result of consideration of goals and information about pupils. Teachers have to rely heavily on their intuition and experience, and this will always be the case, but a framework in which these are used in a conscious process, rather than in unconscious reactions, is likely to result in decisions which are better for all concerned. The purpose of the model, then, is to promote consideration of how decisions might be made and not to describe how they are made.

GATHERING INFORMATION: GENERAL CONSIDERATIONS

It is rather easier to make a case for gathering information about individual pupils than to suggest methods of obtaining information which are not so laborious, time consuming or irksome to teachers that there is a risk of what is gained in feedback being lost in commitment. Any method of providing information must consume some time and it is important for a teacher to see this as time well spent, otherwise the negative attitude to the whole process may defeat its object. But some methods are more demanding than others, and it is the intention in this section to look at the possibilities and discuss each in terms of criteria of suitability for the present purpose and practicability for the teacher.

We might first consider what it is that we would like and then see how far the 'ideal' is met by available methods. What are the ideal features of methods for obtaining information about individual pupils, keeping in mind the context in which it is to be used, as feedback which has to be available constantly and not just on set occasions. It would seem that the ideal method would have the following features:

- suitability for frequent and repeated use
- sufficient flexibility for use at all appropriate times
- ability to be used for individual children
- capacity for providing information about the widest range of characteristics and behaviour
- non-interference with normal working, not taking up learning time
- ability to be carried out without causing anxiety or tension in pupils or teachers
- convenient and not time consuming for the teacher.

To this list should be added the essential requirements of any information, that it should be as valid and as reliable as possible.

Standardized tests

A standardized test is one which has been given to a large number of children in controlled conditions and from the results 'norms' have been established for different groups of children, usually age groups. The result of giving the test to any child can therefore be compared with the 'average' for a particular group.

It is not difficult to see that, though standardized tests may have the advantage of being quick to administer, they match up very poorly to some of the 'ideal' features. They require the pupil to be in a special test situation, either individually (as in reading tests) or as a group (any kind of paper-and-pencil test). Therefore they do take up time, though we should not ignore the learning which can take place during a test, and they require some preparation beforehand on the part of the teacher and probably time for marking afterwards. They are on these counts unsuitable for repeated and frequent use; we could add the danger of inducing anxiety in pupils and the restricted range of behaviours which can be effectively encompassed by paper-and-pencil tests. The reliability of the measurement can be made quite high, but there may be less certainty about what it is that is being measured, that is, its validity. Can it be assumed that the test performance is an indication of ability in normal situations? There is always this uncertainty about what test scores mean but it matters less for some purposes than for our present purpose. When we wish to take action as a result of information about a pupil's abilities or achievement it is important to be sure that the data really refer to these abilities and achievements and not to others. For instance all paper-and-pencil tests depend upon the ability to read and write whatever else they are intended to assess. As a further example, widely used standardized tests of reading ability have been severely criticized in the report of the Bullock Committee. Referring to the Watts-Vernon and National Survey Form 6 (N.S.6.) reading tests, both consisting of items which are incomplete sentences for silent reading, the report states:

We do not regard these tests as adequate measures of reading ability. What they measure is a narrow aspect of silent reading comprehension. . . Both tests are technically *reliable* in the sense they measure the same features to the same degree on different occasions. But their doubtful *validity* is now apparent, in that they measure only in part what they purport to measure.

(*A Language for Life*, 1975, para. 2.13)

A greater scepticism about externally produced tests might therefore be extremely healthy and might result in their being used more appropriately.

Criterion-referenced tests

Criterion-referenced tests give information about a pupil's performance in relation to a specified level of ability or skill or knowledge which is the criterion. The result does not show how a pupil compares with other pupils in the same group, as in the case of standardized tests, but rather how his ability compares with the level of performance which it has been decided represents mastery of a particular idea or skill. Items in these tests are devised so that the score can be expressed as a degree of mastery − 65%, 80% mastery, etc. Results are not compared directly with the average performance of pupils, though in establishing what degree of difficulty is to represent a certain level of mastery normative data are sometimes used. Criterion-referenced tests can be produced externally or by a teacher, and administered to a group or an individual. Some are practical tests and differ little from the children's usual learning activities. They can be used as the occasion demands and can be administered to one child without disturbing others. Examples of such tests are given in the next section.

Although these tests match up much better to the 'ideal' than do standardized tests, they still fall short in several aspects. They are undoubtedly time consuming and for this reason alone could not be used very often. They are also restricted to a few concepts and skills and would have to be multiplied many times if a reasonable range of objectives were to be covered. Even then only cognitive development and skills would be covered; attitudes, interests and personal characteristics would remain largely untouched. As a further disadvantage time is needed for preparation of materials or situations or of questions to be asked. Teachers might argue with justification that more time given to assessing means less time for teaching and there is a danger that the compromise reached is that the teaching becomes narrowed to those aspects of the work which are tested.

At the same time there are advantages for the teacher in having these tests at hand for occasional use, perhaps as diagnostic tools for particular children. They enable a teacher to explore a child's thinking in an activity which is designed to reveal that thinking and had been shown to do so in development trials. When they are externally produced they generally provide results from trying out the test on a large number of pupils and comparison with these helps a teacher to decide whether remedial action is appropriate in the light of the results of a particular child. Thus, used occasionally, individual criterion-referenced tests help teachers to make decisions about certain kinds of learning opportunities which should be provided for particular children. But they cannot be the answer for gathering information about all the children across a wide range of concepts, abilities, attitudes and interests. Tests should be seen as supplements to other methods of providing information which are more flexible, less demanding of time and more wide ranging.

Methods based on observation

These wide-ranging methods are to be found in making use of the observations which teachers are all the time making of children's actions, responses and behaviours of different kinds. Children are displaying their attitudes and abilities all the time in their normal work and many teachers, some more consciously than others, pick up a wealth of data about individuals by listening to the children, looking at the way they go about their work, discussing the work with them and trying to look at things from the pupils' point of view.

While observation – interpreted widely, as more than looking, but also listening, helping children to express their thoughts and feelings and responding – can be seen to have many advantages for the purposes of gathering ongoing feedback about pupils, it also has disadvantages. First the pros: looking back to page 11 at the list of ideal properties of a method for gathering information, we find that observation fares better than any method so far discussed. Pupils are unaware that it is taking place, it takes up no time from learning, can be repeated frequently and causes no anxiety. From the teacher's point of view it requires no preparation of special materials, does not interfere with normal working and provides information about all aspects which are evident in behaviour.

On the other hand, the cons include the criticism that observations are subjective and less reliable than other forms of assessment. There are generally no norms against which to judge whether progress or attainment is satisfactory – though these usually exist in teachers' experience and there is no reason implicit in the method for these not being available. Furthermore, while making observations may not take up a teacher's time, since this is done as part of her normal work, making a record of the observations can be a time-consuming task for out-of-school hours. It should also be mentioned that, although no time is required for preparing materials, a certain mental preparation is needed. Teachers need to have not only positive attitudes towards gathering feedback through observation but also preparation in knowing what to look for in children's behaviours and how to interpret what they find.

The danger of observation being merely a personal reaction, and providing data of little value to anyone else, is so great that if it is to be the basis of a useful method of gathering information, observation cannot remain totally unstructured. It requires a structure which comes from considering the goals of the children's work and from agreeing criteria which can be applied to interpreting children's behaviours in terms of progress towards the goals. What this involves is expressed well by the members of the Bullock Committee:

This will involve a good deal of preparatory activity on the part of teachers, advisers and educational psychologists. The agreed structure should emerge from a programme of meetings and study groups and should be supported by in-service training at both general and school level. We do not underestimate the scale of effort this will require on the part of the authority, but we feel it is fully justified in its benefits.

(*A Language for Life*, 1975, para. 17.9)

The context in which this passage was written was that of children's language education; it could equally refer to any aspect of learning. In the next section we give several examples of ways of using observation for evaluation in several different curriculum areas.

SOME TECHNIQUES AND INSTRUMENTS FOR EVALUATION OF INDIVIDUAL PUPILS

We now take a closer look at the nature and range of methods which have been suggested as having more of the desirable features needed for use in the context of evaluating individuals and give examples of the techniques which can be used.

Criterion-referenced tests

We begin with some methods for obtaining information about specific concepts or abilities. Detailed assessments which are criterion referenced are exemplified by the Nuffield Mathematics Project's *Checking up* guides for teachers. These suggest to teachers situations in which children would show whether they had developed certain ideas or concepts. In so far as these are special situations set up for the purpose of assessment they can be described as tests, but this description suggests a more formal situation than is intended, as this example shows:

The following is a very quick but efficient check-up to see how well the child distinguishes between the ideas of volume and weight. The materials required are (i) two metal cylinders of the same weight and size (say made of aluminium), (ii) a third cylinder of the same size but different weight (say made of copper) and (iii) two glass jars, of the same size and shape, which are about three-quarters full of water. The teacher should take the aluminium cylinders and let one of them sink to the bottom of one of the jars. He then asks the child 'If I put this second cylinder in the other jar, but, instead of letting it sink, I hold it halfway down the jar, will the water rise the same amount in both jars, or will it go up more in one of them?' The same question[s] may be repeated, but this time using one aluminium cylinder and the copper one. First, the copper cylinder is allowed to sink to the bottom and the aluminium one is suspended halfway down, then the situation is reversed.

Children who have not really grasped the concept of volume may say: 'The one that's only halfway down the jar can't push the water up as far as the other one that's gone right to the bottom'. And those who cannot yet distinguish between volume and weight may say: 'The one at the bottom weighs more than the one in the middle because it's sunk – you're holding part of the weight of the other one'.

(Checking up III, page 25)

In this example the information would probably be immediately used by the teacher in deciding what opportunities for further learning to provide for the child, and it also might be recorded with information from other items to give a profile of various abilities and concepts at that particular time. Such a record would indicate the result of each check-up by a sign or a word, not by a score. The information provided by the check-ups is extremely detailed, since each item relates to a different aspect of a concept. For instance, the first book, Checking up I, deals with the concept of number and items concern ability to make comparison between collections of objects in terms of size, quantity and number separately, size and number together, in terms of length, thickness, and length and thickness together, and one-to-one correspondence in a variety of situations.

Similarly detailed information is provided by the NFER criterion-referenced tests on Classification. The test is divided into three main units, in which items relate to 'additive classification', 'multiplicative classification' and 'class inclusion'. Within each unit there are several items, all of a practical nature which pupils can be given in an informal setting. Responses are not written by the pupil but made in terms of actions with materials provided. Individual administration is necessary so that the teacher can ask questions and follow up the answers. There is no overall score for the test or for each unit; the responses to the various items are used to categorize the child as 'able to or not able to classify the given materials by one criterion at a time (with/without help)', 'able or not able to classify the same materials according to a second criterion (with/without help)', and so on.

Kits of materials and a teachers' handbook for assessing children's concepts of area, volume and weight are among the products of the Schools Council project Development of Scientific and Mathematical Concepts in children between the ages of 7 and 11, and provide another possibility for teachers to obtain detailed information about their pupils. In this material assessment is closely linked with teaching and a score is of no value. The handbook aims to help teachers interpret children's responses to the test items and to use these in providing experiences appropriate to the children's ideas. Groups of items relate to ideas such as conservation of weight, logical reasoning and measurement of weight, area and volume.

It would obviously be an immense task to cover in this amount of detail all the concepts which appear among our goals for children's education. Moreover to check on their development in this way would probably take more time than is available for learning. Even then the task of gathering information would only just have begun, since, as we saw on page 10, intellectual skills and concepts are only a part of the data we need for adapting the learning environment. But special situations do not always have to be set up for finding the information since, if normal activities really do provide opportunity for the goals of learning to be achieved, they also provide the chance to see how far development has reached toward these goals. For instance, if mathematics activities provide experiences which help children to distinguish weight from volume it might only be necessary for a teacher to observe children's reactions in these activities to find out about their progress.

A teacher might also look at certain features of the learning environment in searching for reasons why some children may be failing to learn. If much learning is done through individual or group project work an obvious cause of difficulty may be the reading level of the books which the pupils have to use as resources. The Schools Council project on The Effective Use of Reading has given much attention to searching for measures of readability which teachers can easily use, and is 'explicitly interested in discovering whether secondary teachers would be willing to use readability scores to assist them in finding appropriate reading matter for children in mixed ability groups and in interdisciplinary work, where no one teacher knows all the books which are available' (Harrison, 1975, p. 4). There is particular interest in the use of cloze procedure tests which seem, among other purposes, suited to finding out whether particular books are suited to particular readers. In concept the cloze procedure is quite simple: 'The passage for analysis is typed out, but with a number of deletions, and the difficulty of the original passage is gauged in relation to how many of the gaps the reader can fill with the exact word which was omitted' (Harrison, 1974, p. 18). Various studies, discussed by Harrison (1974), have related the cloze score to level of comprehension and, while difficulties remain, it is a productive area of research which can offer firm guidelines to teachers in selecting books which their pupils will be able to read and understand.

The Social Science Research Council's project 'Concepts in Secondary Mathematics and Science' (based at Chelsea Centre for Science Education) is providing teachers with guidelines for analysing curriculum materials according to levels of thinking demanded and matching these to the levels of their pupils' operation. Piaget's stages of concrete and formal operational thinking are taken as the model for describing the demands of various activities in secondary science schemes. Each activity in a programme is studied and classified as requiring mental ability at Piaget's levels 2A, 2B, 3A or 3B. The project has also produced tests which teachers can give to pupils and which result in each pupil being classified as at one of these levels of thinking. If the teacher knows the spectrum of each class, in terms of the proportion of children at level 2A, 2B, 3A etc., she can then choose a curriculum with a level of demand matching thinking of the class (Shayer et al., 1976).

Pupil questionnaires

Information restricted to whether or not pupils are achieving certain objectives is not sufficient by itself, since there may be reasons for the presence or absence of development of certain concepts and skills to be found in the conditions and circumstances of the pupils' activities, in the pupils' perception of the learning environment or in their reactions to it. Among the evaluation strategies proposed for use during the programme 'Man: A Course of Study' (Education Development Center 1970) there is a pupils' opinion survey. This asks questions about reactions to the course, the activities which pupils found hard, easy, most enjoyable, what has been learned most, and how pupils have perceived the demands of the material. The questions are multiple choice and the pupils told how many answers they can tick. For example:

To do well in *Man: A Course of Study*, I have to: (Check 3 answers)
_____ read well
_____ be able to think of a lot of good examples
_____ memorize all the facts in the booklets
_____ ask questions
_____ take part in class discussions
_____ remember everything the teacher said
_____ agree with the teacher
_____ have my own opinion
_____ write well
_____ do extra projects
_____ be able to understand and remember the films

_____try to be as quiet as possible
_____bring in extra information about the animals we are studying
_____answer a lot of the teacher's questions
_____other (What is it? _____)

(Education Development Center, 1970, p. 46)

It is suggested in the teachers' handbook that children fill in the form individually and then discuss their responses in groups. Therefore, as far as the pupils are concerned, the process is informal and provides a starting point for a useful discussion about how different people vary in their reactions to the work. For the teacher it provides insights into the activities as seen from the pupils' point of view.

The self-perception of pupils may influence their reaction to activities, to their peers and to their teacher. A child who sees himself as being good at writing poems, or football, or mathematics may react, on this account, differently to criticism or encouragement than one who does not regard himself as being any good at these things. A teacher who is sensitive to the child's self-esteem will take care not to hurt those who feel they are good performers nor to let others become defeatist about their abilities. A ready way to find out about how children regard themselves is through informal talk, often better outside lesson times, though opportunities for this are necessarily limited. But it is not difficult for teachers to devise a form for occasional use which would reveal some aspects of how children regard themselves. For example Pauline Sears' Self-Concept Scale (in Gordon 1966) provides a list of items relating to physical and mental ability, social relations, personality and school work and asks pupils to put three different questions to themselves about each item. The questions are 'Am I pretty well satisfied with myself in this area?' (pupils are asked to tick YES or NO), 'How much improvement do I think I will make by the end of the sixth grade?' (the form is for fifth graders, and they are asked to say whether they think there will be improvement or not), 'Compared with others in my class, how do I rate now?' (they rate themselves as low, medium low, medium high and high as compared with their class).

Methods involving observation

The examples have so far been of techniques which involve giving pupils special tasks for the purpose of gathering information. It is evident that however informal these special tasks may be they do interfere in normal activities and on this account cannot be used very frequently. Also they produce data which are based on performance or reactions at set times and in somewhat artificial situations; these do not allow for normal fluctuations in interest, concentration and motivation. To obtain a more fair sample of a child's abilities and attitudes it would be better to gather information on several different occasions and in a variety of situations. This is possible when information is collected by observation during normal learning activities. The pros and cons of using observation have already been discussed (pp. 14 & 15) leading to the conclusion that some framework for observation is required if the results are to be any more valuable than general impressions or expressions of opinion. The following examples are of methods which have been developed for gathering information about individual pupils through observation of their spontaneous behaviour.

The Progress in Learning Science project has enlisted the help of teachers in developing checklists for teachers to use, both for picking up information as immediate feedback in helping learning and for recording progress. Items in the checklists were found by a two-stage process of discussions with teachers. In the first stage several working parties of teachers in different parts of the country met to discuss the goals of inquiry-based work in the age range 5 to 13 years. Bringing together the separate deliberations of several groups of teachers of infants and lower junior children resulted in the production of a first draft list of Goals for Earlier Development. Similarly groups of middle and lower secondary school teachers provided Goals for Later Development. In each list there are 24 goals which are abilities, concepts or attitudes: a few examples are: *observing, identifying variables, communicating verbally* and *non-verbally, finding patterns in observations*; the concepts of *area, volume, force, energy, adaptation*; and attitudes of *curiosity, openmindedness, responsibility, willingness to co-operate*. In the second stage discussions with teachers focused upon each of the goals in turn and considered how their development shows in the actions and responses (in other words, the behaviour) of children. Statements of behaviour considered to be representative at progressive levels of development were identified and gradually refined in a series of trials and revisions. Put together these formed the checklists, in which there are three statements under each heading. Examples of the statements relating to nine of the items of the Checklist for Later Development are given on pages 160–162 of Appendix II in the illustrative material.

The items in the checklist are intended to structure observation, focusing it upon significant aspects of children's behaviour and at the same time providing a framework for interpreting the observations in terms of progress towards its goals. As such they are used constantly without any record being made. However, a systematic record can be made occasionally — about two or three times a year — using a record sheet on which the five boxes are reproduced for each child under each heading. Blocking in from the left to the square representing the level reached by a child, and repeating this in different colours on different occasions provides a record of progress. Here is the record of Simon, showing his progress from autumn 1973 to summer 1974.

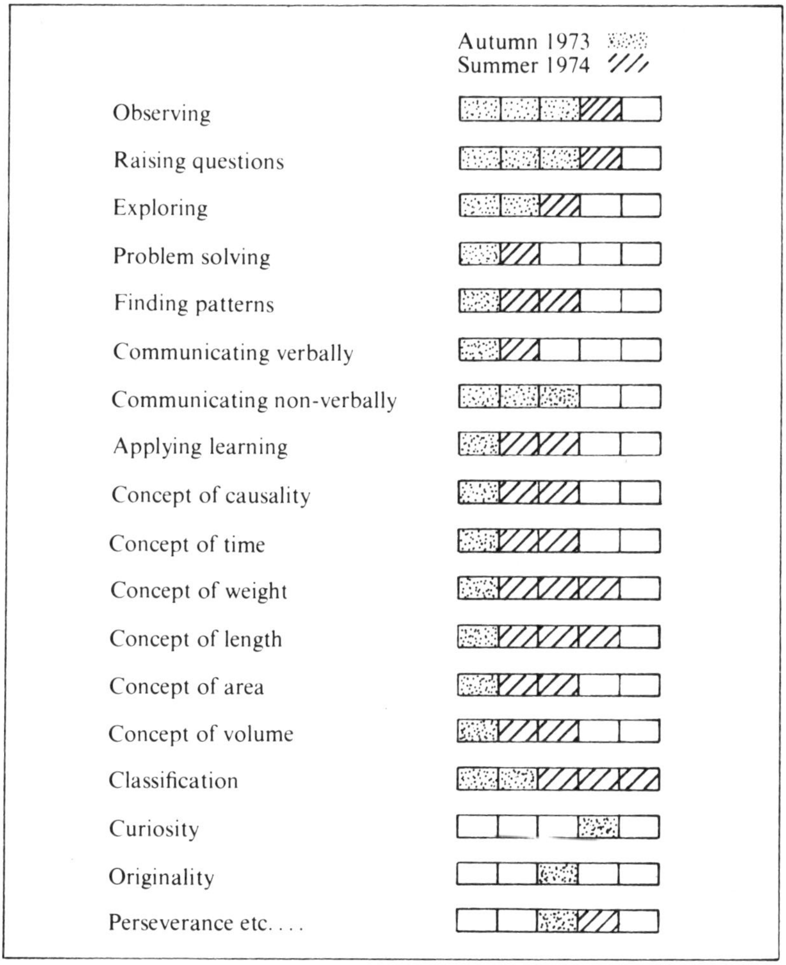

	Autumn 1973
	Summer 1974
Observing	
Raising questions	
Exploring	
Problem solving	
Finding patterns	
Communicating verbally	
Communicating non-verbally	
Applying learning	
Concept of causality	
Concept of time	
Concept of weight	
Concept of length	
Concept of area	
Concept of volume	
Classification	
Curiosity	
Originality	
Perseverance etc. ...	

Fig. 3   Progress record

If this kind of checklist is seen only as a way of keeping records (see Chapter 2 for a discussion on this subject) it would have many shortcomings;

its advantages appear when used as an aid in finding out about children in order to help them. In the case of Simon, for instance, his teacher realized from her observations in autumn 1973 his low level of development of several concepts. She gave special attention to making sure that he had opportunity for the kind of experiences which were matched to his development in these areas and would encourage his progress. (Examples of how she did this are given in the project's book for teachers, *Match and Mismatch*, 1977.) The importance of using the checklist as an aid to diagnosis is made clear in the supporting material produced by the project, some of which takes the form of in-service study material, presenting ideas for discussion about gathering and using information about individual pupils.

Another Schools Council project which has produced material specifically aimed at helping teachers observe and record children's progress is History, Geography and Social Science 8–13. The items in their checklist are the project's objectives which are grouped under the four broad headings of intellectual, social and physical skills and personal qualities (interests, attitudes and values). In a booklet written for teachers entitled *Evaluation, Assessment and Record Keeping in History, Geography and Social Science* the project evaluator has taken each of the objectives and proposed his own breakdown of the subskills which relate to it. There is also a discussion of the implications of each objective for teaching and learning and some hints about how to assess progress towards it. For example:

General objective: the ability to communicate findings through an appropriate medium.
What to look for:
— able to tell another child about his work
— writes a clear account of his work
— can draw a simple map
— tries other methods to communicate findings (e.g. poems, graphs, pictures, music)
— varies his communication according to the projected audience.
(Cooper, 1976, p. 20)

and for one of the social skills objectives (on p. 33):

General objective: to participate within small groups.
What to look for:
— understands the need for rules in a group
— participates in deciding the rules of the group
— can organise a group in such a way as to share roles and tasks among the members

– accepts the role of leader or follower as the situation demands
– appreciates the capabilities, qualities and sensitivities of other members of the group
– can put aside personal goals for the sake of the cohesion of the group.

Commenting on the ways of gathering information about achievement of this objective Cooper writes 'As far as I can see, there are no ways in which the teacher can "test" for the quality of the child's social relationships by any pencil or paper test,' and continues later (on p. 34):

Certainly, it would seem likely that observation would be the most useful tool in the teacher's attempt to assess this general objective. Since some children seem to show different characteristics inside the classroom and out (where perhaps the 'model' pupil becomes a social outcast or a near-bully), the teacher should watch behaviour in as many different situations as possible.

A further example of the use of structured observation comes from a field where almost all other techniques have been found to be inadequate. The Schools Council project on Education of Severely Educationally Subnormal Children has developed a model of observation which first involves general observation, secondly specific observation and thirdly intervention based on the patterns which have been observed. The model is best illustrated through its application to a particular case study which was supplied by Judith Coupe, one of the research officers in the project team. It concerns David, a maladjusted child in a class of 15 in a school for the severely educationally subnormal (ESN(S)). David occupies more than his share of the teacher's time because he throws furniture, hits other children and pulls their hair, so the teacher has to be both trying to control him and constantly on the watch. The team suggested that, since David already demanded a great deal of the teacher's time, an extra ten minutes a day spent observing him would not be a great burden and could help her modify his behaviour. At the level of general observation the teacher was asked to note the following about David's throwing and hitting:

– What does he do?
– When does he do it?
– How does he do it?
– When does he not do it?
– What does he like, for example, a certain toy, praise, physical contact, types of food? (Possible reinforcers)

(Coupe, 1975, p. 3)

Then at the levels of specific observation the behaviour causing most disturbance, in this case hitting others, was studied in more detail using an observation schedule over a period of several weeks. For each event variables were noted such as the time of day, David's location, posture, activity, who were the other children nearby and where the teacher was. Patterns emerged from the specific observations: he was found to hit at certain times in the morning, generally in the classroom, consistently between activities when not handling objects, only when the teacher was more than six feet away, and he hit three children most frequently but never two of the boys.

These patterns led, at the intervention stage, to changes being made in the classroom routine:

(a) Activities were carefully controlled in their duration so as to gradually increase attention spans at specified activities.
(b) As general observations had indicated that he responded well to verbal praise, reinforcement of this kind was deliberately built in to David's activities.
(c) David was given specific classroom tasks to complete between activities/lessons, i.e. monitorial duties of one kind or another.
(d) The two children recorded to be immune from David's previous aggressive outbursts were encouraged to work with him.

(Coupe, 1975, pp. 5 & 6)

Although this is not a situation which every teacher has to face, it is a good example of how regular observation can reveal patterns in children's behaviours which then suggest the likely remedies. There is every reason to believe that conscious and continuing observation of all children would produce evidence which suggests to teachers how they can best match the learning environment to the child. The example of David also adds weight to the advantage which observation has over other forms of assessment in bringing together a number of pieces of evidence gathered in different situations. Thus there is no snap judgement made in one set of conditions giving information which may not be valid in others. We see, too, in this example the value of keeping regular records of observations, which is part of the wider subject of record keeping which is taken up in the next chapter.

At a different level and on a different scale the Headteachers' Association of Scotland, in collaboration with the Scottish Council for Research in Education, in 1973 set up a working party on School Assessments in order 'To consider the form and range of items of information needed to produce for all secondary pupils a comprehensive picture of their aptitudes and interests so as to enable responsible guidance staff to give them the best possible advice on future curricula and/or vocational choice and on appropriate social and leisure activities; and to offer them a common form of statement which will be generally comprehensible and which would be available to them when appropriate.' The statement takes the form of a pupil profile in which assessments are recorded by various specialist subject teachers of a range of intellectual abilities and personal attributes. The information is gathered by observation and assessed in terms of lists of numbered categories which have been proposed for each aspect assessed. For instance, in the case of Oral Comprehension the five categories are:

1. He can accept complex spoken material readily and utilise it. He can remember what he hears for fairly long periods.
2. He can understand complex material with explanation and can usually remember it.
3. He can readily interpret straightforward material, although more complex matter can be taken in with repetition. He has a limited retention of what he hears.
4. He can only readily interpret simple material and has a limited retention of what he hears.
5. He is rarely able to carry out the simplest instructions, even after repetition and explanation; or having understood it he is unable to retain it long enough to act upon it.
   (Head Teachers' Association of Scotland, Notes for English Panel produced by the Working Party on School Assessments, July 1974)

Although in the Scottish scheme the assessments are made for guiding pupils' choice of subjects or further education, there is no reason why the same approach could not be used by teachers for gathering diagnostic information for guiding their decisions in the classroom. The procedure has been devised so that for teachers 'there is a minimum of distraction from their teaching responsibilities'. It also enables teachers to bring all kinds of information together from a very wide range of activities, both in the classroom and in extra-curricular activities.

The use of a system of categories describing the contributions of pupils to group discussions has been suggested for assessing oral interaction in the Schools Council Humanities Curriculum Project (Miller, 1975). They were proposed for use with a full transcript of a discussion but would no doubt be useful for a teacher to have in mind in picking up information about the pupils during a discussion. The 'intellectual objectives of discussion' have been identified and to each of these a negative and positive polarity have been ascribed. In relation to 'The nature of evidence', for example, the poles are: Positive — 'Relates argument to evidence, seeks confirmation from evidence, queries nature of evidence', and Negative — 'Ignores significance of evidence, argues unsupported case, accepts ambiguity in evidence.' In the rest of the scheme there are four pairs of statements relating to various aspects of the intellectual process of discussion and five pairs relating to value judgements and personal positions. The complete list is reproduced in Deale (1975) as well as in Miller's paper.

There are objections to structuring or focusing observations by the use of schedules or checklists, however, which should be acknowledged. While increasing the reliability and validity of the information by defining categories, there is a danger of narrowing the goals of learning to the items on the list. This applies very much less to checklists which are devised by teachers themselves than to ones externally produced. Teachers can build their checklists on all goals they have in mind and, if the list seems too narrow in compass, it may be that the goals are too narrowly conceived in any case, without any influence of the checklist. The criticism of 'narrowing' was considered by the Bullock committee in respect to checklists used for 'screening' children's language development. It was reported that some teachers objected to screening in the infant school because:

> . . . the channelling of teachers' observations could result in an infant school narrowing its aims. It might direct its teaching towards improving the children's performance on the criteria involved in the screening. This point was not accepted by teachers who had experience of operating screening procedures which involved 'channelled' observation. They reported that the checklists offered a useful framework for their normal assessment of children, and that this was in no way distorted by them. Nor, they felt, were their aims and teaching methods adversely influenced.
>
> (*A Language for Life*, 1975, para. 17.6)

It therefore seems that focused or channelled observation has a great many advantages for gathering on-the-spot feedback and for making decisions about meeting the needs of particular children. However, it is limited in value for other purposes, and it may be desirable to use a recognized diagnostic test in cases where a pupil is experiencing difficulties the source of which cannot be observed in normal circumstances.

CONCLUSION

We have considered various ways of collecting information about individual pupils for the purpose of evaluation, that is, in the context of gathering and using data for making decisions about the kind of learning environment which will help a pupil's progress. In this context it has been seen that most points are in favour of methods of gathering information by observation in normal learning activities, using some form of schedule or checklist as a way of focusing and interpreting observations. For diagnosing particular difficulties individual tests may be desirable, and should be as informal as possible. More formal tests have their purpose and do contribute some information useful in the evaluation context but their limitations in this respect have to be acknowledged. End of term tests, for instance, can be useful in telling the teacher about the effectiveness of her work, but it must be remembered that the information is confined to the abilities which can be tested in this way. This restriction has to be kept in mind also when tests are used for monitoring the overall progress of a class or for comparing one pupil's attainment with that of others, though they have greater value in these contexts than as feedback for teachers to use in helping children's progress. Each method of assessment has its particular strengths and weaknesses; it is important that we choose a method best fitted for providing the kind of information required for a particular purpose.

FURTHER CONSIDERATIONS

There are assumptions made in this chapter and issues raised which have not been fully explored and could form starting points for discussion. For example, some teachers have suggested that evaluation is not necessary for the purpose of matching experiences to pupils since the pupils can do the matching for themselves if they are allowed a choice. What is a realistic balance between pupil choice and teacher decision in the selection of learning experiences?

Another point places the discussion firmly in the context of the total set of influences on a child. Many of children's characteristics which have an important effect on their learning are outside the influence of teacher and school (for example, attitudes and values developed at home). Is there value in teachers finding out about things which are beyond their influence and, if so, how might they use the information?

It is noted that teachers are all the time observing children and making use of the information obtained. Is this always in the pupils' interests? What can be done to prevent teachers' decisions being made on the basis of non-relevant information?

The advantages and disadvantages of tests as compared with observation for gathering the kind of information required for evaluation can be explored further. Are assessments based on teachers' observations of pupils inherently less reliable than those based on some form of test? To what extent is it possible to introduce greater reliability by using checklists or other approaches to establishing criteria for assessing behaviour?

After studying some of the techniques and instruments mentioned in the last part of the chapter, their relative benefits for teacher and pupil can be discussed. If there is a conflict between the interests of teacher and pupils which should have priority? Could more be done to enlist pupils' help in providing teachers with the information they need to help with the teaching – learning process?

References

Choppin, R. (1978). *Activities for Assessing Classification Skills*. Slough: National Foundation for Educational Research.

Cooper, K. (1976). *Evaluation, Assessment and Record Keeping in History, Geography and Social Science*. Collins Education and ESL Bristol [for the Schools Council].

Coupe, J. (1975). 'Observation', unpublished teacher's guide from the Schools Council Project in Education for Severely Educationally Subnormal Pupils. (Also will be published in a Schools Council Curriculum Bulletin on the teaching of language and communication to the mentally handicapped.)

Deale, R. N. (1975). *Assessment and Testing in the Secondary School*. Schools Council Examinations Bulletin 32. Evans/Methuen Educational.

Department of Education and Science (1975). *A Language for Life* (Bullock Report). HMSO.

Gordon, I. J. (1966). *Studying the Child in School*. New York: Wiley.

Harlen, W. et al. (1977). *Match and Mismatch*, in-service training materials for teachers produced by the Schools Council Progress in Learning Science Project. Edinburgh: Oliver and Boyd.

Harrison, C. (1974). 'Readability and school', discussion document of the Schools Council Effective Use of Reading Project.

Harrison, C. (1975). 'Measures of readability as techniques evaluation', paper to the Schools Council Evaluators' Group.

Head Teachers Association of Scotland (1974). 'Pupil profiles', notes and progress reports produced by the Working Party on School Assessments.

'Man, a course of study' (1970), in *Evaluation Strategies*. Education Development Center, Cambridge, Mass. USA.

Miller, G. (1975), in *People in Classrooms*, edited by J. Elliott and B. M. MacDonald, Occasional Publication No. 2, Centre for Applied Research in Education, University of East Anglia.

Nuffield Mathematics Project (1972). *Checking-up Guides*. Chambers.

Rosenthal, R. & Jacobson, L. (1968). *Pygmalion in the Classroom*. New York: Holt, Rinehart & Winston.

Schools Council Project on Development of Scientific and Mathematical Concepts in Children (1975). *Area, Weight and Volume: Monitoring and Encouraging Children's Conceptual Development*. Nelson.

Shayer, M., Küchemann, D. E. & Wylam, H. (1976). 'The distribution of Piagetian stages of thinking in British middle and secondary school children', *British Journal of Educational Psychology*, **46**, 164–173.

2 Recording the progress of individuals

John Hayter and Ray Jackson

INTRODUCTION

On the rare occasions when it is necessary to visit the doctor, it is always a considerable comfort to observe that his knowledge of his patients is not entirely dependent on the excellence of his memory. The yellowed and perhaps mutilated card, with its hieroglyphics, allows a quick résumé of the patient's history before a new chapter is opened or an old one is extended. But for such a form of recording, however crude, the doctor could not hope to recall the health details of 3000 or more patients. Normally his filing system is maintained by his secretary, and his recording is brief; normally he sees his patients only occasionally and then one at a time. The records not only serve to enable review, but also form the basis for reports to specialists and hospitals and, providing they are reasonably legible, make it possible for a patient to be well cared for by successive doctors. The system is recognized as necessary and, while there is scope for improvement, it works!

In comparison, the class teacher's task in keeping and using records is complex. Information and data on each child abound, making selection necessary, often in situations where the trivial is easier to record than the significant. Frequent contact with the children allows more information to be carried in the head, without the conscious recognition that in such a form it is difficult for others to use. In addition, there is the sheer weight of numbers — records have to be compiled for groups of thirty and more. An immediate practical decision which has to be taken concerns the time at which data should be added to the storage system. Commonly the updating occurs infrequently, is done under pressure of time, often with unsuitable facilities for preparing and storing the records. The whole exercise becomes a chore — witness a staff room during the writing of reports each term — rather than a necessary and acceptable part of providing a sound education for children who are meeting perhaps forty or fifty teachers in two or more schools over a period of ten or more years.

Since the recorder carries much of the information with him, he is inclined to make little use of his own written records; consequently the value of the records may be a function of the use made of them by those who follow — new teachers, other departments, more senior sections of the school. While undoubtedly school records are used in this way, the lack of experience in making use of records and, probably more important, the disagreement which exists about the importance of particular types of information and the validity of the subjective views of colleagues, result in even the most carefully prepared records remaining unused or at best underused, after compilation.

TEACHERS' ATTITUDES TOWARDS RECORDS

In order to explore the attitudes of secondary teachers towards school records, teachers in some 96 schools were interviewed. The results of this survey are given in Table 2.1.

Table 2.1   Attitudes of secondary school teachers towards records

Teachers	Schools keeping records	Teacher attitudes towards records			Don't know
		Approving	Ambivalent	Critical	
96	81	43	12	20	6
—	100%	53%	15%	25%	7%

Almost 9 schools out of 10 in the survey had records; these included 6 of the 10 grammar schools, 59 of the 60 comprehensive schools, 14 of the 20 secondary modern schools and 2 of the 6 remaining schools.

The teachers who found records useful made the following typical remarks: '... It's good to get another teacher's point of view ...', '... What I like about school records is that they give me valuable information about a pupil's family background and also give an overall picture of his abilities ...', '... I like to look over them to refresh my memory when I expect parents ...', '... as a head of department I find I cannot comment on many pupils unless I consult the record cards. What I seek mainly are Reading Test Scores and the records of the individual's progress with the SRA (Science Research Associates) Reading and Written exercises ...'

Those teachers who found school records of little use in their work tended to make such comments as these: '... I find them unreliable especially the judgements about the pupil's personality and behaviour. These judgements are highly subjective ...', '... I find the primary school record unhelpful since it gives minimum information usually confined to the pupil's reading age and precious little else . . .', '. . . Most of the comments on the records are negative and tend to colour one's attitudes towards the child – sometimes without good reason . . .', '. . . Entries tend to be repetitive . . .', '. . . We usually fill them in at the wrong time of the year – at the end of term – and everything is done in a rush . . .'

These and other comments showed that teachers generally favoured the judicious use of record cards although they often objected to their records and the procedures laid down for completing them. They were particularly worried about stereotyping pupils through the medium of school records. They saw the dangers of the 'halo' effect on assessment, that is, they thought that they might be unduly influenced by the past assessments of the pupil which were already entered on the card. One teacher explained that he purposely never looked at a new pupil's record until after he had been meeting the class for three weeks. Others urged caution here since the youngster might be epileptic, or diabetic or suffer from some other physical disorder that might need attention during these vital first weeks in the school. Such a problem might be overcome if the head looked through all record cards first and alerted the appropriate teachers of children at risk.

Those one in four teachers who objected to keeping records were intense in their opposition. One of these teachers, who had shown a highly traditional approach to teaching in other circumstances, stated categorically: '. . . I've kept records religiously for eight years and not once have I had recourse to use them. . .'

The teachers surveyed generally favoured having more information about their pupils (especially where there were serious physical, emotional and familial difficulties and deficiencies), more information about the pupil's family and some indication of their previous achievement levels and present potential.

Although this survey was not made with a representative sample, it appears likely that the remarks and figures are indicative of widely held attitudes and prejudices. While sceptism may also be apparent in primary schools, it appears that there is rather more uniformity in the records which are kept in response to suggestions or directives from the local education authorities, with the headteacher taking more direct responsibility for the implementation of the authority's policy on records and perhaps personally supervising the updating of the record system.

Primary school records

A co-ordinated approach to record keeping has developed more fully in the

English primary school as indeed have other innovations such as flexible time-tabling, team-teaching, family groupings and so on. Headteachers and class teachers in primary schools evidently felt that they needed a more rigorous system of recording and exchanging significant data than is provided by off-the-cuff opinions, and processed gossip. Further, the need for systemized recording had been accentuated by the breakdown of subject barriers, the teaching of 'fused subjects', the integrated day, and the new organizational patterns occasioned by team teaching and family groupings.

At the primary school level the teacher has unique opportunities to observe the pupil in the classroom and in other settings, learning about him from his written and oral work, his art and craft work, his proficiency at reading, his interests and hobbies, etc. Anecdotal records may be used to give examples of the child's behavioural patterns. So the primary school teacher is in a good position to study the individual pupil in many differing situations. This remains broadly true even in team-teaching organization, since activities are less subject based than in the secondary schools.

Pupils enter the primary school with slight differences in chronological age but wider variations in mental maturity, physical co-ordination, social and emotional readiness for formal school experiences. An early identification of individual differences is an important aspect of any attempt to provide appropriate educational experiences for the child. Further, failure to recognize levels of readiness in the early year of school life may lead to boredom at one extreme and to frustration at the other and indeed may be a major underlying factor in the problems of underachievement, truancy, school phobia, 'drop-outs' and juvenile delinquency. At the start of a child's school life, the teacher has an opportunity to identify levels of maturity through observations, talks with parents, health reports, and developmental records of progress in adjusting to school.

The results of a small survey of records kept by eight primary schools in South Wiltshire indicate the type of information which is often kept for each child. The academic records consist of reading age, IQ and arithmetical standard; standardized tests being used fairly frequently. In addition, significant occasions for the individual are noted together with confidential information where it is felt to be relevant (e.g. home background, court appearances etc.). This record of the child's stay at the school is forwarded to the next school on moving.

There is no shortage of ideas for more innovative record keeping systems; useful methods are described in books by Rance (1971), Foster (1971) and Dean (1972). Each book gives examples of forms which have been found helpful in monitoring a child's progress in a particular skill or which illuminate the pattern of work or developing abilities within a class. In addition to specific items of information recorded on forms, many schools keep samples of a pupil's work which in themselves provide an illuminating record of progress.

The comprehensive system of record keeping developed by Mr D Jackson (headmaster) and staff of the New Ash Green Primary School in Kent is a striking example of a carefully prepared and detailed scheme. The record takes the form of a booklet for each pupil which is kept in a centralized filing system, the records being updated at approximately six-month intervals. The cover provides space for notes on 'Factors concerning individual development' under the headings, 'Home background', 'Physical, Intellectual, Emotional and Social development'; however the main part of the booklet — some 18 pages — lists individual experiences and abilities in basic skills in the areas of speech, handwriting, written language, reading, mathematics etc. Against each item are columns for each of the six years a child would normally spend in primary school; the teacher simply makes a tick where a child has given evidence of the ability or has had a certain experience during a school year. The examples given as illustration in this chapter and in Appendix I show the level of detail which has been achieved. The headmaster, who has permitted us to reproduce these examples, reports that the booklet is being modified in the light of deficiencies which are noted by the staff as it is used. There is consequently a degree of flexibility in establishing the design, which encourages the individual teacher's involvement in using it. The record book has already been found of value in the secondary school to which pupils pass at the age of eleven. Following an evaluation of the use of the booklet over a period of years it is thought that other contributory primary schools may consider the use of a similar system of record keeping.

Records in the secondary school

The case for keeping records for individual pupils when they move to secondary school grows stronger rather than diminishes. Larger schools, more frequent staff changes, increasingly individualized work for pupils all emphasize the need for written records to supplement memories and verbal exchanges. However, in responding to the acknowledged need, the psychological reactions of teachers to an imposed system, are ignored at the enthusiastic implementer's peril. Rational argument must always be related to the likely response of human nature, as illustrated by the case of a headmaster who attempted to tidy up the records of internal examination marks. Scores recorded for each subject against the student's name are often difficult to interpret immediately but some years later their meaning is even more uncertain owing to lack of knowledge of the examination from which they derive,

Table 2.2 Records kept in secondary schools

Custodian of record	Nature of record	User of record	Comment
Headmaster and 'the school'	Report to the Governors	Governors/Managers Director of Education	May be used eventually by school historians.
	Confidential files for records on teachers	Headmaster, LEA, HMI	
	Punishment book	Inspectorate	Required by law. Well maintained, concerned with individuals.
	Headmaster's log book		
	Returns to the DES	DES	
	Visitors' book		
	School reports	Parents	If in book form it may be available for reference by teachers in successive terms – seldom used in this way.
	Attendance register	Headmaster/Housemaster/Attendance Officer	Used as check on truancy
School Secretary, Nurse	Health records of child. Visits to the sick room.	Staff checking on absence. Doctor.	Recording coincides with occurrence. Pupils normally being treated individually.
Careers staff	Personal details, career aspirations, cumulative	Careers staff in offering advice to students, parents	Where developed, may be the most efficiently organized

	record of school attainment.	and in preparing references for employers.	record on students.
Housemaster/Head of Year/Tutor	Personal record card for students. Records of parent interviews, family problems; sporting, social service activities	Successive teachers housemaster etc. in preparation of reports, references	Potentially concerned with the most important issues. All too often inefficiently maintained and spasmodically used. UCCA forms once compiled may be used for record/reference purposes.
	Transfer record sheet	Head of Year/Tutor	Either from primary/middle school or on moving during secondary schooling
Subject Department	Lists of teaching sets.	Department staff	Record of students' progress through sets. Decisions on entry for GCE/CSE.
Class teacher	Mark book – homework and test scores, report comments, occasional checks on lesson attendance.	Class teacher Teacher/Deputy Head	Frequently updated and reflecting individual style of teacher. Of little value in long term but form basis for end of term/year report, discussions with parents.
Student	Probably none. Possibly homework book with record of work set.	Student	Short term value – intended as *aide memoire*.

the results of other students taking the examination, and so on. Following training in the uses of statistical techniques in education, the headmaster introduced a scheme to adopt 'standardized' scores as a record of student performance in each subject at the end of term. While the scheme might have been statistically sound, the reception given by the staff to the handbook which explained how to calculate the scores, and the dubious accuracy (not to mention the antagonistic spirit) with which it was carried out, led one to doubt the wisdom of the innovation. Even where the purpose of a method is clear, there must be some degree of consensus on the value and usefulness of a recording system, unless teachers are to do no more than conform with the requirements of the hierarchy.

What recording systems are to be found operating in a secondary school? What is their purpose and what gaps or deficiencies are apparent? Table 2.2 provides an overview of what might be found within various parts of a school. The records which have been listed include a number that are for internal use, together with others that are for the information of outsiders. The form of the record and the way in which it is completed, must inevitably reflect the needs of these different interest groups. If it is to be an efficient and useful means of communication, the purpose and nature of the system must be understood by the user. The question, 'Is this school's record-keeping system adequate?' needs consideration at two levels. 'Are the records kept efficiently?' and 'Are the records used effectively?'

PROBLEMS OF KEEPING AND USING RECORDS

The efficiency with which records are kept appears to depend as much on the personality of the record keeper as on the appropriateness of the design of the record system used. The teacher who is meticulous about keeping details of housekeeping and the teacher who keeps detailed records of car running costs are both likely to accept an imposed system of record keeping as a normal and useful part of their job. Yet many who find no need for recording the minutiae of their own lives, see no reason to spend precious time making records about the children they teach. Consequently, the efficiency of keeping records will vary with personality and with conviction of the usefulness of those records.

Communicating information beyond the school

Efficiency is of course often spurred by external requirements. Deadlines are set for the preparation of written reports to parents, consequently the record is made with an almost one hundred per cent return even though many teachers may be doubtful about the value of what they write. In addition to the statements of commendation, encouragement or impending doom, the report often contains numerical data which derive from an amalgam of class- and homework, with perhaps a separate score for examination performance. In some schools position in class may still be a feature of both a subject report and a form report; the attractiveness of the simplicity of a number often obscuring the statistical weakness behind the derivation of the number.

Yet to many parents the report is significant, and eagerly awaited or feared. Parents understandably appreciate the facility of written remarks which they can read and re-read, and which may be shown to granny and others. Further, it is a system which they remember and probably regard with some awe from their childhood. Schools which are tempted to reject regular written reports in favour of oral reporting through a child's tutor during a face-to-face interview with parents must reckon with the need to modify parents' expectations, if they are not to weaken one tangible link between parents and school. Even small changes in the system can cause misunderstanding and result in apparent lack of co-operation. This point is nicely made by examples in the Home and School Council Working paper on School reports (1970). The paper describes the reaction of parents to an invitation to write a comment on their child's report before returning it to the school. One headmaster reported that only one of the three hundred reports was returned with a comment from the parent. Meanwhile in a school sited in a 'deprived area in Islington' at least two-thirds of the parents responded each time and sometimes the response rate was as high as ninety per cent. Opportunity to comment was, by itself, not sufficient.

In recent years when schools have reviewed their reporting systems, a mixture of oral and written reports has often emerged as the best means of internal and external communication between subject teachers, tutors and parents. The need for written assessments provides teachers with an opportunity to crystallize their impressions of a child in order to make a worthwhile assessment while the oral report provides for a more productive two-way consideration of the child's progress and needs.

Ever since it moved into new premises in 1969, Bosworth College in Leicestershire has been developing more comprehensive and useful forms of reporting on pupils' progress. A detailed and illuminating account of the development of the system is provided by David Marcus in the Bosworth paper *Reports and Reporting*. He indicates that, after a few years of operation, weaknesses in the initial system became apparent and a working party was established to make proposals for a new approach. The revised system, when adopted, included student self-assessment as a significant element of internal reporting. The student's comments on his progress were confidential to the school and consequently were not shown to the parents. The Bosworth paper is in itself a form of record providing a very useful study of the way in which a school planned, put into operation and evaluated a developing report system.

The issue of effectiveness is more elusive but is certainly more crucial than that of efficiency, since there is no argument for consuming time on the perfect compilation of ill-used or inappropriate systems of recording. Effectiveness must relate to purpose and, since record keeping is time consuming, this should encourage any school to identify very clearly the purpose of its record keeping and to examine whether extra mileage is obtainable from records currently kept. For instance, with written reports to parents — though primarily to inform parents, are they used by the school as a record of a student's progress in a subject or as a person, through his school career? Where reports are bound in a book and this is returned to school after a period in the child's home such a use seems feasible. The increasing use of wallets of subject report slips together with 'no carbon required' paper to produce copies for parents, school and tutor opens the way to a more systematic use of the reports over a period of time. The completeness of such regular reports makes them outstanding as records but, in extending their use, a school staff might feel changes in format and content are appropriate; it may well be that other types of information will be of interest to parents also. Indeed it could be argued that parents should have some say in defining the nature of the information which they are to receive.

As part of its endeavours to increase parents' understanding of educational ideas and the nature of educational provision, the Advisory Centre for Education (ACE) journal *Where* (1974) has provided parents with a checklist of criteria by which to review a child's experience and progress in three broad age bands. The criteria were in fact developed as part of a project carried out by the NFER and the Leeds University Institute of Education who were aiming to establish ways of evaluating teacher training courses. The criteria for each age group are divided into 'subject' categories and a section on language skills for the years up to nine includes the items 'Is your child learning how to listen?' 'Is he experiencing pleasure in what he reads?' 'Is skill in handwriting regarded as important?' While many parents might find it difficult to assess the school's approach and the child's progress with such criteria, such a checklist might well provide an appropriate starting point for establishing communication with parents about what they wish to know.

A particular instance in which there is a need for efficient compilation and effective use of a record occurs when a pupil transfers to a school in a different district. The oral transmission which may be adequate within an institution is then insufficient; but what form of record is appropriate, and how should the receiving school make use of it? Schools might well see local authority advisers

as appropriate consultants in trying to resolve such specification and interpretation problems.

In communicating with employers, schools have again to establish the
nature and form of the information which they provide. Well developed career
departments will be sensitive to the needs of employers and the criteria used
in assessing potential employees, which go beyond a list of CSE or O-level
passes. More and more schools are endeavouring to provide useful information
in addition to a general reference with a statement of academic achievement.
For example, this may take the form of an assessment of personal qualities,
including information on attendance, punctuality and concern over appearance together with the pupil's position on a number of personal quality scales,
e.g. from *gregarious* to *rather solitary*; from *original, shows initiative* to *conventional, doesn't like to be different*. While the danger of taking over the
selection process on behalf of the employer has to be avoided, the explicit
recognition that personal qualities are of considerable importance in future
employment indicates a note of realism in the content of the school's report
to the outside world. The record of personal achievement, described on page
43, is an example of a way in which employees can gain a broad picture of a
pupil's personal and academic capacities.

Records within the school

In contrast with the school-wide nature of the half-yearly or term report,
other records are often confined within particular areas (departments, houses,
etc.) or may indeed be the preserve of an individual. While such compartment-
alization may be desirable in some respects and with certain types of confidential information, the danger of insufficient communication seems more real
than the occasional leakage of quasi-confidential details. Where attention is
concentrated on the class unit the importance of the particular problems and
tensions of the individual may have to take second place to the demands of
uniform progress. Where the child's individual development is of prime
concern and is reflected in the nature of classroom organization and style of
teaching and learning, then it is clearly vital for the teacher to be acquainted
with the pressures and concerns which children may understandably rank
more significant than the school subjects which they study. In the primary
school, where there is greater opportunity for a strong link between teacher
and pupil, there is ample evidence that the environment is conducive to the
communication and use of information. In secondary schools, with perhaps
ten or twelve times the number of teacher/pupil bonds to be formed in any
given year, the problems of communicating information are more daunting
but are increasingly necessary within the context of mixed-ability classes and

individualized teaching methods.

Yet increased information about the children may present teachers with dilemmas enough to tax all their professional skills. What allowances are to be made for the child with overwhelming tensions at home, with another who craves affection, and one who is single minded in his career intentions and whose aspirations find little need for the teacher's own subject? The tidiness and simplicity of the class *en masse* is replaced by the complexity and challenge of variations between individuals.

All this may seem distant from the theme of record keeping, but unless pupils are regarded as fresh from the mould when starting every year of their school life, then knowledge of their abilities, achievements and background generally must be regarded as necessary input at the start of any year and a recognized product at the end of a year. Doctors, or indeed car mechanics, who deal out certain treatments regardless of need at a given age of person or vehicle, are compiling a recipe for disaster. While a caricature of what happens in the classroom, the parallelism should encourage careful thought on catering for individual needs as ascertained from an understanding of the child. Punishments and crimes are not the only things that should be carefully matched.

THE PURPOSE AND USE OF RECORD KEEPING

A number of points are worth bearing in mind when designing the format of record systems and in collecting data. The system of recording should be in accordance with the general objectives of the school and should perhaps be designed by a special staff committee set up for that purpose. (Secondary school counsellors in Stoke-on-Trent, for example, drew up a prototype record card and circulated it to local schools, the first and second drafts were then modified in the light of teachers' suggestions, until some consensus was reached.) Together the school records should form a continuous and comprehensive appraisal of the pupil's educational career, although completion of the records should not overburden the staff with unnecessary clerical work. The recording system should be reviewed frequently so that account may be taken of changes in the school population, the school curriculum, pedagogical techniques, educational theories and philosophies. All information collected should be self-explanatory and should be such as not to give offence to the vast majority of pupils or parents. Current debate on the accessibility and use of school records should serve to clarify thinking further on the purpose, nature and content of school records.

While records may and do serve a variety of purposes within a school, it is pupils and teachers who form the nub of the educational process. It is proposed to concentrate in the remainder of the chapter on the scope of record keeping in contributing to their essential tasks — that of learning and that of encouraging learning and teaching. Not only is this the crucial area, it is also the area into which many current records make least input and the area where in any case superficiality and ineffectiveness lead to rapid rejection by the teacher. Since there appears to be relatively little experience in devising useful systems of record keeping and there are well known dangers in trying to establish uniform systems at a school or within an authority, there are strong arguments for developing a scheme on a small localized scale — in some cases by an individual teacher, more often within a department or within a school, since the use of a commonly agreed system within a unit enables the communication of information to be handled more effectively. The experience of an individual teacher who has tried out his own scheme with his own classes may indeed be a valuable first stage.

The teacher might well start by defining the purpose of his system of records, in terms similar to those which follow:

Purpose	*Notes and examples*
To enable a pupil's progress to be mapped on to the work in a subject during the year.	Where pupils are working on individualized tasks, work cards, etc. the record might take the form of a student/task matrix.
To record mastery of skills identified within a subject.	Skills are listed for each child — items ticked as achieved (e.g. New Ash Green record book, see Appendix I)
To record work completed.	Page reached or books read in primary context.
To provide record for subject/ class teacher in the following year.	Must be in format understood by recipient. Abstraction from records of current year may be an advantage, e.g. 'The following pupils are unable to add fractions'.
To provide information for decision making on an appropriate course for students — in determining stages in current course (short term) — in planning future studies (long term).	Indicators of readiness for particular pieces of work might be identified and listed for each child. For example see 'Progress in Learning Science' checklist Appendix II. Valid progress details over several terms. Standardized scores of value particularly if easy computation facilities available.
To identify and record significant personality, behavioural characteristics.	Might be achieved with a listing of behaviour patterns (co-operation, care of property, degree of anxiety over work, etc.)

To understand more fully the nature of activity, use of resources, etc. within a classroom.

Likely to be a short-term study to provide evidence for making decisions about allocation of resources, different organizational patterns, etc. Pupils may record and display information as part of their work.

EXAMPLES OF RECORDING SYSTEMS

It may be of value at this point to consider, in greater depth, some record keeping systems which have been developed to meet particular objectives.

(i) Methods of recording to enable a pupil to maintain a record of his own progress

In the listing of records kept within a secondary school, it was noted that records kept by students were seldom used. Since this approach would seem to have considerable potential for development, it justifies a more detailed discussion.

Whether cleaning shoes, climbing mountains or learning mathematics, the majority of people like to be aware that they are making progress. In order to recognize significant progress, it is necessary to have some idea about what has to be achieved and to be aware of milestones *en route*. At the simplest level, children learning to read are often led through a series of simple readers, their position in any text being marked by a card bearing a page number. A simple form of record keeping — meaningful to the child and of value to the teacher.

Table 2.3   Pupil's work card

GEOMETRY   NAME _____

Tasks	G1	G2	G3	G4	G5	G6	G7
Completed (put a tick)	✓	✓		✓			
Date	4.6.74	20.6.74		3.7.74			
Worked with	Roy			Jane			

As children grow older they are able to appreciate in some way the scope of a whole course. Aspiring secretaries recognize in the contents of a shorthand manual that which must be learned before the end of the year. However, the magnitude of the total task may be overwhelming and the format in a book may obscure the stages through which a student must pass. A more careful analysis of the concepts and skills would be of help. In designing any recording method it is desirable to aim to make it encouraging to the pupil, avoiding where possible forms which show progress only over a long time or are too complex and may act as a disincentive. A system of learning which involves work cards makes for an easily understood form of record keeping with children marking the tasks which they have completed on a grid of the sort shown in Table 2.3. The majority of students will probably not keep such a record efficiently without frequent reminders and some persistent training. Pupils have too often come to accept the teacher's judgement on quality and rate of work as being the only one of importance. To appraise their own work critically may be a new experience and one requiring the sympathy and initially the active involvement of the teacher.

A major experiment in the field of pupil kept records has been carried out in Swindon and Wiltshire Schools since 1970. Called the Record of Personal Achievement (RPA, see Notes, p. 46), this was designed for 14–16 year-old pupils of all abilities and aptitudes by many teachers working with the Swindon LEA. Also involved were employers, personnel assistants, careers officers, lecturers in colleges of education and colleges of further education. The objectives of the recording system are to identify the pupil's achievements in family life, citizenship, leisure and work. The scheme aims to acquaint pupils with their own strengths and weaknesses. In emphasizing the former and minimizing the latter it is hoped that the scheme may help develop the pupil's self-esteem and self-confidence which is particularly lacking in pupils who are socially disadvantaged. Further, the scheme provides opportunities for success to pupils who are not ordinarily adept at school activities of an academic nature.

The method used provides an immediate and continuous record of all successful achievements both inside and outside the school. These activities are entered in a permanent record which is presented to the pupil when he leaves school. The essence of the method is that the pupil may choose what he thinks is a successful achievement and records the facts which must then be certified by a responsible adult. Records may be made of individual and group activities, course work, lectures, visits, service to others, time keeping, assignments, creative activities, reading, oral work, individual physical performances, team sports, leisure pursuits, writing, music and drama and works experience.

No competition is encouraged and neither are comparisons made between pupils. It is hoped by the compilers of the scheme that due weight will be given to a number of individual qualities which are masked by current recording and assessment systems. These include: physical fitness, appearance and bearing, the ability to communicate, concern for others, courtesy, punctuality and regularity, diligence and perseverance, the ability to work with others, reliability, the ability to carry out instructions, the ability to manage money, independence, initiative and willingness to develop and to continue with new interests, curiosity and creativity. The scheme has attracted the attention of the Schools Council which has funded an evaluation study. Some sample pages from the Record of Personal Achievement are shown in Appendix III.

(ii) Recording designed to enable the teacher to understand more clearly the stage of development of children within the class, in order to plan more effective and appropriate learning experiences

Piaget's ideas on concept development have caused teachers to rethink their approach to the teaching of many subjects. The concepts inherent in elementary science and mathematics have received particularly close attention and it is necessary to identify important concepts when establishing a new programme. However, it is one thing to identify the concept and its relation to others; it is quite another to establish a child's readiness to cope with that concept. This particular problem emerged during the work of the Schools Council's Science 5/13 Project and gave rise to a further project, Progress in Learning Science, which has developed checklists to help teachers identify the level of ability and of thinking achieved by individual pupils. (See Chapter 1, pp. 18–20.) Extracts from the checklist for Later Development are given on pages 22–26 together with an example of how these can be recorded in a way which reveals areas where progress has or has not been made.

(iii) Recording to help the teacher understand the balance of activities of children within a class operating an 'integrated' day

Rance (1971, pp. 46–47) describes a method which involves the use of 'pie' charts each to represent a week's work for each pupil. Each pie chart is divided into quarters representing subject areas (Mathematics, English, art and craft, other activities). Each of the quarters is further subdivided into five segments representing the days Monday to Friday. After each day's work in the subject, part of the appropriate segment is coloured in proportion to the amount of time spent on that topic (see Fig. 3, p. 21).

Such a technique gives a quickly identified map of the work completed by individual pupils. Any imbalance between subject allocations may be identified and the pupil's work pattern modified as necessary. Although it is suggested that this record system should be kept by the teacher, it seems unlikely that many teachers will be prepared to devote the time required for use with a whole class. However with some modification there would seem to be no reason why pupils in the later years of junior school should not build up their own records. An alternative type of record keeping system for this situation is described by Annabelle Dixon (1971), who encourages her pupils to maintain the records with only minimal support from the teacher.

Any system of this type may be part of the ongoing work of the class teacher but alternatively, it may be used as a 'private' research instrument used for a short period of time. While its completion may be too time consuming to contemplate making use of it for a long period, it may have great benefit in illuminating difficulties in classroom organization or in the learning process which are present, but only perceived in a general way before analysis.

THE WAY FORWARD

Many schools are in the process of reviewing their systems of record keeping and it could be very beneficial if others followed the example of Bosworth College in providing a record of the evolution of their own system. At the same time several large scale surveys of current practice are being undertaken. In 1973—74 the Department of Education and Science carried out a survey on record keeping and inter-school liaison in nearly 200 schools throughout England. In Scotland headteachers have more recently been involved in a study of assessment and recording. The working party involved set itself the aim of producing an assessment and recording scheme which makes maximum use of the information readily available to teachers through observation of their pupils and minimum demands on teaching time. By establishing criteria for the assignment of grades they aimed also to remove some of the problems of interpreting grades given by different teachers. (Some details are given in Chapter 1, p. 25.) Published reports of both the DES and the Scottish studies are anticipated. In 1976 the Schools Council agreed to fund a two-year project to be undertaken by the NFER to examine present methods of record keeping in the primary school and to develop systems appropriate to the curriculum content, methods and organization of the contemporary primary school.

Surveys of record keeping systems may provide a useful picture of the state of current practice and may reveal interesting and novel systems. However, acknowledging the problem of record system transplants, many schools will wish to use the experience of others alongside an examination of the current practice and needs of their own institution.

It may be desirable first to examine the variety of systems operating within an institution and to map the use made of them. Apart from any official systems, what personal recording systems have teachers adopted over a period of time? Is there any evidence that the efficacy of personal or official systems is examined from time to time? Could greater use be made of the records which are kept at present? Further, are the particular points of contact (e.g. between schools) where communication could be eased by appropriate record systems? To what extent is continuity over time an important consideration in using record forms?

In planning new approaches to record keeping how might parents be involved in decisions regarding the nature and form of records which are to be submitted to them? How far can pupils maintain their own records — from candid comments on their own progress to the more mundane checking of tasks covered. What are the possibilities of designing some recording system to provide useful information for planning more effective work in the class-room with one's class, in using resources and in distributing time and energy? While it is unlikely that any system of keeping records will totally satisfy those who make use of it, the current concern and developmental activity may well lead not only to more systematic individualized educational provision but will also provide a greater awareness of the goals of the teaching and learning process at the centre of it.

References and notes

Dean, J. (1972). *Recording Children's Individual Progress*. Macmillan.

Dixon, A. (1971). 'What kind of records', *Forum*, **13**, No. 2, pp. 45–46.

Foster, J. (1971). *Recording Individual Progress*. Macmillan.

Home and School Council (1970). *School Reports* (Working Paper), pp. 5, 12.

McAlhone, B. (1974). 'Checklist on your child's schooling' I, II & III, in *Where*, Nos. 91–93, April, May & June 1974. Advisory Centre for Education, Cambridge.

Marcus, D. (1973). *Reports and Reporting*. The Bosworth Papers 3, available from the Bosworth College Bookshop, Leicester Lane, Desford, Leicester-shire.

Rance, P. (1971). *Record Keeping*. Ward Lock Educational.

Record of Personal Achievement, Swindon Education Committee. (All inquiries to the Organizer, Curriculum Study and Development Centre, Sanford Street, Swindon, Wiltshire.)

3 Classroom accountability and the self-monitoring teacher

John Elliott

ACCOUNTABILITY AND SELF-EVALUATION

The aim of this chapter is to examine the nature of whatever relationship exists between general notions of self-evaluation and the more specific ways in which teachers might be held accountable for what goes on in their classrooms. It is increasingly the case that a variety of social institutions and groups — ranging from those of central and local government to various minority groups representing the more sectional interests of parents and pupils -- are claiming the right to at least some measure of control over what teachers actually do in classrooms. (If a teacher is to be 'called to account' then each claimant has an equal obligation to explain the nature of his interest. For example, in law it is necessary to establish the principle of *locus standi* — each party to an action must possess an interest in the outcome before an action can proceed — and in this case too the 'claim' must be legitimate.) In this respect one of the common denominators uniting these often widely disparate groupings is the demand for some systematic form of 'teacher accountability' within which context the evaluation of teachers is frequently perceived to function as an instrument of social control.

There are already disturbing signs in this country that teachers may be required to conform to ill advised systems (see p. 52) of accountability similar to those currently being operated almost universally in the USA (see Clegg, 1975) and it is therefore a matter of some urgency that the emergence of such movements is accompanied by a rigorous analysis of what is involved when evaluating teachers in such contexts. For example, various interested parties may already influence, or attempt to influence, what teachers do in their classrooms. A prima facie case thus already exists for proceeding with an assessment of the extent to which teachers may, in fact, be held responsible for meeting (or failing to meet) such demands.

Notions of accountability within the context of teacher evaluation require at least a minimal ascription of responsibility to teachers for what happens to their pupils. However, one can distinguish between two types of 'responsibility' relevant to the evaluation of people (see Feinberg, 1968) each of which possesses a degree of correspondence to qualitatively different kinds of evaluation. There is, for example, a certain conceptual discreteness between how much a particular *action* can be considered as causally responsible for certain consequences, and the extent to which a *person* can be held culpable for the consequences of his actions.

The difference is one of attribution for, in the first case, it is the action itself (rather than the actor performing it) that is evaluated; in the second case the converse is true, since the evaluation is of the actor himself rather than the action. If these distinctions are valid, then the evaluation of teaching cannot be equated simply with the evaluation of teachers because the one involves ascribing responsibility to actions rather than to those people who perform them, and the other involves ascribing responsibility to persons rather than to their actions. The distinction is not only important but also one that is almost totally ignored in the dominant accountability systems now emerging in this country.

Perhaps the best way of exploring the relationship between these two evaluative paradigms is by means of an example outlining the potentially different interpretations that could be placed on the statement 'the teacher is responsible for his pupil's failure to reason independently'. This proposition will be examined from the separate perspectives involved in assessing causal responsibility and assessing culpability that were outlined above.

Assessing causes

The statement could be interpreted as implying that a teacher's actions are capable of causally influencing a pupil's performance, in this instance the failure to reason independently. However, the difficulty here is determining the extent to which the actions of a given person, Smith the teacher, can be considered as causally responsible for a particular effect on Brown the pupil. As Feinberg has argued within the context of ascribing causality to actions in general:

Which 'contributor' to an event is to be labelled the cause of that event . . . is always a matter of selection, often an occasion for decision, even for difficult judgement, and is generally 'relative' to a variety of contextual considerations. (Feinberg, 1968, p. 112)

This proposition enables one to proceed with the hypothesis that pupil performance, contrary to the assumptions implicit in many accountability schemes, can be influenced by a multiplicity of factors interacting together.

Which of these factors is subsequently identified as *the cause* is not so much a matter of discovery but rather a matter of selection in the light of contextual considerations. The most fundamental of these is perhaps the relationship between the actions of a teacher and his role responsibilities in a given situation.

In the terms of our example, let us suppose one external evaluator believes teachers to have a responsibility to protect and develop the activity of independent reasoning in their classrooms. Ascertaining pupils to be successful (or not, as the case may be) in this task a teacher would then be expected to proceed to search out ways in which his conduct influences pupils' learning. If, on the other hand, a second evaluator believes the responsibility for protecting and fostering independent reasoning lies elsewhere, then he would be expected to focus his search for causes in another more appropriate direction. However, let us suppose yet a third evaluator believes that for teachers to be responsible for fostering attitudes of punctuality and thrift has utility for society as a whole. What if the teacher does not understand himself to be under such an obligation? Whilst this evaluator (on finding that pupils were unsuccessful in these areas) would search for the cause in the actions of the teacher, the teacher may proceed to argue that his actions cannot be the cause because he is under no obligation to develop such attitudes. Indeed, he may suggest that the cause of this failure is rather to be found in the way parents rear their children and that, as a consequence, the development of such attitudes is the parents' responsibility not his.

We thus have a teaching situation about which different evaluators disagree, not because of the facts, but because of the differing perspectives from which they viewed the particular action in progress. The values of the evaluator are therefore seen as directly impinging upon the activity of attributing causes to particular effects.

Moreover, disagreement about the extent to which a teacher may be held responsible for what happens in his classroom arises not only from the conflicting values of those doing the evaluating but from different beliefs about the range of influence his actions can reasonably be expected to achieve in normal circumstances. Thus, Evaluator A may tend to ascribe causal responsibility to a teacher's actions, if these fail to bring about certain learning outcomes, because he assumes the production of these outcomes is normally within the teacher's powers to control without too much difficulty. On the other hand, Evaluator B may have no such tendency, believing that it is unreasonable to expect this degree of control. At the same time Evaluator B may distinguish between a responsibility for *promoting* certain learning outcomes and a responsibility for *preventing* them. For example, whilst a teacher may not necessarily have a responsibility to develop certain concepts (although he may be obliged to try) one can conceive the possibility of his having a responsibility to avoid imposing constraints on the development of these concepts. Such a distinction enables the teacher to fulfil the latter require-ment without responsibility for exerting a positive influence on the develop-ment of the appropriate concept. Thus, one may posit a situation in which pupils fail to develop the concepts, even though the teacher has fully dis-charged his responsibilities. The distinction rests on the belief that although it is normally difficult to exert a positive influence on the learning of concepts it is much easier to exert a negative influence.

Assessing culpability

An alternative interpretation of the statement 'The teacher is responsible for his pupils' failure to reason independently' may suggest the concomitant notion that the teacher is to blame for bringing about this failure. For example, 'The teacher indoctrinated the pupil' implies that the teacher is to blame for preventing pupils from reasoning independently. The extent to which people (as distinct from their actions) are considered more or less blameworthy usually involves one of the following grounds (see Feinberg, 1968, p. 102):

a) *The quality of intention expressed by their performance*
   e.g. Teacher A says 'Do you all agree?' in a deliberate attempt to 'pre-vent the expression of divergent ideas'. (Wrong intention)
b) *The degree of care and effort expressed in their performance*
   e.g. Teacher B says 'Do you all agree?' knowing it could 'prevent the expression of divergent ideas'. (Negligence)
c) *The degree of skill displayed in their performance*
   e.g. Teacher C says 'Do you all agree?' in a more or less conscious attempt to protect the expression of divergent ideas but in so doing unknowingly prevents their expression. In other words, what a person intends not to happen in fact happens in consequence of the very method selected to prevent it. (Lack of skill)

Each of these grounds suggests different levels of blame. For example, blame is drastically reduced but not eliminated if a teacher can show that his preventing the expression of divergent ideas was due to lack of skill rather than wrong intention. And obviously, a negligent teacher who brings about defective acts out of a lack of concern for the consequences of his action is less blameworthy than one who brings them about deliberately, but more blameworthy than one who brings them about while trying to prevent them.

It follows that people ought not to be considered as worthy of blame (or praise) merely on the evidence of what happens because this evidence is insufficient to establish the extent to which the person is culpable. Moreover, it is always possible for a person to proffer either a justification or an excuse for what he had done which, if valid, might not merely reduce blame, but remove it altogether. In terms of justification one could argue that, although normally the teacher has a responsibility to avoid bringing about a particular state of affairs, the circumstances in this instance were rather special and required him to take that course of action for the sake of another, overriding, responsibility.

For example, a teacher may argue that although he prevented his pupils from developing their understanding of issues about abortion in society, he felt justified in doing so since it protected some of them from suffering severe emotional disturbance beyond their powers to cope with at the time. Again, a teacher might legitimately argue that, although he normally had a responsibility to avoid bringing about a particular action, there might be special circumstances constraining the nature of the classroom activity. In this latter case the circumstances might not justify his action for the sake of some further overriding principle, but rather they are a plea for the recognition of circumstances restricting his freedom of action. He may, for example, have been an unwilling agent in bringing about a particular effect because of external duress or even physical constraint. Alternatively, it would not be difficult to imagine special factors in the situation making it difficult for the teacher to foresee the ultimate consequences of a named course of action.

Accountability

I shall now try to relate the foregoing analysis of the concepts of evaluation to the concept of accountability. Implicit in this attempt is the proposition that a person becomes accountable to others whenever he is capable of rendering an explanatory account of his conduct if obliged to do so by another deciding to attribute responsibility to him for the consequences of his actions. Such accounts may confirm that he is indeed responsible for the results of his actions, or alternatively constitute an attempt to remove or reduce blameworthiness by showing (either by way of justification or excuse) that in the circumstances he could not be held culpable for what he brought about. Moreover, within accountability contexts the evaluation of a person's culpability should be capable of challenging those excuses and justifications furnished by the person himself.

Teachers thus become accountable to others when they are obliged to evaluate external evaluations of their culpability: 'Calling to account' specifies an evaluative paradigm within which a person participates in the process of evaluating the extent to which he is blameworthy. Here I am not necessarily arguing that external evaluation always calls teachers to account, for one can clearly blame teachers without giving them the right of reply. I am simply asserting that the concept of accountability implies the right to self-evaluation. The concept thereby specifies a fair procedure since teachers are in a good position to evaluate their culpability. They have direct access via introspection to their own intentions in, and beliefs about, the classroom situation. They are in a good position to assess the freedom of action open to them in such situations and it is for these reasons that observers' evaluations must pass the test of the teachers' judgement. (This is not to imply that first-person evaluations are infallible, for people can describe their intentions and situations inaccurately despite their ideal position to do so accurately. Nonetheless, external evaluations employ 'second-order' constructs and this raises problems of interpretation. For example, Shipman (1974) expresses concern that people often have trouble recognizing themselves and their activities in reports written about them, and that external reporters should worry about this more than they do.)

What then is the relationship between the concept of accountability and the assessment of the consequences of teaching? If teacher accountability means that a teacher is able to provide an explanatory account of his activities when obliged to do so by a challenge, then it is worth looking in more detail at the procedures by which accountability is established. First, the challenger must establish a reasonable *prima facie* case to which to ascribe blame. This will involve, at least in part, an accurate assessment of whatever consequences flowed from the teacher's actions in the situation. If culpability is based on an inaccurate assessment then an obligation to answer is not established, for a teacher may reasonably argue that he is not obliged to account for consequences his actions have not brought about. Second, the ability to render an explanatory account presupposes that the teacher is aware of the consequences for which he is being held culpable, and that a *prima facie* case has been established requiring him to account for them. If the teacher is not consciously aware of the consequences of his actions then he is in no position to explain them to others. The concept of accountability thus implies that both outsider and teacher are aware of the consequences of the latter's actions.

Some limitations of current accountability systems

House (1973) argues that the dominant accountability systems in the USA possess certain shared characteristics:

First there is a small set of prespecified goals. Second some measure of output is established . . . often only one measure like achievement scores. Third, people with good results are rewarded or people with bad results are punished. The output measures are maximised with little concern for limits or side effects.

This model makes four assumptions relevant to the present argument:

a) That teachers have a responsibility to bring about only a limited range of outcomes.
b) That achievement scores can be used to assess the consequences of what teachers do in classrooms.
c) That teachers can be praised and blamed simply on the basis of causal evaluations of the consequences of their actions.
d) That teachers have no rights of participation in evaluations of their culpability.

The first assumption is the subject of a later discussion and therefore I intend for the moment to concentrate on how my previous analysis relates to the remaining three. The assumption that achievement scores provide a reliable indication of teaching effectiveness is demonstrably false, for such tests may assess what pupils have learned or even that they have learned what was intended, but they do not and cannot assess that what has been learned is a result of what teachers do. There are, of course, numerous factors operating in the classroom that influence pupil performance and which are difficult to control (e.g. those related to social background, peer group norms, and school ethos) and recourse to achievement scores alone must fail in an attempt to explain which factors in a given situation are the cause of learning or learning failure.

Robert Stake, in his paper on this topic, is among those arguing that major differences in test scores cannot be explained by differences in teaching method, pointing out the fact that achievement tests were designed as predictors of future academic success rather than measures of teaching effectiveness. However, test scores might be capable of discriminating effective from ineffective teaching if it were true that all classroom situations are easily manipulable by teachers, yet even if this were normally true, which I doubt, it may not be true for particular situations. Therefore, although a particular teacher's pupils scored high on tests, at best this would only make it probable that his teaching was effective. Accountability systems relying on tests mistakenly and conveniently make the assumption that teachers are omnipotent in their classrooms!

A more appropriate way of determining the consequences of teaching may be via case studies of teacher-pupil interactions: in other words, evaluations of teaching are appropriately based on the study of what is actually happening in that teaching situation. As Joseph Schwab (1970) argues, this approach on a large scale:

will require new mechanisms of empirical investigation, new methods of reportage, a new class of educational researchers, and much money. It is an effort without which we will continue largely . . . ignorant of what real consequences, if any, our efforts have had.

In this country such an approach has been pioneered in the sphere of curriculum development by The Schools Council Humanities Curriculum Project, The Ford Teaching Project Unit 2 Research Methods (see p. 89) and The Schools Council Progress in Learning Science Project (see Appendix VII).

Even if assessments of the consequences of teaching were less dubiously based it remains true that ascriptions of praise and blame are not necessarily entailed by such assessments. Current accountability systems assume that teachers are to be held culpable for bringing about learning failure, yet I have argued that blame is only justifiably ascribed if there is evidence of lack of skill, negligence, or wrong intention. The particular circumstances in which a teacher is operating may be such that no amount of good intentions, effort and normal skill would enable him to avoid bringing about certain consequences as a result of his teaching.

Finally, this conflation of consequential responsibility as between the action and the person withholds from teachers the opportunity to excuse or justify the actions they perform. Any genuine concept of accountability must contain the implicit right to such opportunities for it is patently unfair that the administration of rewards and punishments should occur prior to teachers' own self-evaluations. Genuine accountability protects the teacher from the unfair and primitive forms of evaluation those accountability systems described by House appear to embody. He suspects, quite reasonably, in my view, that the motives behind the establishment of so many of these systems is to cut down costs rather than improve teaching effectiveness.

For what are teachers accountable?

We are now in a position to assess the above question concerning the responsibilities of teachers in respect to their pupils.

According to House (1972) the dominant system of accountability in the USA operates with a 'productivity' model. Teachers are praised and blamed for actions which maximize or fail to maximize utility for the most powerful groups in that society. I have already argued that the system described by House does not qualify as a genuine form of accountability on the grounds that it does not involve any evaluation of the evaluation by the evaluated.

Rather it involves an authoritarian and unfair system of evaluation which any genuine form of accountability would rule out. It could of course be claimed that this objection is met by a productivity model of accountability in which the evaluated have opportunities to evaluate the evaluation.

However, I would argue that this is not so, for even if we replaced the criterion of productivity for society's most powerful groups by utility for society as whole, this could never furnish an adequate framework for determining the extent of teachers' responsibilities. The utilitarian approach, as Rawls (1971, p. 26) has pointed out, constructs the well-being of society out of the net balance of satisfactions gained by its members. In as much as the satisfactions of some members of society can be balanced against the dissatisfactions of others it is always possible that the maximization of utility for society can be to the disadvantage of some of its members. For the utilitarian, productivity for powerful groups may well equate with the maximization of utility for society in general.

The utilitarian model of accountability further fails to take into account the requirements of social justice. House (1973) contrasts the 'productivity' model with what he calls the 'responsive' model operating in less dominant accountability systems. The teacher operating within a 'responsive' paradigm has a responsibility to ensure that all concerned benefit from the outcomes of his actions, albeit unequally, and in so doing the requirements of justice are seen to replace those of utility as a criterion of accountability. House (1973, p. 15) argues that the dominant accountability systems in the USA make unjust demands on teachers and quotes the plight of minority groups as an example supporting his case:

For some time many minority groups have been incensed with middle class domination of the school and the lack of response to their needs. This is quite different from a plea for greater productivity. Increased productivity in fact may be incompatible with increased responsiveness. Great concentration on raising achievement scores will make the schools less sensitive to minority communities. Less tangible goals become extraneous.

With House I believe that in any genuine system of public accountability for teachers the requirements of *social justice* rather than the *maximization of utility* should govern teacher evaluation and self-evaluation. As Rawls (1971, pp. 3–4) argues, we know intuitively that:

. . . justice denies that the loss of freedom for some is made right by a greater good shared by others. It does not allow that the sacrifices imposed on a few are outweighed by the larger sum of advantages enjoyed by many. Therefore in a just society the liberties of equal citizenship are taken as settled; the rights secured by justice are not subsequent to political bargaining or to the calculus of social interests.

For Rawls (1971, p. 62), justice demands that:

all social values — liberty and opportunity, income and wealth, and the bases of self-respect — are to be distributed equally unless an unequal distribution of any, or all, of these values is to everyone's advantage.

Injustices are thus defined as inequalities that do not benefit all, and House's 'responsive' mode of evaluation does not therefore demand an equality of response to various groups in society. What is required is preferably a response benefiting all rather than one depriving any, however unequally that benefit might be distributed.

So far I have described and elaborated on House's two models of accountability which I shall now refer to as:

1. Utilitarian Accountability
2. Democratic Accountability

(If the reader wishes to understand the development of my views in this respect he should read 'Putting the judgement back into evaluation', *SAFARI Interim Papers*, No. 2, Centre for Applied Research in Education, University of East Anglia, 1977.)

In my view teachers have a responsibility not to maximize utility for society but to consider the interests of a wide range of social groups, since the narrow range of outcomes measured in current accountability systems reveals them to be not only unfair to teachers but also socially unjust.

However, even this model of *democratic accountability* as it stands is inadequate if it appears to ignore the teachers professional freedom to pursue educational ideals and values, and implies total dependency on the values of the wider society. In the past society has recognized the right of teachers to be professionally accountable to their peers for intrinsically educational values like 'the development of rationality and a concern for truth' (see Sockett, 1976). This right has given teachers something of the status of a profession. I do not wish to imply that teachers have developed a system of *professional accountability*: merely that society has recognized their right to develop one if they choose. In my view teachers have not strengthened their professional status by neglecting this right. Had they not done so, they would now be in a much stronger position to resist the imposition of *utilitarian forms of accountability*. As House has pointed out, doctors have developed a strong system of *professional accountability* and are thereby able to resist the onslaughts of the current 'accountability' movement in the USA.

In advocating this third *professional model* of teacher accountability I am not arguing for an insular approach. A democratic model can incorporate the professional model in the sense that it acknowledges the freedom of teachers as a profession to pursue their own interests as educators as well as their duty to satisfy the interests of outside groups in society. One could argue that a system which did not bestow this freedom would be socially unjust, for justice requires that a teacher be responsive to the interests of a variety of social groups including those of his own profession. Such a system requires that the teacher does not pursue his own professional interests in ways which prevent him from protecting and fostering the interests of other social groups, and that he does not pursue the interests of any or all outside groups in ways which prevent him from protecting and fostering educational values like rationality and objectivity. For want of better terminology I will call this model a *democratic-professional* model of teacher accountability, as it clarifies the fact that *just actions* do not require teachers to sacrifice their professional interests and to become totally dependent on the interests of other groups in society.

Within a *democratic-professional* system of accountability teachers can be called to account not only for failure to maximize utility for a particular group or society as a whole but also for failure to protect a plurality of interests in society including those of their own professional group. Justice therefore requires that teachers evaluate the outcomes of their actions in the light of the interests of a variety of social institutions and groups.

TOWARDS A METHODOLOGY OF SELF-EVALUATION

Self-monitoring

In this section I shall attempt to outline a theory of method for self-evaluation within a democratic-professional system of classroom accountability. The ideas will be largely based on my work with Clem Adelman in the Ford Teaching Project (Elliott and Adelman, 1976), but will also draw on the experience of others in the fields of classroom research and teacher education. The Ford Teaching Project was an attempt to help 40 teachers in 12 East Anglian schools to develop their competence at self-monitoring in the classroom. In self-monitoring the teacher becomes aware of the consequences of his actions and the extent to which he can be held responsible for them by reflecting about his practice. Self-monitoring not only implies self-evaluating one's responsibility for what happens to pupils but doing so objectively. Inasmuch as self-monitoring implies objectivity it involves the teacher overcoming subjective obstacles to giving accurate accounts of his actions.

Let us look briefly at the relationship between self-monitoring and accountability. By self-monitoring a teacher is able to evaluate accurately whether he brings about the sort of consequences others might hold him accountable for, and whether they would have a reasonable *prima facie* case for imputing responsibility and ascribing blame. In this way he not only monitors his accountability by assessing the consequences of his actions, but places himself in a position to render an explanatory account when challenged to do so.

Stages in self-monitoring

It is possible to view the self-monitoring process in terms of three logical stages:

1. Identifying those actions which are performed directly at will rather than indirectly via the consequence of some prior action, e.g. 'asking a question' as opposed to 'eliciting information'.
2. Assessing the consequences of those actions one performs directly.
3. Assessing one's culpability for the consequences of one's actions, e.g. the extent to which one can be blamed for what happens to pupils.

How then can a busy teacher set about the task of self-monitoring through each of these stages? I say busy, because we must remember that the primary task of teachers is to 'bring about learning'. Therefore the methods of self-monitoring adopted must help rather than hinder the performance of this task. Such methods should help teachers select from the mass of data available that which is most relevant to assessing their accountability.

Self-monitoring direct actions

Teachers should initially try to monitor those direct actions which are likely to influence pupils' performance. In order to select such actions it is not necessary actually to determine their outcomes. There are *prima facie* reasons why some kinds of actions rather than others are likely to exert a marked influence on pupil performance. Goldhammer (1969, Chapter IV) in his work on the 'Clinical Supervision of Teachers' and the Ford Teaching Project used similar criteria. The following are perhaps the most important for purposes of self-monitoring:

1   Frequency of recurrence
The teacher should select persistent and recurring elements in his conduct. These *patterns* are most likely to reflect the salient features of an enduring persistent 'self'. Pupils' responses to teaching will be very much influenced by their knowledge over time of persistent tendencies in their teachers' conduct. For example, if a teacher changes topic very infrequently during discussions they will feel freer to bring him back to the point they want to discuss than

if he changes topic frequently. Isolated elements of conduct express less stable aspects of a teacher's 'self' and are therefore more changeable than frequently recurring elements. It is the least changeable aspects of the 'self' expressed in frequently recurring elements which are bound to have the biggest impact on pupil learning. Frequent repetition over time has cumulative effects so that the influence of later actions will be greater than that of earlier actions within the same category. In selecting actions against this criterion the teacher develops a view of his own personal identity over time. The greater this knowledge of self extending into the past, the greater will be his capacity for objectivity in the present. Such knowledge makes it difficult for a teacher to escape from the realities of his present behaviour. It enables him to anticipate tendencies to behave in certain ways so that he will find it difficult not to look for them in his present conduct. When a teacher becomes aware of patterns in his behaviour this provides guidelines for future self-monitorings.

2   *Normative significance*

Patterns which proximate to norms of behaviour among the teaching profession or certain sections of it are more likely to influence pupil learning than patterns which are relatively unique to individuals. The cumulative effects of collectively salient acts will *prima facie* be far greater than patterns which are relatively unique to particular individuals.

For example, a teacher who engages in a question-posing rather than a didactic pattern of teaching is unlikely to foster independent learning markedly if the vast majority of his pupils' past and present teachers have collectively reinforced in them dependent attitudes through didactic teaching.

3   *Theoretical significance*

Patterns which are significant in terms of a theory of teaching are prima facie more likely to influence pupil performance than patterns which have not been found to be of theoretical interest. For example, in 'Flanders Interaction Analysis' the categories 'direct' and 'indirect' are claimed to be significant for pupil performance (see Flanders, 1969). Advocates of discovery methods claim that the categories of 'explicit indication' and 'implicit indication' of objectives is significant (see Nuthall and Snook, 1975). The Humanities Curriculum Project claimed that 'giving opinions' and 'refraining from giving opinions' is significant. Generalizations and statistical correlations derived from educational folklore and research can all be utilized to pick out patterns which are strong candidates for causal appraisal of outcomes.

4   Structural significance

It is usually possible to detect a super-ordinate pattern which picks out the structurally significant features found in a number of subordinate patterns. By structurally significant features I mean features of the primary aims expressed in the sub-patterns. For example, Ford Project Teachers tended to subsume their patterns of direct action under either of two bipolar categories labelled *structured – unstructured*. These labels picked out two different sorts of structure in the teaching. Structured acts of teaching expressed aims related to the products of learning. Unstructured acts expressed aims related to the manner in which pupils learned. If you like, one category picked out product objectives and the other process values.

Patterns which are related together in terms of some category of structural significance are likely to exert a collective influence on pupil performance which is far greater than isolated patterns.

Perhaps the most important criterion of those mentioned above is that of frequency or patterning. But the more additional criteria a pattern satisfies, the greater the confidence one can place in its causal significance. The collective application of these criteria enables a teacher to monitor his actions selectively and economically so that in applying them he focuses awareness on those actions which are most likely to exert an influence on how pupils perform.

Criteria for teachers' self-monitoring the consequences of their actions

In order to self-monitor consequences a teacher needs to assess the causal significance of the patterns of direct action he identifies. For example, he may discover that constantly switching the topic of discussion results in pupils being unable to develop their ideas in depth.

As I suggested earlier, not all possible states of affairs in the learning situation can be described as outcomes of teaching. Assessments of the causal significance of teaching patterns are relative to the teachers' responsibilities to foster or prevent some outcomes rather than others. Such responsibilities furnish criteria for selecting relevant outcomes of teaching patterns from the mass of data available. It is therefore important for a teacher to clarify what his responsibilities are in the teaching situation (see Downie et al., 1974, Chapter V).

Within the democratic-professional model of accountability responsibilities fall into two main clusters. First, there are a teacher's responsibilities to foster and protect those distinctively educational values for which he can be held accountable by his professional peers. Secondly, there are responsibilities to produce outcomes which benefit all groups within the larger society. I argued that outcomes which benefited members of a particular interest group should meet the overall requirement of social justice, i.e. should not deprive members of other groups.

Thus a teacher needs to know what possible outcomes of his actions might deprive his various audiences in society and what educational values define his professional responsibilities as an educator. In other words, he needs to help his audiences spell out as precisely as possible what their interests are. These criteria then provide him with a method for evaluating the consequences of his actions. Later I shall describe a method for clarifying these criteria. Meanwhile I should like to suggest a set of criteria for monitoring one's responsibility as an educator for fostering and protecting distinctively educational values.

During the course of the Ford Project it became clear that teachers' judgements on one another's performance were using criteria closely connected to 'self-directed learning'. They argued that as educators their teaching ought to aim at 'enabling independent reasoning' in pupils. Teachers did not claim that this should be their only aim, but simply that they should not pursue other goals at its expense. Moreover, there seemed to be an important difference in kind between these other goals and 'enabling independent reasoning'. The former referred to developing knowledge and skills as a result of learning. The latter didn't easily fit into the category of a learning outcome or product, but appeared to pick out the way in which pupils learned rather than what they learned. Rather than merely establishing their beliefs or acquiring skills on the authority of the teacher, the pupil did so on rational grounds by reasoning out why a belief was true or why a particular method was likely to get the best results.

It was R. S. Peters (1968) who first suggested that 'educational aims' embodied clusters of values and principles of procedure specifying not so much the content of teaching, but the manner in which this content was learned and transmitted. In other words, 'aims' specified criteria for what was to count as an educationally valuable process of teaching and learning. Peters contrasted such 'aims' with intended learning outcomes of educational processes which may not be in themselves intrinsic values of education.

The views of Peters were first used in practical curriculum design by Lawrence Stenhouse, the director of the Humanities Curriculum Project. Stenhouse (1969), writing about his design of the project said:

We adopted a research plan based upon the specification of a procedure of teaching which should embody the values implied in the aim in a form which could be realized in the classroom. This means that the changes which we specify are not changes in terminal student behaviour but in the criteria to which teachers work in the classroom. These changes are defined by enunciating certain principles of procedure or criteria of criticism which are expressions of the aim. They are, if you like, specifications of a form of process.

From a logical analysis of the aim of 'understanding controversial issues' Stenhouse and his team derived that notorious principle of 'procedural neutrality' as well as others, including the less notorious 'protecting divergence' (see Pring, 1973).

It is my view that the objectives versus principles of procedure debate posits a false dichotomy between two conceptions of aims. It is valuable in as much as it highlights an important distinction between two ways of talking about education. But these two ways of talking are not necessarily inconsistent with one another. The distinction gives us a perspective for exploring the relationship between teachers' responsibilities to the larger society and their peculiar responsibilities as educators. The various kinds of knowledge and skill they are obliged to foster through learning are determined by conceptions of the instrumental value of education within the larger society. On the other hand, teachers' obligations to foster and protect such values as 'rational autonomy', 'a concern for truth', and 'independent reasoning' in the process of achieving socially valued knowledge are determined by professional conceptions of the educational process itself. Such conceptions refer to the manner in which socially valued knowledge and skills should be learned and transmitted. Distinctively educational aims impose limitations on the extent to which teachers ought to control pupils' thinking in the pursuit of socially valued knowledge.

The assumption that teachers can clarify their teaching responsibilities by breaking their aims down into more precise specifications of learning outcomes is somewhat misconceived when the aims refer to values and principles of procedure regulating the teaching—learning process. So, in the Ford Teaching Project we tried to help our teachers clarify their idea of 'enabling independent reasoning' by analysing the educational values and procedural principles it implied. We hoped that this analysis would help teachers understand their responsibilities to protect and foster distinctively educational values.

The aim was analysed first into the educational values which must be realized if pupils are to 'reason independently'. These values specify the freedoms or rights pupils ought to exercise in the learning situation:

(a) To identify and initiate their own problems for inquiry.
(b) To express their own ideas and develop them into hypotheses.

(c) To test their ideas and hypotheses against relevant evidence.
(d) To defend rationally their own ideas, and to submit the ideas of others, to reasoned criticism. (Freedom of discussion)

In order to exercise these freedoms two sets of conditions may be necessary. First, pupils must be free from external constraints on their exercise. In other words, certain negative freedoms from constraints are necessary conditions of exercising the positive freedoms listed above. Secondly, the existence of these negative freedoms may not be sufficient to enable the exercise of the positive ones. Pupils must also possess certain intellectual capacities to exercise the latter. They may be free from constraints, for example, on the expression of ideas but still unable to express them because they lack concepts in which to express ideas. The first set of conditions we called *extrinsic enabling conditions* and the second set *intrinsic enabling conditions.* It follows from this that a teacher aiming to 'enable independent reasoning' is under a moral obligation to implement certain principles of procedure requiring him to refrain from imposing constraints and to attempt those indirect actions which foster pupils' intellectual capacities.

Negative principles refrain from

1. preventing pupils from identifying and initiating their own problems.
2. preventing pupils from expressing their own ideas and developing their own hypotheses.
3. restricting pupils' access to relevant evidence and drawing their own conclusions from it.
4. restricting pupils' access to discussion.

Positive principles help pupils

5. to develop the capacity to identify and initiate their own problems.
6. to develop their own ideas into hypotheses that can be tested.
7. to evaluate evidence in the light of its relevance, truth and sufficiency.
8. to learn how to discuss.

The values specify those conditions of learning which teachers have an educational responsibility to bring about. The principles of procedure specify those indirect actions the teacher has to refrain from or perform in order to implement these conditions. They therefore furnish criteria for monitoring consequences of teaching and determining the extent to which his responsibilities as an educator have been met.

Our analysis was not based solely on armchair reflection. It was performed in the light of: (a) discussions with teachers about the values and responsibilities encapsulated in their conception of 'aims'*, and (b) a study of the criteria applied in teachers' judgements about their own and other peoples' classrooms. This empirical information allowed us to test our logic against the practical logic of our teachers and vice versa.

Self-monitoring the consequences of teaching

It is one thing for a teacher to know what consequences he has responsibilities to avoid or attempt, but quite another to monitor the extent to which such responsibilities have been met. In other words, he may know the criteria but be unable to apply them to his own actions. In the Ford Teaching Project we found this a major difficulty with our teachers. How, for example, does one monitor the extent to which one has 'prevented pupils from expressing their own ideas'? The problem is largely one of having access to the relevant evidence. Test situations do not furnish such evidence because they do not provide information about how teaching actually influences what is learned and how it is learned. The fact that pupils are able or not able to demonstrate their learning in test situations says nothing about how the teacher influenced either the content or process of their learning. How does a teacher get access to this sort of evidence?

It might be argued that pupils' responses to teachers' actions can be inferred from evidence of observable behaviour. For example, there will be behavioural indications if pupils are 'prevented from expressing their own ideas'. The teacher should observe pupils' overt responses to his actions. As an example, the teacher frequently says 'Do you all agree?' and pupils frequently reply with silence. Can one infer from this that the teacher 'prevents pupils from expressing their own ideas'? This interpretation assumes: (a) that silence for pupils means 'we are not free to express our own ideas', and (b) that pupils understand the teacher's statement to mean 'you had better agree with that'. But suppose the pupils interpreted the teacher's meaning as 'I am trying to find out what your ideas are on this issue', in which case the response 'we are not free to express our own ideas' is rendered less intelligible as an interpretation of silence. A more plausible interpretation would be 'we do not have any ideas on this issue'. How pupils interpret an action places

* For excerpts from some of these discussions read *The Language and Logic of Informal Teaching* (see p. 89).

certain logical limitations on what can count as an intelligible response to it. It is only if one's assumptions about pupils' interpretations of actions are correct that one is likely to infer the meaning of their responses accurately.

If teachers and pupils are agreed about how the former's actions are to be interpreted — so that certain overt behaviours constitute typical expressions of intent or meaning — then teachers may be able to make accurate inferences from pupils' overt responses. Thus, if 'Do you all agree?' typically means for both teachers and pupils 'I am trying to find out what your ideas are.', then it is likely that silence can be accurately interpreted as 'We don't have any ideas on this issue'. However, if saying 'Do you all agree?' typically means for the teacher 'I am trying to find out what your ideas are.' and for the pupil 'You had better agree with me.', then the former is likely to misinterpret the silence, and thereby describe incorrectly the consequences of his actions as 'exposing ignorance' rather than 'preventing the expression of pupils' ideas' (albeit unintentionally). In the circumstances, the latter is likely to be the more accurate description.

In the Ford Teaching Project teachers frequently made inaccurate assessments of the consequences of their actions because they too easily assumed that pupils shared with them the same rules for interpreting teacher behaviour (see *The Stranger in the Classroom*, ref. p. 89). In order to self-monitor the consequences of their actions teachers require access to pupils' interpretations and the meanings of the pupils' behaviours, as well as to observable data. But how is access gained? The answer is simply 'via pupils' own accounts of their responses'. The pupils after all are in the best position to know the meanings of their behaviours and how they are related to interpretations of what teachers do. Honest accounts from pupils provide evidence for self-monitoring by the teacher of the consequences of his actions.

Of course, one has to face the fact that pupils' accounts are not necessarily reliable. They may either consciously or unconsciously distort their accounts in order to present the teacher with a false view of his behaviour. When we asked teachers in the Ford Project to elicit pupils' accounts for themselves we found that pupils normally tended to ascribe to the teacher the sort of identity they believed he wanted. They would do this either because they liked him and did not want to hurt his self-image, or because they feared his reactions to criticisms of his performance.

I have cited two ways in which teachers can get access to the interpretations and meanings which need to be understood to self-monitor consequences of teaching. One is via observation of pupil performance and the other via pupils' introspective accounts. The teacher needs constantly to check his own accounts of the consequences of his actions against those of his pupils.

However, both the teacher's observations and, as I suggested previously, the pupils' accounts may be unreliable. Pupils' accounts may be coloured by their feelings and fears about the teacher. Teacher's observations may be severely distorted by their tendency to ignore that which suggests a gap between the values they profess and their practice.

The latter can be countered to some extent by the use of observers. Such people are, by virtue of their detachment from the action, in a better position to observe behaviour accurately. The teacher can therefore check his own observations against those of the observer. For example, it has been my experience that teachers tend to overestimate the extent to which pupils contribute to class discussions. An observer is in a position to chart who contributes and to what extent, and feed these observations back to the teacher. The observer is also in a good position to check whether or not the observational data cited by pupils exists. For example, if pupils argue that the teacher was repeatedly 'asking for agreement' by saying 'Do we all agree?' the observer is able to check the extent to which this overt behaviour recurred during a lesson. So a teacher can get access to the evidence he requires to assess his own responsibility for consequences by using pupils' and observers' accounts of what is going on.

In the Ford Teaching Project we tried to get teachers to check their own accounts of their actions against the accounts of pupils and observers. We called this method *triangulation*.* The method rests on the view that each party — the teacher, the pupils, and the observer — is in a special position. The teacher is in the best position to know 'what he means' by what he does. The pupils are in the best position to explain how they responded to the teacher's actions. The observer is in the best position to collect accurate data about the observable features of both the teacher and pupils' conduct. From our experience it is possible to use triangulation material to check the objectivity of teachers' accounts, using the following guidelines:

1   The accuracy of a teacher's account should be doubted if the observer disputes the observable evidence cited in support.
2   The accuracy of a teacher's account should be doubted if the pupils dispute his interpretation of their behaviour.
3   The accuracy of a teacher's account should be doubted if it implies no gap between his professed values and his practice and is confirmed by pupils.

The last criterion stems from the fact that teachers will tend to distort

* For a general account of the role and function of triangulation in the study of social action read pp. 235–238, Chapter XI, in Harré, R. and Secord, P. F.

their own accounts in order to place their actions in a favourable light, and pupils will tend to avoid accounts which are critical of teachers (in their presence). The three criteria together suggest that one may place highest confidence in accounts which imply a gap between aspirations and practice, and are confirmed by observers and pupils.

Something needs to be said about the role of the observer in the triangulation. In the Ford Teaching Project his job was to help teachers monitor their own behaviour and its consequences in the classroom. In constructing accounts of behaviour and consequences the observer used teachers' rather than his own conceptions of their role responsibilities. He also tried to avoid ascribing praise and blame in the way he constructed accounts from his observations. In other words he tried to produce accounts which were neutral with respect to whether the teacher was culpable — had brought about certain outcomes intentionally or unintentionally, with care and effort or negligently, skilfully or unskilfully. Consider the following hypotheses developed from observations of Ford Project teachers:*

(i) *Changing topic*
When teachers change the topic under discussion they may prevent pupils from expressing and developing their own ideas, since pupils tend to interpret topic changes as attempts to get conformity to a particular line of reasoning.

(ii) *Positive reinforcement*
Utterances like 'good', 'interesting', 'right', in response to ideas expressed by pupils can prevent the expression and discussion of alternative ideas, since pupils tend to interpret such reinforcement as attempts to legitimize the development of some ideas rather than others.

(iii) *Selective critical questioning*
When teachers ask critical questions of some pupils rather than others they may prevent the former from developing their ideas, since such questions will tend to be interpreted as negative evaluations of the ideas expressed.

(iv) *Leading questions and statements*
Questions and statements containing information about the answer the teacher 'has in mind' may prevent pupils from developing their own ideas since they will tend to interpret such acts as attempts to constrain the direction of their thinking.

* For a full list of these hypotheses see Unit 3 of the Ford Teaching Project publications (see p. 89).

(v) *Inviting consensus*
When the teacher responds to pupils' ideas with questions like 'Do you all agree?', 'Anyone disagree with that?' he will tend to prevent the expression of divergence because pupils will interpret such questions as attempts to impose a consensus view.

(vi) *Question/answer sequences*
When the teacher always asks a question following a pupil's response to his previous question, he may prevent pupils from introducing their own ideas. They may interpret such patterns as attempts by the teacher to control the input and sequencing of ideas.

(vii) *Introducing factual information*
When teachers themselves introduce factual information, either in verbal or written form, pupils may be prevented from evaluating it, since they will tend to interpret such inputs as attempts to persuade them to accept the veracity of the information.

(viii) *Not inviting evaluation*
When teachers do not invite pupils to evaluate the information they are studying pupils will tend not to criticize it because they interpret the situation as one in which the teacher does not want criticism.

These hypotheses are about the observable behaviours of the teacher. They concern outcomes which are relevant to the values the teachers professed and possible explanations of how pupils come to respond in the ways cited, i.e. via their interpretations. But, none of these hypotheses about defective actions necessarily ascribe blame. A teacher in changing topic may be trying to prevent the development of pupils' ideas or he may be doing so quite unintentionally. If he does so unintentionally he may have predicted the possibility of this outcome but made no attempt to safeguard against it (negligence), or he may have tried his best but failed. If he had tried his best but had failed to control the outcome which was normally controllable, he may be blamed for lack of skill. But none of these kinds of culpability is implied by the hypothesis on 'topic changing'. By generating such hypotheses observers can describe the teaching without implicitly or explicitly ascribing praise or blame. The teacher can then use them to check his own accounts. If the hypotheses give the teacher reason to doubt the accuracy of his own account he can try to resolve the discrepancy by checking the observer's interpretations and inferences against transcripts or recordings, and pupils' accounts of their interpretations and actions.

Why might an observer restrict his role simply to constructing accounts of teaching behaviour and consequences rather than trying to determine praise and blame? The reason lies in the fact that observers who are aiming to locate moral responsibility for defective acts reinforce tendencies to distort the facts of the situation to escape moral blame. It is only when the objective attitude among teachers is highly developed that such observers are likely to call forth 'answering accounts' based on objective assessments of behaviour and consequences. There are implications here for the development of accountability systems. As we have seen, in accountability contexts, ascribing responsibility presupposes that the teacher is able to recognize an obligation to explain the consequences of his actions. In other words, he is aware that his actions have consequences which require some explanatory account. Thus an accountability context for the determination of culpability is not established unless the teacher is able to monitor objectively the consequences of his teaching.

In an accountability context the evaluator who is concerned to assess culpability has a responsibility to protect the teacher's ability to monitor the consequences of his own actions. Otherwise the context is destroyed. It is difficult for him to exercise this responsibility when the teacher is anxious and defensive in his presence. Our experience in the Ford Teaching Project suggests that self-monitoring consequences may best be developed 'outside' an evaluatory context where the observer aims to assess culpability. Instead, the observer helps the teacher to monitor behaviour and consequences and leaves him free to form his own judgement about the extent to which he is to blame for them. Freed from the feelings of defensiveness and anxiety generated by the prospect of possible disapproval, the teacher is able to look at his own performance more objectively. As a result he will come to recognize consequences for which an observer would be quite justified in calling him to account. When a teacher develops this ability imaginatively to place himself in an accountability context it becomes possible for observers to determine culpability in a way which protects his capacity to self-monitor accurately.

So we must make a distinction between the role of observers 'within' accountability contexts and their role in establishing the conditions which make it possible for teachers to operate in such contexts. In the Ford Teaching Project the central team adopted this latter role. We might label it the role of the 'outsider'* to pick out the fact that the observer operates outside the accountability context he is helping the teacher to establish. We found that people generally associated with this context — headteachers, professional

* Central team members were also described as the 'strangers'. However, the role of the 'outsider' is not quite the same as that of the 'stranger'. The latter can operate 'inside' on an accountability context. What picks him out is not so much being outside the system of praise and blame as that his strong feelings towards the individuals in the classroom might prejudice his judgements.

colleagues, college supervisors, inspectors, and parents – are not the best people to perform the 'outsider' role. Teachers are not easily convinced that such people are operating 'outside' their normal roles. University researchers are more suitable because, rightly or wrongly, teachers tend to view them as outsiders to the system. Within the Ford Project teachers were initially less defensive with central team observers adopting 'the outsider' role than with fellow teachers as observers. Later they became less defensive with other teachers and here there was a marked progression from teachers serving in other schools to colleagues in their own schools. This progression can probably be explained by the greater intensity of competition between teachers in the same school than between teachers from different schools.

The Ford Project tended to move through two phases. In the first phase teachers worked with the 'outsider' as an observer helping them to self-monitor and leaving them to evaluate their moral responsibility for themselves. In the second phase teachers began to use each other as observers within a developing system of professional accountability. The emergence of this second phase did not dispense with the need for the assistance of the 'outsider'. Practitioners and the observers concerned with morally evaluating them will always tend to select and distort their observations to fit their biases towards defence and criticism respectively. The 'outsider's' continuing role is to make his accounts available to both parties so that they can be compared with their own. Teacher-observers in the Ford Project were able to compare their own accounts of a colleague's performance not only with his account but with that of the 'outsider'.

In this second phase of the project the 'outsider' tended to relate to the teacher in a different way from the first phase. Initially when teachers lacked methods for self-monitoring the 'outsider' took many initiatives. He asked for observation opportunities, elicited accounts from teachers and pupils, and supervised checking procedures. In the second phase teachers requested observation, spontaneously produced their own accounts, interviewed their own pupils and the 'outsider', and cross checked accounts.

Self-monitoring culpability

I have already outlined three criteria for self-evaluating culpability; namely, those of intention, care and effort, and skill. What I am concerned with in this section is the question of how teachers can guard against deceiving themselves about the intentions, qualities of will, and degrees of competence expressed in their actions.

Collecting value judgements

Here the teacher gives a variety of audiences independent access to classroom data and uses their judgements of his culpability to check his own introspections. There are ontological reasons why other peoples' judgements of culpability can help in self-evaluation. People construct their moral identities from the evaluations of others rather than introspection alone. If they were denied access to such evaluations or believed they were being constantly deceived by others they would find it impossible to construct any stable moral identity. There are also not unrelated epistemological reasons. (For well argued ontological and epistemological reasons for agents' checking their judgements against those of an audience see Wood (1973), pp. 196–199.) The honest reactions of others serve as a check on self-deception and assist the development of an objective attitude towards oneself. In this respect a teacher's collection of value judgements about himself serve a similar function to triangulation in self-monitoring acts and their consequences.

In adopting this method the teacher takes the initiative in trying to establish an accountability context for his work. He invites various audiences to 'call him to account' by giving them access to his classroom. Seen in this light an accountability system is not something imposed by others, but something he generates from a need to be objective about himself in the classroom.

Within a democratic-professional system of accountability judgements need to be collected from a wide range of audiences: fellow professionals, inspectors, pupils, parents, etc. Judgements from such diverse audiences not only help teachers to check the objectivity of their own accounts but provide data for reflecting about the criteria which ought to govern them. Thus if a teacher is blamed for deliberately 'preventing the expression of ideas' the ascription implies that he ought to refrain from such behaviours. From an analysis of the value judgements collected, the teacher can determine various audiences' conceptions of his role responsibilities.

Within the Ford Teaching Project value judgements about teachers were collected from only two audiences: fellow professionals and pupils. The range of audiences would therefore need to be extended in any highly developed system of democratic-professional accountability. However, the foundations of such a system have, I believe, been established in the project.

Classification methods

How are the various patterns of teacher behaviour to be classified? Teachers need a set of categories for self-monitoring their patterns of behaviour in the classroom. We found that Ford Project teachers already possessed at the beginning of the project sets of shared categories which enabled them to monitor their performance in the light of distinctively educational values. These provided the conceptual basis for a professional system of account-ability. Although the categories were shared, not all teachers used the same terms to label them. For example, some teachers used the term *structured* and others the term *subject-centred* to label things in the same category. So the central team suggested that, for purposes of communication, where the labels were interchangeable only one should be used.

The categories fall into three sets. The first set picks out patterns of teacher influence on the learning situation. Here the crucial distinction is the extent to which teachers' actions prevented pupils from reasoning independently. If they tend to do this then teaching is labelled *formal*. If they tend not to it is labelled *informal*.

The second set classify teachers' primary aims. When aims primarily express preselected learning content, teaching can be labelled *structured*. When aims are not primarily items of pre-selected content teaching can be labelled *unstructured*. Unstructured aims pick out an emphasis on the manner in which pupils should learn rather than on what they learn. They refer to primary intentions to help pupils direct their own learning. Self-directed learning may also be a subsidiary aim within a dominantly structured approach. Structured-unstructured simply label primary aims.

The third set of categories classify teaching methods according to the degree of control attempted over pupils' thinking. *Directed* methods label a high degree of attempted control over pupils' thinking. Pupils' thinking is expected to conform to teachers' preconceived plans. *Guided* methods label a lower degree of attempted control. The teacher tries to exert some positive influence on pupils' thought processes but in doing so is concerned at the same time to protect or foster their powers of self-direction.

The teacher 'guides' when he tries to respond helpfully to problems in the learning situation posed by pupils, e.g. by making suggestions, asking questions, etc. *Open-ended* methods label a very low degree of attempted control over pupils' thinking. They constitute attempts to remove situational constraints on self-directed learning, rather than attempts to exert any positive influence.

The three sets of categories used by Ford Project teachers can be represented as follows:

1. Situational categories	Informal		Formal
2. Primary aim categories	Unstructured		Structured
3. Method categories	Open-ended	Guided	Directed

By combining categories we were able to produce a comprehensive typology which makes it logically if not practically possible to identify ten types of teaching. This typology was not fully developed until after the work in schools officially terminated. It is a development from the schema of types which characterized the range of aspirations held by the project's teachers. This schema is outlined in *The Language and Logic of Informal Teaching*, p. 28. It contained five types but because it defined our teacher's aspirations it ignored the types which their actions might fall under quite unintentionally.

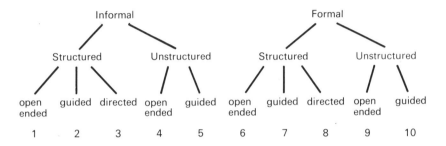

The typology takes into account both intended and unintended outcomes of teachers' actions. Types 3, 6, 7, 9 and 10 indicate gaps between intentions and practice, while 1, 2, 4, 5 and 8 indicate the realization of teacher intentions. Take 7 and 8 as examples of each group. In 7 'structured-guided' indicates an attempt to protect self-directed learning in pursuing pre-selected learning outcomes. The third category 'formal', however, indicates that the attempt failed. In 8 'structured-directed' indicates an attempt to make pupils thinking conform to the teachers' preconceived plans for bringing about pre-selected learning outcomes. The third category 'formal' indicates that the attempt does indeed make pupils' thinking dependent on the teacher (according to the definition of 'formal' given above). Notice that each set of categories in the typology has a hierarchical relationship with the other sets. Methods can be subsumed under primary aims but not *vice versa*. Methods and primary aims can be subsumed under situational outcomes but not *vice versa*.

It is obvious that the categories in the typology are determined by Ford Project Teachers' conceptions of their responsibility to protect and foster independent reasoning in classrooms. The distinctions they make are significant variables with interactions influencing pupils' abilities to reason independently. Thus, the degree to which teachers pursue pre-selected learning outcomes may affect the degree to which they try to control pupils' thinking, which in turn may influence the extent to which the learning situation provides a context in which independent reasoning can take place.

The typology helps teachers to monitor both the consequences of their actions and their culpability for consequences in the light of a particular conception of their professional responsibilities as educators. It enables teachers:

(a) to classify their direct actions under categories which are structurally important, i.e. 'structured-unstructured'.

(b) to classify consequences of teaching which meet or fail to meet their role responsibilities, i.e. 'informal-formal'.

(c) to assess their culpability for consequences by subsuming their actions under a category which picks out the manner in which they were performed, e.g. 'open-ended' and 'guided' pick out desirable intentions while 'directed' picks out undesirable intentions or negligence.

Describing which particular type identifies a given teaching situation will involve all three stages of self-monitoring I have outlined in this paper. Let us take four examples to illustrate this:

1   The ascription of 'informal-unstructured-guided' will involve classifying direct actions (unstructured) and their consequences (informal). Since 'guided' methods can be ascribed to the teacher he can be praised for desirable intentions with respect to consequences.

2   The ascription of 'formal-structured-directed' will involve classifying direct actions (structured) and their consequences (formal). Since 'directed' methods can be ascribed to the teacher he can be blamed for either undesirable intentions or negligence (lack of care) with respect to consequences.

3   The ascription of 'formal-structured-guided' is more complex. The consequences the teacher brings about (formal) are defective but they are brought about unintentionally since the ascription of 'guided' indicates desirable intentions. However, since they may be brought about through lack of care or skill the teacher may not be completely free of blame. The ascription of this type therefore exonerates the teacher from blame in one respect but leaves a question mark about whether some degree of blame can be ascribed on other criteria. Negligence and lack of skill are perhaps more difficult to assess accurately and the open-endedness of the typology in these respects is perhaps, therefore, acknowledgement by teachers of the complexities involved in assessing culpability rather than an indication of its inadequacies.

4   The ascription of 'Informal-structured-directed' must be a rare event. It classifies consequences in terms of desirable features. But the ascription of 'directed' indicates that the teacher is blameworthy for intending undesirable consequences.

I hope I have said enough to indicate how the typology can be used to self-monitor consequences and culpability. It provides, I believe, a conceptual basis for a professional model of accountability. This is certainly not sufficient for what I have called a democratic-professional model. However, implicit in the typology is a strong acknowledgement of responsibilities owed in society. The structured-unstructured dimension indicates the degree to which teachers pursue learning outcomes which are valued in society. The open ended-guided-directed dimension helps teachers to monitor how much control over the production of socially valued knowledge is consistent with protecting independent reasoning. Within the context of democratic-professional accountability the typology helps teachers monitor the extent to which maximizing benefit to other social groups is compatible with meeting their distinctively educational responsibilities.

Implications for the Bennett Report

What I have said in this section has certain implications for any critical assessment of the controversial Bennett Report on *Teaching Styles and Pupil Progress*. Bennett (1976) classified teaching styles into three main types: informal, formal, and mixed (between formal and informal). He argued that 'The effect of teaching style is statistically and educationally significant in all attainment areas tested'. The attainment areas largely fall within what can loosely be called 'basic skills', namely, reading, mathematics, and English (grammar). He concluded that in all three areas pupils of informal teachers progress less than those of formal teachers, and in reading less than of both formal and mixed teachers. The differences claimed in performance between formally and informally taught pupils were very large indeed, ranging from three to five months in reading and mathematics, and four to five months in English.

If valid, such results should indeed cause grounds for deep concern among informal teachers. However, some differences in progress in learning skills between formal and informal teachers should be expected, and I would claim will be expected by teachers themselves. The fact that informal methods are not so efficient as formal methods in maximizing skill acquisition is only a reason for ascribing blame from the utilitarian standpoint that the ends alone justify the means. But this very standpoint is itself rejected by the informal teacher who is unwilling to use means which fail to protect the ability of the pupil to reason things out for himself. If the informal teacher faces the alternatives of maximizing progress in terms of the products of learning or protecting the rational autonomy of the pupil, his values require him to sacrifice efficiency at the former for the sake of the latter. Bennett's research is based on the assumption that efficiency in maximizing learning outcomes is the only criterion against which to evaluate teaching. He therefore compares and contrasts two teaching approaches against a criterion which is only wholly acceptable to the practitioners of one approach (the formal). He evaluates the informal teacher against the formal teachers' standards alone. His research lacks any understanding of, and sensitivity towards, the educational stand-point of the liberal progressive movement within the teaching profession. It is perhaps significant that his 'subjects' were given no 'right of reply' prior to the publication of his report.

Nevertheless, Bennett's results should still give informal teachers grounds for concern. One wonders if such a gap in basic skill development is necessary in order to protect the rational autonomy of the child. I believe it is not, and that the major problem for classroom research lies not so much in evaluating the differences between informal and formal approaches as in evaluating the differences that exist between different types of informal teaching. Unfortun-ately, Bennett's typology of teaching styles, even in its original form of categorization into twelve types, masks the latter differences. In other words it is too crude to deal with the problem. His research design is based on the assumption that a single teaching variable (i.e. informality — formality) is of greater significance than the interaction between a number of teaching vari-ables. However, at the end of his report he comments:

It therefore seems to be curriculum emphasis and organisation rather than classroom organisation factors such as seating, grouping, and degree of move-ment and talk, which are crucial to pupil performance.

He comes to this conclusion from reflecting on the fact that one informal teacher in his sample defied the general trend and achieved the best results. The one 'successful' informal teacher, from Bennett's account, seems to me to fall into the informal-structured-guided type in the Ford Teaching Project typology. It was our experience that few teachers implemented this type of teaching. It requires a teacher to reconcile his accountability to society with the humanistic values of liberal education in difficult circumstances such as high teacher-pupil ratios, and therefore demands the highest degree of skill. I suspect that many of Bennett's informal teachers adopted the easier and less skilful approaches of informal-unstructured-open-ended or informal-unstruc-tured-guided which sacrifice accountability to society for accountability with respect to the values of a liberal education. The latter approach does require a high degree of skill as well, but with respect to a method for achieving a single aim (protecting and fostering rational autonomy) rather than with respect to a method for achieving two distinct sorts of aims as is the case with informal-structured-guided.

For me the implication of the report is a call for better in-service training for informal teachers and not for a reversion to formal methods. Bennett is not unaware of this as a possible implication. He refers to 'the possibility that the results may not reflect badly on informal methods themselves, but on the way these methods are put into practice . . . It seems generally accepted that to teach well informally is more difficult than to teach well formally . . . The education of teachers, like the education of children, would seem to need much closer examination.'

It is a pity that Bennett's failure to pinpoint the significant teaching variables prior to his research has resulted in this lack of clarity about how to interpret his results. It only helps to intensify the unproductive polarization which exists between traditionalists and progressives. The Ford T typology which was developed with teachers suggests that the differences of approach between informal teachers are as significant for pupil progress in the basic skills as the differences between formal and informal teachers. Bennett's emphasis on similarities between informal teachers masks the significant differences between them. He should have spent more time studying teachers' perspectives prior to designing his research. Drawing their intuitive understandings of classrooms together, which incidentally he pours scorn on at the beginning of his report, would have helped him to develop more sophisticated ways of categorizing the complexities of teaching. In turn this greater sensitivity to complexities would have resulted in less ambiguous interpretations of findings and I suspect would also have promoted greater dialogue between traditionalists and progressives. After all it is this dialogue which is required in any professional—democratic accountability procedure.

SELF-MONITORING TECHNIQUES

In the previous section I tried to move towards a methodology of self-evaluation for teacher accountability. In this final section I shall describe some techniques for implementing the methods described.

Keeping field notes

The technique of keeping field notes is essentially a way in which teachers can continuously record their accounts of their actions. Notes should be made as soon as possible after action has occurred. The greater the time lapse, the more difficult it will be to reconstruct accurately. Memory distorts over time and teachers tend to forget or repress what has happened.

During a lesson time is very limited for making notes, and it is important that the teacher's anxiety to write things down does not interfere with the requirements of teaching. However, during any lesson there are hiatuses which provide an opportunity for making notes. For example, a teacher may during the course of a classroom discussion gradually become aware of his tendency to interrupt a pupil whose views he strongly disagrees with. Not too much lapse in concentration is needed for him to note that:

10.30–11.00   Interrupted Bob J. at least six times when he was trying to argue for reform of the abortion laws.

After the lesson, or at the latest during the evening of the day on which it was given, the teacher can organize, expand and add the notes made during the lesson.

Frequently during the Ford Project we observed teachers checking their actions in 'mid course', an indication that they were beginning to self-monitor. But on interviewing the teachers later, many were unable to recall these moments of awareness. Field notes are an aid to this end. They allow a teacher to reflect about his past 'self', and thereby make plans for modifying its expression in future action. Fred Walton, a Ford Project teacher who constantly used this technique, summed up its value as follows: 'Broadly speaking the field note book provides evidence which helps me to make informed judgements in the classroom. This enables me to formulate strategies which will bring about a desired change.' (Bowen et al., Ford Unit 2, p. 21.)

Ken Forsyth and John Wood, two teachers also involved in the project, summed up the advantages and disadvantages of field notes as follows (see Bowen et al., Ford Unit 2, p. 35):

Advantages

1. Very simple. No outsider (observer) needed at all.

2. Good ongoing record. Used as a diary it gives good continuity.

3. First-hand information can be studied conveniently in teacher's own time.

4. Acts as an *aide-memoire*.

5. Helps to relate incidents, explore emerging trends, etc.

6. Very useful if teacher intends to write a case study.

Disadvantages

1. Need to fall back on aids such as question analysis sheets, tapes and transcripts.

2. Conversation impossible to report by field notes.

3. Notebook works with small groups but not with whole class. Initially time consuming.

4. Can be highly subjective.

Field notes need refer not only to what the teacher does directly. They can contain on-the-spot evaluations of outcomes on, and observations of, pupil performance. Here is an extract from the field notes of Brian Iredale, another Ford Project teacher, in which the noted significance of teacher talk for pupils leads to him reflecting about the nature and manner of his verbal contributions and their outcomes:

Self
(1) Accused of talking too much on an occasion when the whole session was given to attempts to:

    (i) Go over work-in-progress
    (ii) Review what we have done
    (iii) Reaffirm our aims
    (iv) Agree to simple rules

I reflect that on the many occasions when I talk very little as teacher to class, and as teacher to sub-group within class and to individuals, what is perhaps being referred to is a very concentrated, eliptical and sometimes cryptic way of speaking, exuberant, quick, volatile, impatient of slowness or inattentiveness or disinterest distractingly exhibited. This reduces the effectiveness of much talk-presented data except perhaps when it is put over on a formal occasion — but how? How does it come about that sometimes in speaking to whole or sub-groups, it fails through such factors and class attentiveness lapses; at other times class attentiveness is high. Yet how much is taken in on each kind of occasion? Are there some who do take in on 'low' occasions, and some who hardly take anything in on 'high' occasions? (Iredale, 1975, Ford Unit 4, p. 20)

Tape recordings

Recordings capture the data from which one can reconstruct one's actions. Field notes cannot contain what one is not aware of, or what is forgotten or repressed. Recordings are, therefore, valuable supplements to field notes because they can bring about a retrospective awareness of one's actions or help one to recall what has been forgotten or repressed.

    Here is an account by a middle school teacher of her first experience of listening to a tape recording of her lesson:

My first experience of tape recording was very casual. It seemed vaguely like a good idea. I had no specific aims. The play-back of a class discussion was a shattering blow!

I had no idea how much discussion was dominated by me, how rarely I allowed children to finish their comments, what leading questions I asked, and how much I gave away what I considered to be 'right' answers. This experience resulted in my completely rethinking my teaching approach (which I'd always believed was very child-centred), and I taped a series of discussions to record and monitor my own progress. The results were reasonably good. I completely revised my questioning techniques, cultivated non-committal comments and talked less and less. One interesting side-effect was the initial hostility of the class when I withdrew verbal support and refused to 'give away' answers, etc. (Bowen et al., 1975, Ford Unit 2, p. 9)

Some researchers have argued that video and other forms of visual recordings are preferable to tape recordings on the grounds that the latter do not collect the visual data of non-verbal behaviour. However, as Stenhouse (1975) points out, this difference is probably far more important for observers than for the teacher. Teaching is necessarily mainly a verbal activity and the main data will concern speech. An observer may need to place teacher 'talk' in its non-verbal context in order to infer the intentions and meanings it embodies. But the teacher is in a different position from the observer since only he has access to what he had in mind. The 'talk' recorded is not used as a basis for inference. It simply brings to consciousness the intentions and meanings it indicates. Consequently he has no need of all the data that the observer required for his inferences. The teacher simply needs sufficient data to recall the significance of his actions.

Tape recordings also have possible advantages over video recordings for the self-monitoring teacher. They are less obtrusive and do not require the services of a third party. There are certain problems of tape recording in informal classrooms where pupils are sitting in small groups and the teacher moving among them. However, a cassette recorder with a shoulder strap and microphone, either built-in or attachable to the teacher's body, can go a long way to solving the problem.

Ken Forsythe and John Wood list the advantages and disadvantages of tape recording as follows (see Bowen et al., Ford Unit 2, p. 29):

Advantages	Disadvantages	Notes
1. Very successfully monitors all conversations within range.	1. Buying one!	Acclimatize children to presence of tape recorder.
2. Provides ample material with great ease.	2. Nuisance to carry about.	Be selective over what is transcribed.

3. Versatility – can be transported or left with a group.

3. Transcription largely prohibitive because of time involved.

Advantageous to have a battery operated cassette recorder with built-in microphone.

4. Records personality development (of teacher).

4. Masses of material may provide little of relevance.

5. Can trace development of group activities.

5. Can disturb the children; can be inhibiting.

6. Continuity can be disturbed by the practical problems of operating.

7. Nothing visual – does not record silent activities.

The ideal use of a tape recorder is to study the recording in conjunction with a transcript. The latter allows the teacher to dwell on particular aspects in depth. Unless he is an audio-typist or has access to one, he will have to transcribe by hand. This is so time consuming that he will need to be very selective in his choice of extracts. Perhaps the least time consuming use is to listen and make a note of those actions which fit all or some of the criteria listed earlier, for example, frequency, structural significance, etc. If there is time a teacher might transcribe by hand examples of the patterns noted down.

Tape-slide recordings

One useful modification to tape recording is tape-slide recording, particularly as a technique for eliciting various audiences' judgements of teachers. Here the 'outsider' takes photographs during a lesson to provide a visual context for the talk recorded on cassette via a radio microphone worn by the teacher. The camera is attached to the cassette recorder via a pulsing device so that, on playback, the recording activates the slides at the appropriate moments. The technique was developed by Clem Adelman (see Walker and Adelman, 1975, pp. 132–134) and was used extensively by observers in the Ford Project. The photographs are taken on a number of criteria related to the techniques function to help audiences make informed judgements about teachers in class-rooms. Walker and Adelman describe these criteria as follows:

... the underlying question in the cameraman's mind is 'What does an out-sider listening to the sound tape recording need to see to understand what is being said?'. The pictures show who is talking to whom, whereabouts, and what objects are being referred to. They chart increases and decreases in listeners and speakers, the introduction of new objects, changes in space use and so on, the rate depending on the fineness of the data that the observer considers may be needed. (Walker and Adelman, 1975, p. 132)

In the Ford Teaching Project the technique of tape-slide recording enabled teachers to carry their classrooms to their audiences. Sometimes tape-slides were shown to fellow teachers, to pupils, and occasionally to parents. Video-tape recordings can also be used for the same purpose, although the necessary hardware is more expensive and less widely available for both recording and playback. Such recordings have one great advantage over direct observation. They make one's teaching accessible to large audiences. Reliance on direct observation limits one's audience to two or perhaps three people.

Normally a teacher's various audiences have great difficulty in getting themselves into a position to make the sort of judgements which establish his accountability. As I argued previously, accountability is only established if the audience is able to make some accurate assessment of the consequences of teaching in the situation. Yet, with the exception of pupils and sometimes a few colleagues engaged in team teaching exercises with him, a teacher's audiences have no direct access to first-hand evidence of his performance. People make judgements on the basis of test and examination results or verbal reports from others who are supposed to have 'inside' information, for example, pupils, heads of department and team teaching partners. The former are generally thought to be more reliable than the latter, but as I have argued a teacher cannot necessarily be held responsible for everything his pupils learn or fail to learn. Blaming a teacher for bad test results can easily involve the self-deception of refusing to acknowledge one's own responsibilities as a parent or colleague for poor performance on the part of the pupils.

Heads and fellow teachers often base their judgements on the reports of those who are closest to the teacher, generally those provided by pupils, and heads of department. Sometimes their judgements are based on evidence of a teacher's public conduct within a school. I have known at least one head and staff group who misjudged a teacher's competence in the classroom because they evaluated him on the basis of his administrative inefficiency on routine school matters.

Parents tend to base their judgements on accounts provided by their children, and the general community from hearsay derived from contact with parents, school staff and press reports claiming to have penetrated the school corridors and classroom walls. The less second-hand the information is the more reliable it is believed to be. Thus pupil reports have recently become a major source of information for the press in its reportage on life in classrooms. In the Ford Project many teachers stated that they feared the judgements of their pupils far more than those of any other audience precisely because they were in the best position to make informed evaluations of their performance.

Within the present system of relationships between teachers and their various audiences, pupils have enormous power because they have access to information everyone wants. Pupils can use their position as 'insiders' to harm their teachers professionally. Although it is true that they are in the best position to know what is going on, it is also true that this position gives them the power to deceive others about their teacher's classroom performance. The reliability of inside informations implies honesty on the part of the insider.

The problem has become so big in schools that a professional code has had to be invented to cope with it. In most schools teachers are required to refrain from questioning pupils about the conduct of other teachers and must not allow pupils' reports to count in their evaluations of their colleagues. In some ways this is unfortunate. As participants in the teaching–learning process, pupils are in an extremely good position to provide reliable information about what their teachers do. What is required is a technique which permits the checking of inside information for bias and distortion. Here independent access to classroom data through tape-slide recordings can be of assistance. Thus, if pupils argue that certain behaviours of the teacher inhibited their learning, their account can be checked at least with respect to whether or not the behaviours cited were actually performed by the teacher.

Taking one's classroom to one's audience changes the balance of power between different audiences in the enterprise of evaluating teachers. No longer does a head and his staff have to rely exclusively on the information provided by those closest to the teacher such as his head of department. Nor do those outside the boundary of the school as an institution have to rely exclusively on the reports of insiders or the press. And, of course, for the honest teacher, classroom tape-slide recordings enable him to appeal to independent evidence in assessing his answerability and constructing his own accounts of his performance. They can, therefore, function to protect him against unfair ascriptions of blame.

The use of tape-slide recordings as a basis for collecting judgements of a teacher's performance not only limits the power of any particular audience to determine the judgements of others, including that of the teacher as his own audience; it also serves as a check on the subjectivity of informants, and the teacher himself. Also, if those with some direct access to his classroom know that the information they provide can be checked against independent evidence, they are more likely to give information they honestly believe to be accurate.

Interviewing

The Ford Project began to develop interviewing as a technique of two-way hypotheses testing. First, the teacher formulates accounts of his actions prior to the interview and then frames questions to his audience which are designed to test these hypotheses against their judgements. During this procedure the teacher refrains from disputing his audience's accounts as they emerge. Any signs of defensiveness on his part will make them nervous about responding honestly. His role is to question, listen, and if necessary seek elaboration and clarification of what is being said. The interview will be focused but open ended in the sense that the teacher will draw his audience's attention to possible patterns in his behaviour but not express explicitly or implicitly his own views about whether his conduct illustrated these patterns or the extent to which he is to blame for them.

Secondly, the audience interviews the teacher. The purpose of this part of the interview is to give the teacher an opportunity to answer the accounts he has elicited from them. The audience's own views will be clear to the teacher so that they cannot hide their judgements. However, the questions asked should again be focused and open ended. They should be focused on what the audience's views are about, and open ended inasmuch as they should express the intention of testing these views by indicating that the teacher is free to disagree with them. The audience should also refrain from arguing with the teacher as his answering account emerges.

This two-way interview helps to establish an accountability context in which the teacher (a) invites his audience to call him to account by eliciting their accounts and (b) answers them through having his own account elicited. The technique protects the teacher from being too threatened by giving him a measure of control through his questions over what his audience says. This may result in a lack of depth and detail in his audience's accounts. But, such as they are, they are likely to be expressed more honestly than those offered to a perceptibly anxious teacher. Even if this is not so honest, accounts which the teacher finds unbearable are unlikely to produce honest replies from him. The technique is designed to get the maximum honesty possible by reducing the level of the teacher's anxiety in front of his audience. The effects I believe are cumulative. If the teacher achieves a measure of objectivity, albeit at the sacrifice of depth and detail on one occasion, he is likely to increase his capacity for objectivity on the next occasion.

These evaluations are particularly important when pupils are the audience. It will be difficult for the teacher to elicit pupils' interpretations and meanings separately from the judgements they imply. Their accounts will provide data of both kinds. Yet we found in the Ford Project that, of all the audiences' judgements, those of pupils were most feared. Also, pupils were usually extremely fearful of the results of honesty about their teachers. Any situation which reduces anxiety for both is likely to produce honesty from both. We found this two-way interview with pupils could only be initiated gradually through the intervention of the 'outsider' who:

(a) Interviewed pupils with the teacher's permission and preferably with some of the teacher's questions in mind.
(b) Allowed pupils to control what was fed back to the teacher.
(c) Chaired the session in which pupils elicited the teacher's answering account.

Where teachers demonstrated through this exercise that they were capable of listening to pupils and admitting the validity of some of their evaluations, they were able to establish their trust and begin to implement the two-way technique without the intervention of the 'outsider'.

Using observers to collect data

Earlier I tried to show how *observable data* collected by observers could be used by teachers to check their accounts of their performance in the classroom. It is therefore important that the data should be collected in a form which the teacher can use. In order to ensure this, it is necessary for the teacher to insist on certain procedures and observation techniques. The following guidelines are adapted from Goldhammer's (1969, 89–90), and Walker and Adelman's (1975, pp. 9–13) work on observation methods in the classroom:

1. The teacher should expect the observer to collect observable data which are relevant to evaluations of his actions in the classroom. Therefore, it is necessary for him to make sure that the observer accepts this task and understands his conception of his role responsibilities prior to observation.
2. The teacher should expect the observer to record in writing the observable data. 'Abstractions and inferences from the data should be bracketed, for example, "Johnny chewed his pencil", "Andrew passed notes to Sally"

should be separated out from the inference "the children seemed bored". If the lesson's pace precludes complete, continuous recording, it is generally better to capture specific episodes in their entirety than to collect otherwise piecemeal and fragmentary notes.

3. The teacher should expect a post-observation conference with the observer in which he has access to the written record and where the observer supports statements like "You used many complex and un-defined technical terms" and "You did all right" with verbatim data. "Get whoever observes your lessons to talk about what they see . . . if neces-sary adopt the stance of the interviewer, asking all the time for instances and examples. Don't let the observer ramble off into anecdotes or un-necessary theory, but keep him/her to the point." ' (Walker and Adelman)

4. The teacher should expect the observer not to interfere with his teaching. 'In the event that children approach him spontaneously with questions, he should explain . . . that his job is to write down what is happening in the class, and the like.' (Goldhammer)

'As an observer it is easy to find yourself "playing teacher", scanning the class and "fielding" all the glances that pupils throw your way. By returning glances and "staring out" pupils the observer can often estab-lish a public image of himself as someone who "knows what is going on", or "has eyes in the back of his head . . ." For most observational purposes it is perhaps best to accept a pupil's glance without staring back. To avoid all eye contact, or to "field" it all, makes you an object of curiosity and highly intrusive.' (Walker and Adelman)

'The observer's physical position in the classroom ought simultaneously to be minimally distractive to the pupils and to provide him with a different vantage point from the teacher's unless, for specific reasons, other arrangements have been made in advance.' (Goldhammer)

'Generally you want to be in a position where you can observe most but intrude least in the activities of the class . . . It is important to avoid coming between people who might want to communicate with each other, or to block access to important resources.' (Walker and Adelman)

The observer will be helped to maintain his role if the teacher clarifies it to the pupils prior to the lesson.

In this paper I have tried to outline both a philosophy and a methodology of self-evaluation which is consistent with teacher accountability in the class-room. In doing so I have tried to pinpoint the inadequacies of what currently pass for accountability systems. Implicit in much of what I have said is the view that a genuine accountability system is something negotiated between the teacher and his audiences. It is a system he freely participates in to support the development of his own self-awareness by checking his tendency to self-deception. As such, an accountability system is not just a way audiences can control what teachers do. It is also an instrument teachers can use to improve their own performance in the classroom.

ACKNOWLEDGEMENTS

In writing this paper I owe a tremendous debt to Hugh Sockett, Barry Mac-Donald, Ernest House and Stephen Kemmis. Hugh and Barry alerted me to the subtle ways in which crude and unjust ideas about teacher accountability were beginning to emerge in this country with increases in centralized political control over our education system. Discussions with Ernest, well known for his attacks on accountability in the USA, made me aware of the need to develop a positive account of teacher accountability. Stephen read the first draft of this paper and prompted me to construct a further draft out of the ashes of his criticisms.

John Elliott, on behalf of Classroom Action Research Network, has given permission for the Ford Teaching materials to be quoted in *Evaluation and the Teacher's Role*. (The Ford Teaching Project publications are listed on p. 89.)

References

Bennett, N. (1976). *Teaching Styles and Pupil Progress*. Open Books.
Clegg, A. (1975). 'Battery Fed and factory tested', *Times Educational Supplement*, 11.7.75.
Downie, R. S. et al. (1974). *Education and Personal Relationships*. Methuen.
Elliott, J. and Adelman, C. (1976). 'Innovation at the classroom level: a case study of the Ford Teaching Project', Unit 28, Course E203. The Open University.
Feinberg, J. (1968). 'Action and responsibility' Chapter VI in *The Philosophy of Action*, ed. Alan R. White. Oxford University Press.
Flanders, N. (1969). 'Intent, Action and Feedback' in *The Nature of Teaching*, ed. Lois Nelson. San Francisco: Blaisdell.

Goldhammer, R. (1969). *Clinical Supervision: Special Methods for the Supervision of Teachers*. Holt, Rinehart and Winston.

Harré, R. and Secord, P. F. (1972). *The Explanation of Social Behaviour*. Basil Blackwell.

House, E. R. (1972). 'The dominion of economic accountability' in *Educational Forum*, November 1972.

House, E. R. (1973). *The Price of Productivity: Who Pays*? Urbana, Ill: Center for Instructional Research and Curriculum Evaluation, University of Illinois (mimeo).

Nuthall, G. and Snook I. (1973). 'Contemporary models of teaching', Chapter 2 in *Second Handbook of Research on Teaching*, ed. R. M. W. Travers. Rand McNally.

Peters, R. S. (1968). 'Must an educator have an aim?' in *Concepts of Teaching*, eds. C. J. B Macmillan and T. W. Nebon. Rand McNally.

Pring, R. A. (1973). 'Objectives and innovation: the irrelevance of theory', in *London Educational Review*, **2**, No. 3.

Rawls, J. (1971). *A Theory of Justice*. Oxford University Press.

Schools Council (1970). Humanities Curriculum Project. *The Humanities Project: an Introduction*. Heinemann Educational.

Shipman, M. (1974). *Inside a Curriculum Project*. Methuen.

Sockett, H. (1974). 'Teacher accountability' in *Proceedings of the Philosophy of Education Society of Great Britain*. **X**, July 1976. Basil Blackwell.

Stake, R. 'Measuring what learners learn'. Urbana, Ill: Center for Instructional Research and Curriculum Evaluation, University of Illinois (undated mimeo).

Stenhouse, L. (1969). 'Controversial value issues in the classroom' in *Values and the Curriculum* (1970). Washington DC: National Educational Association (CSI).

Stenhouse, L. (1975). *An Introduction to Curriculum Research and Development*. Heinemann Educational.

Walker, R. and Adelman, C. (1975). *A Guide to Classroom Observation*. Methuen.

Wood, D. (1973). 'Honesty', Chapter IX in *Philosophy and Personal Relations*, ed. A. Montefiore. Routledge.

FORD TEACHING PROJECT PUBLICATIONS
(Available from the Cambridge Institute of Education, Shaftesbury Road, Cambridge)

Unit 1   Patterns of teaching

The Language and Logic of Informal Teaching
    by John Elliott and Clem Adelman
Primary School 'The Tins'
Primary School Elective Tasks
Primary School Science
'Paper Structures' – Middle School
Social Studies in a Secondary School

Unit 2   Research methods

Support for Research-Based Inquiry/Discovery Teaching
    by Donald Cooper et al.
Ways of Doing Research in one's own Classroom
    by Beris Bowen et al.
Classroom Action Research
    by John Elliott and Clem Adelman
The Stranger in the Classroom
    by John Elliott, Clem Adelman and Karen Sitte, et al.
Three Points of View in the Classroom – generating hypotheses from classroom observations, recordings, and interviews by John Elliott assisted by Dave Partington
Team Based Action Research
    by Len Browning et al.
Self-Monitoring Questioning Strategies
    by John Elliott assisted by Tony Hurlin
Eliciting Pupils' Accounts in the Classroom
    by John Elliott, Clem Adelman and Michael Collins, et al.

Unit 3   Hypotheses

The Innovation Process in the Classroom
    by John Elliott and Clem Adelman
Implementing the Principles of Inquiry/Discovery Teaching: some hypotheses
    by Clem Adelman, et al.

Unit 4   Teacher case studies

A Third-Year Form Tries to Enter a Freer World
    research into ways towards inquiry/discovery working by Brian Iredale
The Castles Group
    by Ken Forsyth
Inquiry/Discovery Learning in a Science Classroom, and *The China Project*
    by Anne Rumsby and Roger Pedler
Question Strategies: A Self Analysis
    by Tony Hurlin
Identifying Problems and Strategies in the Classroom
    by Roger Pols, et al.

4 Organization for learning

David Hamilton and Joan Hickmott

Consider these four examples of organizational change:

1   Craighill Comprehensive School is situated on the outskirts of a large
northern city and serves a mixture of private and public housing. The school
comprises a central three-storey building surrounded by satellite units for
home economics, science and craft. The science department is a one-storey
block made of sixteen laboratories built around a central store, a lecture
theatre, a workshop and a darkroom. When the school was opened the five
science staff were recruited to teach an integrated course to the first two
years. Although the first cohort of teachers was appointed on this basis, none
of them had previously taught together; and only two of them had had any
prolonged experience of integrated science.

2   Hopedale is a comprehensive lower school in the east midlands. Until
1966 the first-year intake had been grouped into classes of different presumed
ability. When the Nuffield O-level schemes were introduced in that year, the
three science teachers found that there was less need to create ability groupings. Using the Nuffield approach, they gradually evolved a science programme
suitable for mixed-ability classes throughout the three years of the school.

3   Hurstmount Primary School was opened in 1967 to cater for the needs
of a growing commuter village in the south of England. By June 1972 a 'bulge'
of 9–11 year olds had reached the top of the school and were timetabled to
be taught as two parallel classes. During the summer holidays various staff
changes had left these children with one full-time and two part-time teachers.
To overcome a possible imbalance in teaching time these three teachers
decided to pool the entire seventy-four children and work alongside each
other as a team.

4   In June 1971 over 400 pupils and 20 teachers moved out of the over-
crowded 19th century village school at Greenholm and began a very different
life in an open-plan primary school built nearby. As none of the teachers had
been to any other open-plan schools, the move was greeted with mixed feelings.

Each of these brief case histories describes the advent of an educational innovation. In all cases these changes represented a radical departure from the *status quo*. Furthermore, unlike other curriculum innovations, these developments were much more than a mere updating of textbooks or the introduction of new syllabuses and equipment. Instead, they foreshadowed a fundamental restructuring of the pedagogy previously employed in these schools. Thus, despite their apparent diversity, these innovations share a common attribute; each one seeks to break down the barriers between, respectively, subjects, pupils, teachers and classrooms.

In many instances innovations like these are described as organizational changes; that is, they are regarded as a framework of practical means rather than a cluster of educational ends. To adopt a communications metaphor, organizational forms are the transducers in the educational system. They act to change one form of energy (aims) into another (pedagogical practice). Clearly, different organizational forms operate in different ways in different settings. To extend the metaphor: some may amplify the original signal, others may have a muting effect. Still others may introduce elements of distortion. In exceptional circumstances, some may even extinguish the signal completely. Although this characterization is an oversimplifcation, it helps to demonstrate the mediating role played by organizational forms. In practice, of course, all three elements (aims, organization and enactment) are inextricably interrelated. Thus, to evaluate an organizational change using educational criteria is also to consider the ideas that fostered its development and the patterns of teaching that it promotes. Above all, such innovations must be studied in the context of the day-to-day life of schools, teachers and pupils. In these terms, then, forms of organization are not abstract entities but crucial components in the realization of educational aims in practice.

This chapter aims to extend these ideas by examining them in the context of contemporary discussions about curriculum evaluation. The first part outlines the reason why curriculum evaluation has begun to look more closely at organizational forms. The second section outlines a series of general evaluation strategies that might be used to examine them. And the third part considers, separately, each of the organizational forms described at the beginning of this chapter.

Throughout, the intention is not merely to indicate questions to address or procedures to pursue. These have a limited use since they are rarely applicable in every situation. Rather, the main thrust of this chapter is to provide the reader with a range of critical probes which can help not only to map out the surface contours of curriculum change, but also to penetrate a little more deeply into the underlying and more uniform bedrock.

EVALUATION AND ORGANIZATIONAL FORMS

In the early and mid-1960's curriculum development in Britain was conducted along accepted and established lines. Groups of experienced teachers and subject specialists were given the task of producing a technology of texts and equipment which, in effect, could carry the new ideas in an unchanged form through the school system. Within this framework curriculum development sought to update the syllabuses already used within the schools and, as a result, paid very little attention to certain other forms of school or classroom organization that were emerging at that time.

Later, however, curriculum development began to take into account these parallel movements and gradually incorporated them into its rationale. In essence, curricula were redefined in broader terms — using new patterns of organization (e.g. non-streaming), modes of learning (e.g. self-paced) and types of assessment (e.g. diagnostic rather than performance tests). One effect of this change in emphasis was a move away from producing materials and teachers' guides as the main agencies of change towards, for example, a greater interest in teacher training (or retraining). By their new but firm focus, these second generation developments also acknowledged the potent influence of teachers and the critical importance of the teaching process.

In its turn, curriculum evaluation has responded to these changes and moved away from a reliance on input—output techniques (cf. pre-tests and post-tests) and, instead, has tried to gain greater understanding of the relationship between organizational forms and the multiplicity of classroom transactions that they generate. In this respect, curriculum evaluation has been forced to consider innovations that have not merely produced, but also encouraged a diversity of process and outcomes. Variety has become the bread of curriculum life, not just the exotic spice.

Is it possible, then, to analyse such outcomes as the move towards mixed-ability teaching in the secondary school or open plan design in the primary school? In most cases they cannot be considered in conventional terms; there are no centrally developed lists of objectives or statements of goals to use as measuring rods. Nevertheless, the merits of open-plan schooling and mixed-ability teaching are still the subject of continuous debate. What, if anything, can be done to unravel the complexity of these phenomena? Has the first generation evaluator any expertise or insight to offer? In line with the overall stance of this book, an attempt will be made to answer this question by suggesting approaches that might be applied to real-life settings by non-professional evaluators.

AIMS AND GENERAL STRATEGIES FOR THE EVALUATION OF ORGANIZATIONAL SETTINGS

Commonplace among the contemporary canons of evaluation is the notion that there are decision makers in education at all levels: from pupils and parents to inspectors, administrators and politicians. While each of these groups has an obvious interest in the organization of schooling, the grounds for their interest may vary. Thus, the possible initiators and audiences of an evaluative inquiry are extremely diverse. They might include parents anxious to select a school for their children, college lecturers seeking up-to-date material to document current practice, advisers interested in the suitability of specific curriculum materials, headmasters planning to restructure the curriculum within their own schools, students searching for a first appointment to match their aspirations, and teachers seeking promotion through posts that have been advertised. All these people, and others, have a practical interest in reaching a heightened understanding of the workings and ramifications of school organization and curriculum change. All of them, too, plan to act upon that information. Clearly, though, the questions posed by such inquiries will differ in important respects since each person will employ different (but overlapping) perspectives.

If the agreed purpose of an evaluation exercise is to construct an information base for decision making, a first useful evaluation task is to penetrate the ideas that fostered the organizational form in its present setting. For example, what were the precipitating factors? Was it set up to address an educational or an administrative problem? As noted above, this material can provide a backcloth against which the organizational form can be examined; that is, it can be assessed against its own criteria. At the same time, however, it is important to remember that the original blueprint may have changed beyond recognition. The fact that a method of organization no longer achieves its initial aims does not necessarily mean that it is failing. New circumstances may have arisen (e.g. a change in catchment area) or hidden benefits may have been uncovered. (Contact with a local college of education may have provided equipment on loan.)

A second strategy is to look for the displacement effect caused by the innovations. As vehicles of change, innovations almost certainly introduce new features into the context of the school, and prompt a range of unintended and unanticipated consequences. For example, open-plan schooling may promote conflict with parents accustomed to traditional forms of organization; the stream of visitors attracted by the glamour of new schemes may make inroads into teachers' preparation time; and teacher turnover within an innovating school may be increased because its staff become attractive to other schools. In some instances, the interruption effects may be short lived. But in certain cases they may have a prolonged impact (e.g. design defects in open-plan schools).

A third general consideration that might underpin the evaluation of organizational forms comes from a recognition that schools are also human institutions. The issues they confront are not merely organizational, economic or educational, they are also human problems to be addressed and overcome. Thus, in aggregate terms, this human factor (typified by differences between teachers) may be insignificant when examined across schools, whereas in individual settings it may loom much larger and swamp the niceties of curriculum change. Consider, for example, the difficulties encountered by schools with a high pupil turnover that try to introduce very idiosyncratic forms of organization requiring lengthy periods of pupil induction. Or consider schools where attempts at bold curriculum change are neutralized by the diffidence of the head teacher. There is, of course, another side to this picture: personal idiosyncrasies may enhance rather than rule out the effects of organizational change. Indeed, in an educational climate that encourages grass-roots development, schools and individuals that 'do not follow the course as suggested' may become the solution rather than part of a curriculum problem.

One final element useful to the evaluation of specific settings is to examine the context which envelops the school. What are the legal, financial and denominational limitations (and potentialities) relevant to the work of the school? How do these penetrate the classroom? How are they linked to the catchment area and its pupils (cf. the difficulty of organizing after-school activities in rural areas where the school bus leaves at 4 o'clock)? What resources are provided by the local education authority (advisers, film library, teachers' centre)? How important is this hidden subsidy? And so on − the list is deliberately left open.

FOUR EXAMPLES

Curriculum integration

The cluster of organizational changes in schools that are commonly known as integrated, inter- or multi-disciplinary curricula usually relate to attempts at realigning or redefining the boundaries of school curriculum. At the minimum this may simply involve a new terminology (e.g. 'combined' science'). More usually it implies a more profound reorientation; deeply rooted and cherished notions about the nature of education are brought into question. For example, the adoption of integrated studies may reflect a belief that the traditional school curriculum is no longer an accurate mirror of the prevailing structure of knowledge. This, in turn, casts doubt on the organization of the timetable, the structure of teacher training, and the criteria used for entrance to higher education. Hence, changes in the organization of learning are something more than a reshuffling of the timetable. Other more potent influences are abroad. What are these factors? How can they be analysed?

First, it is sometimes helpful to establish what, in fact, is being integrated. At what level (or levels) are the aims of integration to be expressed: in the content of the syllabus (physical-chemistry); among the staff or pupils (team teaching, open education for blind children); in the allocation of time and space (the integrated day, open-plan schooling); or at a conceptual level (as in thematic curricula like *Man: A Course of Study*)? Certainly, these requirements make differential demands upon the organizational flexibility within a school and among its teachers.

One way to explore these demands is to compare the old and new modes of organization in terms of the boundaries that are transgressed or the distinctions that become blurred after integration has taken place. Here are two hypothetical examples. It could be argued, for instance, that 'social studies' (e.g. an amalgam of history, geography, sociology and economics) is more integrated than 'combined studies' (history and geography), since it includes subjects not normally on the curriculum. That is, it not only blurs the distinctions between school subjects, it also broaches the barrier dividing school and non-school subjects. Similarly, 'creative arts' (from poetry to woodwork) may be more integrated than 'arts and crafts', since it not only blurs the traditional distinction between vocational and non-vocational subjects, but equally confuses the distinction between mental and manual disciplines, single- and double-period subjects; and male and female curricula. By analysing integrated studies in these terms it is possible to gain provisional access to the assumptions that govern them.

As these examples suggest, the variations of integration are infinite. So, by definition, are their possible permutations and combinations. Many experiments at integration develop from a major rethink of the curriculum. It is not surprising, therefore, that they are often linked to other educational changes (e.g. the atrophy of the 11+ examination, or the development of comprehensive schooling).

Second, it is often useful to ask who controls the integration; and, thereby, examine the superstructure of educational responsibility, authority and power that surrounds it. What form does the control take? For example, do all the subjects that are 'integrated' have an equal say in planning the courses, or does a pre-existing structure of specialist responsibility linger on and act as a hidden constraint?

Perhaps the clearest illustration of this superstructural effect is provided by the public examination system. Its dominating influence on school curricula (as shown by the reluctance of universities to recognize certain examination subjects) may preclude integration, while in other cases (as in the introduction of CSE Mode III) its impact may facilitate organizational change. Similarly, the present training, reward and career structure of teaching is hierarchical. As such, it may conflict with the egalitarian ethos implied by 'team teaching' or with the supposed parity among subjects implied by '*inter*-disciplinary studies'.

The power of the superstructure need not always act against integration. It may just as easily be brought to bear to bolster an innovation through, for example, the provision of extra equipment, the allocation of additional pre-paration time, or the disbursement of personal privileges (such as exemption from class duties). An appreciation of facts such as these can go a long way to provide an accurate interpretation of the organizational pattern under review.

A third investigational strategy pertinent to integrated studies is to explore the history of the innovation – in particular, to ask why it was established. Where did the initiatives come from? How has it subsequently changed? In-formation of this kind may explain why certain innovations are claimed to be successful when, to a casual outsider, they may appear to be falling far short of the original aims. Organizational changes take place for a diversity of reasons – sometimes not always explicitly framed or even consciously under-stood. For example, integrated studies may be organized to promote minority subjects like geology or Italian or to share the work of inexperienced or diffi-dent teachers. They may also be initiated using less obvious criteria: to foster the cross-pollination or educational ideas and practices, to demonstrate the inadequacies of an old school, to offset a lack of qualified staff, to project the tired image of an old school. In these last two instances the integration becomes an end in itself – an organizational rather than a pedagogical solution.

A final investigational probe is to place the integrated mode or organiza-tion in the temporal context of a child's school career. What does the child encounter before and after these experiences? Are the transitions smooth, or do they interrupt the child's schooling (not necessarily a negative feature)? How major are the disjunctions? What are their key features? If the integrated studies are sandwiched in this way, how do they retain their autonomy?

Mixed-ability grouping

Like the adoption of integrated studies, mixed-ability grouping usually implies a major reformulation of accepted modes of organization. Similarly, the term retains a broad spectrum of meaning and is equally widely used in primary and secondary education.

In attempting to probe its content and form, a number of questions can be posed which can help to unravel the apparent complexities. As before, it is useful to begin by asking what is meant by 'mixed-ability' randomized grouping? Banding — randomized grouping within broad ability categories? Or random grouping — with separate provision for 'slow learners'? As a corollary, it is also relevant to establish how the 'mixing' was conducted — on the basis of age? feeder school? home area? alphabetic order?

A second inquiry might concern the enactment of mixed-ability teaching. Does it apply to all subjects? For the entire school day? How is it reflected in the materials and methods of teaching and in the assessment of pupil progress?

These questions can provide an indication of the preparation that has gone into developing and updating the scheme and, for instance, can help to distinguish pragmatic from considered attempts at mixed-ability teaching. Another issue that might be fruitfully explored is the extent to which these changes have influenced working relations among the staff. *A priori*, the existence of a common syllabus for all children makes the likelihood of inter-staff communication more likely. Does this occur? Does the 2E teacher feel her status is improved by the advent of mixed-ability teaching? Or is she now forced to 'compete' with the other teachers? Mixed-ability teaching may also undermine a staff hierarchy based on the assumption that good teachers teach high-ability classes. Is this hierarchy abolished, driven underground or replaced by a different form of relationship?

A third approach to the analysis of mixed-ability teaching is to examine the conception of 'mixed ability' retained by the teachers. Does it stress the differences or similarities between children? How do these ideas relate to the education that is offered by the school? (For example, a pedagogy based on differences between pupils is more likely to use individualized than cooperative methods.) Is there consensus among the staff?

A fourth avenue of inquiry is to seek information about the future plans for the school. This may give some indication of the teachers' responses to mixed-ability teaching. Is it to be maintained, extended, modified or abandoned? What are the reasons given for the proposed changes?

Team teaching

By its very nature, team teaching is a move away from the traditionally accepted role of a class or subject teacher. Hence, an important basic question to establish is why the team teaching was introduced. Was it implemented to solve a problem (the need to 'carry' a weak teacher); was it a logical response to a shortage of resources; did it arise naturally from a group of teachers wishing to pursue an integrated course of study; or was it the result of a particular style of building?

A second focus of inquiry is to ask what form does the team teaching take. Is it restricted to certain children, teachers, subjects or times in the day? How is the team constituted? Is it built round shared skills or specialized knowledge? Is there a division of labour, power and prestige? Or do the staff have equal shares in the work and responsibility? What is the team's relationship to the head teacher?

A third approach is to consider the organization of inter-staff and inter-pupil relationships. In what way do the teachers and children manage the social complexity of teaching? Is the team teaching unit regarded as an entity in itself or is it just a cluster of groups and classes who join together for certain activities? How is the unit subdivided; are the groups all the same, and do all the children have opportunities to work with all of the team? Are all the children shared or do the teachers have a special interest in specific children within the unit?

A fourth investigational probe is to examine the school-based provision made for maintaining the coordination and coherence of the team. Is any school time allocated for team discussions and advance planning? What hidden subsidies does the team enjoy (auxiliaries, secretaries, volunteer parents)? Is there any way in which centralized but accessible records are kept? What are the opportunities for individual members of the team to indulge their own interests?

A final strategy is to look at the team teaching in a wider context. Has it been accepted and understood by the parents? What steps have been taken to gain their cooperation and overcome their apprehension? Are regular meetings held for parents?

Open plan schools

Of the organizational forms already discussed open plan schools involve the most visible form of restructuring within school. However, 'open plan' is merely an architectural term and need not imply any specific form of educational organization. Nevertheless, the originators of open-plan schooling in Britain were greatly influenced by the type of education that took place in one- or two-teacher rural elementary schools. Group methods, the integrated day, vertical grouping and so on had been used in these settings since the demise of 'payment by results' in the late nineteenth century.

One approach to the analysis of an open-plan school is to locate its design (or, in the case of a modified school, its redesign) within the gradual evolution of open-plan schools. What type of thinking is reflected in the layout? Was it planned round a notional class grouping? Was it intended to house other organizational forms (e.g. team teaching)? How much space is allocated for sharing? Are there any specialized areas (e.g. for music)?

A second consideration might be to examine how much educational planning went into the design. Was it built to an (inflexible) standard design or were local variations incorporated? Did the teachers have any say in the proceedings?

A third possibility is to discover how the present form of organization differs from the original conception. Has the school population increased or decreased? Have there been any changes in space utilization? Has this led to any changes in school policy?

Further insights might be gained by asking to what extent has the open-plan design been an educational facilitator or inhibitor? Do teachers feel better able to communicate among themselves or do they feel more vulnerable to the criticisms of their peers? Does the absence of physical boundaries make the teachers and children more responsive to the opportunities offered by the open-plan design? Or does the flexibility promote a uniformity of approach?

A fifth and final question might be to investigate whether other educational boundaries have been removed by the advent of an open plan. What boundaries are used to divide time? Are subject boundaries relocated? Are work and play, home and school, teachers and pupils strongly delineated?

CONCLUDING REMARKS

This chapter has tried to construct short lists of questions that might be useful 'starter packs' in eliciting information about the workings of different forms of school or curriculum organization. No attempt has been made to provide detailed checklists since this would merely camouflage the difficulties in conducting such an investigation. Evaluation is not simply the process of gathering information. Rather, it is concerned with the appraisal of a specific educational practice by collecting information about that practice which is relevant to the value systems shared by those interested in the study.

In so far as this chapter builds only upon imaginary examples, it inevitably lacks a degree of definition. Yet, paradoxically, this deficiency also points to perhaps the most important tasks for anyone conducting an evaluation.

Without a detailed knowledge of the situation and without an equally detailed knowledge of the values that are relevant to the participants or observers an evaluation is, indeed, impossible. By itself, information is valueless. Thus, the information-gathering task is only part of a complex interacting process that is focused jointly by the cumulation of knowledge about the situation and by the attendant value systems. What are the aspirations or beliefs that fostered the organizational form? What ripple, backwash or displacement effects followed its introduction? How important to its functioning are the competencies of teachers and pupils? Are there any hidden subsidies received by the organization? Whether making considered decisions about the management of school classrooms or the transformation of school systems, the process of evaluation is the same.

5 Making curriculum decisions

Keith Cooper

Clearly there are a number of general dilemmas which, because they face all teachers, irrespective of their subject specialisms, may be thought of as belonging to the whole curriculum. What principles should govern the selection of curriculum content? To whom, at what stages and in what form should it be made available? How should the curriculum be planned, organized and evaluated? What modes of teaching and learning are likely to prove most effective? (Schools Council 1975, pp. 8–9)

Decisions about the curriculum are at the root of all teaching; teachers have to make curriculum decisions every day of their working lives. Sometimes it is clear that this is what they are doing. Perhaps they are attending a staff meeting, or working on a new environmental studies scheme, or taking part in a meeting of a curriculum study group. The issue which faces the teacher in these situations could vary from whether the school should adopt mixed-ability teaching to the choice of a textbook, or the decision as to whether the work published about the evaluation of primary French did or did not imply that French should be abandoned forthwith. More often, probably, it is not at all obvious that the teacher is making a decision about the curriculum when she decides in a primary school to do art in the afternoon rather than the morning, or chooses a new reading book for Jane. In the secondary school, similar decisions might be whom to enter for GCE, CSE, or for no examination at all; which textbook to use with the class today; or whether to give a piece of work a mark out of ten or to write comments but no mark. Some of these choices may appear to be matters of administrative convenience or simple classroom management, but each of them makes a greater or lesser contribution to the range and form of the curriculum content available to the individual pupil. They are no less curriculum decisions than the design of a science scheme would be.

It is not the purpose of this chapter to go through all possible decisions about the curriculum and give precise indications for their resolution. It would in any case be impossible to achieve that aim, since each decision is necessarily taken within a context which defines the problem uniquely. What can usefully be done, however, is to look at the elements which seem to be present in all situations when teachers make decisions about the curriculum, in the hope that a prior awareness of factors which may not be apparent at the time will help in making the decision.

THE INFLUENCE OF VALUE JUDGEMENTS ON CURRICULUM DECISIONS

The most pervasive, but least acknowledged, factor in the making of any decision by teachers as individuals or in groups is the values held by those involved. At some levels, as for instance a governmental decision to legislate on comprehensive schooling, there would be no argument about the importance of the values held by those making the decision. At other levels the case is not so clear cut. One might imagine, for instance, that value questions have little to do with the writing or choosing of school textbooks. Consider this example, however.

Imagine what would happen in a school if a Social Studies text were introduced that described the growth of American civilization as being characterized by four main developments:

1. Insurrection against a legally constituted government, in order to achieve a political identity;
2. Genocide against the indigenous population in order to get land;
3. Keeping human beings as slaves, in order to achieve an economic base;
4. The importation of 'coolie' labour in order to build the railroads.

Whether this view of American history is true or not is beside the point. It is at least as true or false as the conventional view *and* it would scarcely be allowed to appear unchallenged in a school book intended for youth.

(Postman 1973, pp. 88–9)

If this American example seems remote, it would be possible to imagine similar passages from books written in England about Welsh or Scottish history which would be totally unacceptable in those countries, or books about the Reformation or the British Empire which would similarly shock or upset.

The reality of the basis of educational decision making was caught by the Schools Council Working Paper No. 53 on *The Whole Curriculum 13–16*.

The truth is, of course, that in so far as people's views diverge on a great many social, political, philosophical and other questions, so too will their views about what kind of school curricula are desirable and attainable.

(Schools Council 1975, pp. 17–18)

There are few decisions about curriculum content which do not touch on some area of legitimate difference of view, and which do not therefore involve some judgement of relative value. Less obviously, perhaps, the same is true of decisions about how to put the curriculum into practice. A decision to adopt mixed-ability teaching could possibly be based primarily on evidence about greater efficiency in bringing about learning; but it is also rooted in a conception of the nature of education. In the same way, it is (at least in part) a reflection of a teacher's values when she decides to give a numerical mark (using the same criteria for all the children) to each child's work rather than merely writing comments which refer to the individual child's previous standard of work.

It is all very well to suggest that values are a fundamental element in all educational (and therefore all curriculum) decisions. The acceptance of this view raises a number of questions which are very difficult to answer. If our own values permeate our teaching, are we justified in imposing those values on our pupils — however unwittingly we do it? Where our personal values are in conflict with those of the school, the local community or society as a whole (however these are determined), where should our choice lie? Are there ways in which our teaching can also take into account the values held by the pupils? There is no easy answer to any of these questions. They have not been the subject of wide debate within the profession or in the community generally; the nearest we have come to such a debate is to deplore the value base of those with whom we disagree. Without such discussion, however, the individual teacher is likely to continue to be in a very exposed position.

Perhaps the only acceptable way forward is for us to acknowledge the inevitability of the value-based nature of curriculum decisions, and to regard it as a matter for discussion rather than deprecation. If we were able to become more aware of our own values, and were prepared to be open about them, it might perhaps become possible for others (whether teachers, pupils or parents) to become open about theirs, and for understanding to increase. Complete agreement is not possible, and compromise will not necessarily be beneficial. In the long term, we may well wish to encourage our pupils to define their own values, and therefore be able to interpret their educational experience accordingly. 'The curriculum is also a reconciliation of diverse and often conflicting claims and the balance which is achieved between them can never be a perfect or definitive one.' (Schools Council 1975, p. 18)

THE INFORMATION BASE FOR CURRICULUM DECISIONS

A second important element in all decision situations is information. Other chapters in this book have been about the collection and storage of information; but there is no point in either collection or storage unless there is some potential use for it – some occasion when the possession of information will make a decision easier or in some way better. It would seem as well, however, for us to be clear about the role of information in decision making. It is a common assumption – not just for education but for all situations involving decisions including at the governmental level – that decisions are potentially easy when the decision maker has at his disposal all the relevant information. Life is not as simple as that, however. Sometimes we do not even know what information would be relevant to the situation even if we could get it; even when we think we know what is potentially relevant, we are rarely in a position to obtain as much information as we would like.

The possibilities have been neatly represented graphically in Braybrooke and Lindblom (1963). They use two main criteria for categorizing decision settings – the importance of the decision and the information available. The authors suggest that, if these criteria are seen as intersecting dimensions, particular decision situations can be placed somewhere in one of the quadrants; but they regard most educational decisions as falling somewhere in the quadrant of relative unimportance and low information available. Braybrooke and Lindblom spend some time working out a strategy for making decisions in this context.

Even if we accept that we will always as educators be needing to make decisions in situations when we have a relatively small part of the information we would ideally like to have, our emphasis must be on 'relatively'. It is usually possible to find out more than we already know. If we take the example of the infant teacher wishing to give Jane a new reading book, it is possible that the teacher is happy to know that Jane has finished book 2, and to give her book 3. It would be possible, however, for the teacher to spend some time analysing the sub-skills of reading; finding out which of these sub-skills Jane has mastered and which she has not; analysing the available books in terms of the contribution each makes to the development of each of the sub-skills; and matching Jane's needs with the book which seems best to cater for them. The teacher would still be far short of a position of complete knowledge, for instance about Jane's response to particular styles of writing, or about her motivation towards reading. Nevertheless the teacher would, in the second situation, be using considerably more information than in the first. It is at least possible that the reading book Jane finally got in the second case would develop her reading ability more effectively than would have been possible in the first case, where she was automatically given the next book in the same series.

It will immediately be apparent to all teachers that, in spite of the possible benefits to the child which may accrue from the collection of more information in the way suggested, there are considerable costs for the teacher in terms of her own time and the education of the rest of the class. Indeed, this thought will probably have occurred several times already to most readers of this book. The constraint of time will be considered again later; we are concerned here with the possible range of information from which the teacher may, if she wishes, select. In many cases, of course, decisions may have become a matter of routine, with the possible options highly restricted and the indicators for a particular decision clearly set out. Where the school enjoins the use of only one set of texts in a particular area (whether a reading scheme or a science text in the secondary school) there can be no debate over what happens when the end of one book is reached — the child or the class starts on the next one in the series. While we may recognize the routine nature of such decisions, however, it is important to note that the routine applies only within an agreed context which is — at least potentially — open to change. If the school buys another reading scheme, so that the teacher has a choice of book to follow the one which has been finished, or if the Head of Science feels able to encourage teachers to cover the agreed topics in any order, then these decision areas cease to be routine, and information becomes more important. Ways in which information can be collected appear in the other chapters of this book. There may, however, be other sources which the teacher can use.

Very occasionally the teacher will find that something has been published which is relevant to the situation she faces. In this context, the situation most written about is probably that of the option system for fourth- and fifth-year pupils in the secondary school. This is frequently discussed either as a technical exercise (as in the chapter called 'Curriculum planning' in Rogers 1971) or as an organizational contribution to the raising of the leaving age (for example Schools Council Working Paper 33, *Choosing a curriculum for the young school leaver*). Richardson (1973, 1975) goes into some detail about the discussions in the school which led up to the framing of the option system, and is thus a rare example of consideration of the value implications of decisions about choices available for these pupils. It is true that the timetable is the embodiment of the educational philosophy of the school — but only occasionally, it seems, is that philosophy actually discussed before the timetable is drawn up.

One other area in which the teacher can use published work to help in the decision making is in the use of materials or ideas from national curriculum development projects. The information varies from accounts written by teachers using the project (e.g. Baranowski 1974; but these accounts sometimes seem written as publicity for the project, as in *Teachers Talking* (1974) from the Schools Council project Geography for the Young School Leaver, or in most of the articles about projects in the Schools Council's *Newsletter*, formerly *Dialogue*); through articles by teachers which take a more critical approach (for example the comments on the Schools Council Humanities Curriculum Project in Elliott and MacDonald 1975); to the reports of the evaluation of the project.

The usefulness of this material varies enormously, but the teacher interested in the work of a project will probably find it worthwhile to look at the information available. The evaluation report on the Schools Council *Breakthrough to Literacy* teaching materials (Reid 1975), for instance, gives evidence about the use of the materials with a small sample of children and teachers; on the basis of this, Reid makes some important observations about the way the suggested use of the materials might be modified, and points where the teacher might need to take special care (such as in the use of the materials by slower learners, and in the need for attention to be paid to the teaching of the mechanics of handwriting).

More often, probably, there will be no published evidence about materials or ideas the teacher is considering. In this case, the teacher will need to make her own analysis of the material in question. What are the aims and objectives (if any)? What extra resources are required? Is any particular form of classroom organization implied? Can the children read the material? Will the teacher's own role have to change significantly? Each teacher will readily compile her own list of such questions. As well as looking at the material in this way, the teacher might also consider undertaking what has been called 'an analysis of curriculum potential' (Ben-Peretz 1975), to look beyond the immediately implied or directed use of the materials or ideas to their possibilities if adapted or used in combination with other ideas the teacher has.

CONSTRAINTS ON CURRICULUM DECISIONS

A third relevant consideration in curriculum decision making is that of the constraints or the context within which the decision has to be made. No decision can be made in a total vacuum, and both collective and individual decisions have to be made in the awareness of the context. The constraint which many teachers feel most acutely is that of time. The most common response to the ideas or suggestions about curriculum which are made to teachers is that there is no time to do it – or at least, that the time required would mean that other teaching would suffer. There are two different dimensions of time as it affects teaching and curriculum decisions. One is time with the children – teaching which can only be done with the pupils there. This sort of time is strictly limited by the hours the children attend school and the number of days in the year the school is open. Since it is reasonable to assume that all this time is already taken up with some activity, it is obvious that a suggestion for the introduction of some new activity means that it must take up time occupied with other activity – so something must go to make room for it.

This is a very real problem. Most teachers would not admit that any of their time with the children is wasted on non-educational or trivial activities, so the introduction of anything new is replacing something which is felt to be of value. It must be said, however, that we should not take as a necessary truth the proposition that, as teachers, our time with the children is all valuably spent. A regular analysis of what we do with the class could well show that there are at least some activities which fit better under the label of 'child-minding' rather than education. We might, of course, wish to justify this on the grounds that neither children nor teachers can or ought to work at full capacity through the school day and school year. Such a justification would, however, require considerable evidence in its favour for it to convince parents and education committees.

Even if we could identify some areas in our current work when the children are either not fully engaged, or are busy at work of little educational value, and we could use this time to implement new ideas, the problem of whether to replace activities we consider educationally valuable with other activities we believe to be more valuable, will not disappear. In practice, the onus seems to be on the proponents of innovation to justify its inclusion rather than on others to justify retaining existing activity. Yet it often seems to be the case that there is less evidence about the value of existing work than about the innovation, and the worth of what is done now is taken for granted. What will be needed is the working out of educational priorities at the individual, school, community, local authority and national levels, perhaps using the ideas on the collection and use of information for decision making outlined in *Curriculum Evaluation Today: Trends and Implications* (Tawney 1976).

Time spent in contact with the children is only one dimension of the time constraint as it effects teachers. The other – at least as important – is the time available for work which must be done when the children are not present. It is usually this time which teachers claim not to have enough of when they reject an innovation. This claim does not always seem to be related to actual out-of-school activity, however; it is probably more related to the individual teacher's conception of what the job entails, and what can count as her own time. Arrangements for curriculum innovation which are going to demand considerable use of time out of school hours might perhaps take more account of teachers' notions of what is reasonable.

Even when the teacher does not see time as a constraint on a curriculum decision, it is likely that the available material resources will limit the possible work she can do. If one of the choices in a situation involves the provision of extra money, and another does not, there is very likelihood that the latter alternative will be preferred. More usually, however, decisions which involve extra resources mean choosing priorities from the available options in the same way that priorities need to be decided over the use of time. In the case of material resources, however, it may be that some redistribution can be done within the institution as a whole rather than just within the individual teacher's allowance. In this case, as in others, decisions will arise which affect not only individual teachers or single departments, but the whole school.

Where priorities have to be decided for a group, it seems that final decisions emerge only after a process of negotiation between the interested parties. In the case of the allocation of money, this negotiation might be straightforward bargaining for amounts; but it happens in other decision situations as well. In the case of the formation of a new Humanities Department at Nailsea School, for instance, Richardson's account (Richardson 1973) makes this apparent. In 1969, after a pilot course in humanities with the first year pupils, there was much discussion as to whether humanities should be extended to the second year for 1969/70.

The immediate result of these enquiries about the future of the humanities course was that its status in the curriculum was left somewhat undefined. As far as the 1969/70 session was concerned, it was — as an official part of the curriculum for all children — still confined to Year I. Thus, if the staff, as they separated for the summer holidays of 1969, were having to question some of their old assumptions about the autonomy of department heads, they also took away with them some evidence that Denys John [the Head] too recognized the limits of his autonomy, since they had been able to prevent, or at least to postpone, the extension of the humanities course into Year II. He had scarcely concealed his own desire to see the course continued for the children who were moving into the second year in the autumn; nevertheless he had bowed to the doubts of those who were opposing this by agreeing that further thought be given to the matter before any decision was made. On the other hand, he did have his way over the extension of the teaching to be done in mixed-ability groups for the second year children; for English, history, geography and religious education, along with art, crafts, music and physical education, were now to be taught in tutor groups. This meant also that the 'general subjects' or remedial groups ceased to exist as teaching groups . . . . At the same time, humanities gained a toe-hold on the second year; for Graeme Osborn and Bob Jarratt, with the backing of Reg Clarke, had been able to persuade the heads of the departments concerned to allow them to teach with their own two second-year groups a further course in place of separate courses in English, history, geography and religious education. It seemed that, in this area of the curriculum, there had been a kind of unconscious bargaining going on. (Richardson 1973, pp. 80–81)

This process of negotiation could be paralleled from the experience of most teachers, certainly in secondary schools; and it is not always unconscious. It is worth considering, however, whether the idea of decisions arrived at after negotiation applies also to the classroom. Situations arise where the teacher is reminded of the adage about leading a horse to water but not being able to make it drink. In these circumstances, decisions which are to be effective may well have to be 'negotiated' rather than imposed.

There are other ways in which particular decisions have effects wider than appeared at first. When the Schools Council Humanities Curriculum Project (HCP) is introduced, for instance, it may be that one or two individual teachers are trying to implement the idea of non-directive teaching with the fourth or fifth year pupils. It seems likely that pupils would not wish to accept non-directive teaching for a small part of the week, and directive teaching for the rest. Problems would arise for all the teachers in the school, with some pressure on those not involved in HCP to become less directive in their teaching, and perhaps stronger pressure on those trying to implement HCP to remove the source of the discontent. In a different way, decisions about curriculum in one part of the school or the education system affect other parts. When primary schools decide to teach French or new maths, this clearly has considerable implications for teachers in the secondary schools. When Nuffield Science courses for O- and A-levels were introduced, changes were forced on the science teaching in the whole of the secondary school.

One final consideration needs to be looked at. Every curriculum decision taken by a teacher, whether as an individual or as a member of a group, is located somewhere in both formal and informal decision making structures. These structures necessarily act as constraints on decisions, since they will define the area within which the teacher has been given responsibility (in the case of the formal structure) or feels that she has responsibility in the case of the informal structure. In many large secondary schools, such as Nailsea (Richardson 1973) the formal structure for decision making has been expanded, by the use of committees and working parties, so that there is little need for an informal structure. Each teacher could (in theory at least) give a precise description of her various areas of responsibility and influence. In small schools such a formal structure rarely exists, and responsibility can be a matter of custom. This situation seems to have the effect of expanding the teacher's responsibility for the individual pupil, but of limiting her influence on decisions affecting the whole school.

Whatever her position within the decision making structures, however, and whatever her awareness of them, the teacher cannot escape the need to make decisions, of greater or lesser moment, about the curriculum which is to be available to the children she teaches. This chapter has suggested that all her decisions are necessarily taken in the light of the values of those involved, of the information available, and of the constraints which operate on it.

FURTHER CONSIDERATIONS

One of the major points made in the chapter is that many of the issues touched on have not been the subject of debate within the profession, and ought to be. One of the areas in which such debate is most urgent is the place of values in our teaching. How acceptable is the claim that decisions at class-room or school level are influenced by the values of those involved in taking them? If values affect decisions, are they transmitted to pupils through the effects of the decisions? If so, is this thought acceptable or should there be some attempt to avoid it? Can the teacher take into account the values of the community, and of society as a whole?

Previous chapters have suggested a number of kinds of evaluative information, and ways to collect it. What is the relevant information a teacher would require to make a decision about, say, the change from a traditional to a modern mathematics course? Would the information be readily available, and if not, what steps could be taken to find it? If the information is not obtained, is it better to leave things as they are? The general question refers to decisions closer to the classroom as well. Suppose a teacher decides to spend less time on marking both in class and at home in order to have more time for discussion with individual pupils, what information could she obtain which might help her to justify the reallocation of her time?

References

Baranowski, M. (1974). *A Pilgrim's Progress through the Project*. Occasional Paper No. 2, Schools Council History, Geography and Social Science 8–13 Project, Liverpool University School of Education.

Ben-Peretz, M. (1975). 'The concept of curriculum potential', *Curriculum Theory Network*, 5, No. 2, pp. 151–159.

Braybrooke, D. & Lindblom, C. E. (1963). *A Strategy of Decision*. New York: Free Press.

Elliott, J. E. & MacDonald, B. M. (eds) (1975). *People in Classrooms*. Centre for Applied Research in Education, University of East Anglia.

Postman, N. (1973). 'The politics of reading', in *Tinker, Tailor, . . .* , N. Keddie (ed). Harmondsworth: Penguin.

Reid, J. (1975). *Breakthrough in Action: an Independent Evaluation of 'Break-through to Literacy'*. Longman.

Richardson, E. (1973). *The Teacher, the School and the Task of Management*. Heinemann Educational.

Richardson, E. (1975). *Authority and Organization in the Secondary School* (Schools Council Research Studies). Macmillan Education.

Rogers, T. (1971). *School for the Community*. Routledge.

Schools Council (1971). *Choosing a Curriculum for the Young School Leaver*. Working Paper 33. Evans/Methuen Educational.

Schools Council Geography for the Young School Leaver Project (1974). *Teachers Talking*. Avery Hill College of Education.

Schools Council (1975). *The Whole Curriculum 13–16*. Working Paper 53. Evans/Methuen Educational.

Tawney, D. (ed) (1976). *Curriculum Evaluation Today: Trends and Implications*, Schools Council Research Studies. Macmillan Education.

6 The evaluation of the school as a whole

Ray Jackson and John Hayter

Is **X** a good school? Which is the better school, **Y** or **Z**? The generality and possible inappropriateness of the questions does not stop them being asked. While specific questions about curriculum, internal organization, methodology and materials may be generally regarded as of proper concern and relevance to the professionals within education, the interest in assessing the school as a whole extends over a much wider population. The parent selecting a school, the pupil selecting an institution for A-level work, the local education authority responding to inquiries about possible visits to schools by visiting dignitaries, the house agent advising prospective buyers, all make and use more or less sophisticated evaluations.

Parents, teachers, children, educationalists and citizens — often think and talk of the school as a single entity and set up questions which appear to invite simple and concise answers — almost in the form of a score out of ten or a description in not more than one sentence. While one might doubt the validity of any brief response given by a member of one interest group to another member of the same group, the reply is fraught with even more interpretive difficulties when the questioner and the respondent are from different interest groups. For the unexpressed dimensions of the whole school depend to a considerable degree on the viewpoint of the observer. While the pupil's judgement may be in terms of the attitude of the school to uniform, the quality of school meals and the quantity of sports facilities, that of the teachers may reflect their view of the opportunity given by the school for professional judgement and for development and of their relationship with the headteacher, while local residents may be reacting to the language, appearance and behaviour of the children on their way home from school.

Although none of these viewpoints would be recognized as adequate for providing the anticipated judgement on a school, it seems important to acknowledge their existence and the fact that many decisions are made on the basis of such slim and arguably partisan evidence. Is it valid then to think of evaluation in the context of the whole school? Before dismissing the notion

113

as inevitably superficial or impractical, it is necessary to examine the crucial terms — 'whole school' and 'evaluation'.

THE MEANING OF 'WHOLE SCHOOL' AND 'EVALUATION' IN THIS CONTEXT

It has already been suggested that the perceived 'whole' school depends to a considerable extent on the viewpoint of the observer. An important distinction can be made between those who might be regarded as insiders (e.g. teachers, pupils) and those who are outside (e.g. local residents, inspectorate). However, significant groups straddle this divide often having to reconcile a mix of resulting viewpoints (e.g. parents, managers). Siting the interest groups physically in relation to the school buildings provides an incomplete though not necessarily an inappropriate analogy. The detail and the pattern of which the insider is aware are unknown to the outsider who relies to a large extent on samples of exterior features and activity.

As well as the viewpoint of the observer his own system of values adds colour, relief and a second perspective to what is seen. Members of a particular group have, as it were, been equipped with a variety of viewing devices — rose coloured spectacles for some, magnifying glasses and binoculars for others; some, it might be thought, have periscopes with distorting mirrors. So, for example, one might find among the group of school managers of a local comprehensive school one who received her own education in an independent school and who sends her own children to an independent school, and another who has campaigned in the locality for the introduction of comprehensive education. In addition, there is a whole range of values relating to student/ staff relations, attitudes to discipline, the nature and purpose of education and the condition and future of society.

The discussion thus far perhaps only emphasizes the fragmentation of views about the whole school, which is already recognized as a complex and many faceted phenomenon. Yet it seems as well to recognize that individuals in each group carry a picture of the school with which they are involved. The picture is not necessarily a static one, since new experiences and developments will add to an increasingly complex jigsaw, but nonetheless the personal image exists. Further, and crucially, individuals within groups and also members of different groups need to communicate from time to time, often in order to reach decisions relating to the school. In this consideration of the whole school it therefore seems more useful to use that term to describe **all the educational provision, activity and influence of the institution** within a very wide encompassing boundary. We should thus be recognizing that no single view of the components exists, that no simple summation process will produce a measure for the whole, and that all we can expect to achieve is to study various aspects of a school. However, in any such study we would be endeavouring to ensure that such aspects are considered in relation to other elements within the whole school boundary.

What then are possible meanings of evaluation in the context of the whole school? In spite of the arguments which can be amassed to undermine the notion of a simple test of quality of an institution, there appears to be a lurking attraction for a straightforward, easily administered approach. This may lead too easily to a 'something is better than nothing' justification for an inadequate approach or to reliance on a single measure of performance such as O- or A-level achievements. It may be helpful to consider first the difference in emphasis between a basically judgemental as opposed to an essentially diagnostic approach. The former is perhaps the natural expectation, addressing questions such as 'Are specific school objectives being achieved?' and 'Is the academic performance of pupils satisfactory?' In such areas implied or established criteria may be used to provide answers even though they may need to be appropriately qualified. The limitations of such an approach in the field of curriculum development have been recognized increasingly in the light of the complexity of the phenomena, of which only some outcomes are considered, and in terms of the value of such evidence once it is provided. The so called 'agricultural-botany' model of evaluation (Parlett & Hamilton 1976), in which carefully matched groups are submitted to different treatments, has been regarded as less appropriate in many situations than an approach which endeavours to increase understanding of the ongoing process by means of a variety of evidence including reports from participants in the system with differing perspectives. Any judgemental quality is consequently seen as part of a larger whole, which endeavours to 'illuminate' the situation for observers, in particular those who are in a position to make decisions. Such an approach is of more of a diagnostic nature. Not viewed as an end-of-session examination but rather as a state-of-the-nation review which will perhaps lead to modifications of strategy, content and methodology at a later stage.

General inspections of a school or the consideration by an education authority of the possible closure of an institution may be easily recognizable as situations involving an evaluation of the whole school. However, it will be more useful to broaden the definition of evaluation in respect of the whole school to **include the gathering, analysis and interpretation of a wide range of evidence relating to various aspects of the school's aims, functioning and achievements.**

Evaluation as interpreted here should be purposeful in the sense that it is concerned with providing information and evidence for particular individuals and groups who are in situations requiring them to make decisions. Teachers, managers, parents, local education authorities are clearly groups in such a position and this approach assumes an active role for the eventual recipients of the evidence in clarifying the questions to which they are wanting to address themselves with the help of evidence.

Before providing a brief survey of what has already been achieved in the way of evaluation with respect to the whole school, it is worthwhile to attempt to identify particular decision areas and to clarify the principal decision makers involved.

DECISION AREAS REQUIRING EVALUATIVE INFORMATION

Having allowed our concern with the whole school to include aspects of the school in relation to the work of the total institution, there is a danger of fragmentation into an almost endless list of elements. However, it is suggested that a number of fairly broad decision areas can be identified where in each case evaluative evidence will be desirable. Important areas appear to be those relating to:

1   Parental choice
2   Maintaining standards
3   Attributing responsibility
4   Planning development
5   Understanding the working of an institution
6   Resolving conflict
7   Pupils' decisions

A full discussion of each of these is not possible within the scope of this chapter but brief notes are provided in the form of a table (Table 6.1) in order to indicate the nature of the issues within each decision area.

EVALUATION FOR WHOM AND BY WHOM?

Groups of decision makers may be delineated in a variety of ways; four groups are suggested here as significant in any consideration of decision making with respect to the whole school. These are (i) consumers (parents and pupils), (ii) professional educators (class teachers, head teachers), (iii) administrators (LEA's, DES) and (iv) society in general. The decision areas identified earlier may be linked with these groups as tentatively indicated in Table 6.2 (p. 118).

The linking of elements is in no sense absolute and readers may question the inclusion or exclusion of ticks. It is worthwhile noting that, although two groups may have an interest in the same decision area, the questions posed by the groups are unlikely to be the same and are likely to require a different

Table 6.1   Decision areas for evaluative evidence

1 **Parental choice**	Parents are required to make choices within the curriculum and may wish to exercise choice over the school attended by their children. The principle of choice is established in general terms in Education Acts but seldom acknowledged so openly at decision points; it often appears administratively convenient to keep demand/insight low. Yet a curriculum that is largely school determined suggests differing patterns, with, it is likely, differing appeal for parents.
2 **Maintaining standards**	The function of the most widespread and longest running evaluation activity as developed by Her Majesty's Inspectorate. The balance of judgement and advice may vary. In particular, decisions regarding the efficiency or otherwise of independent schools is an activity clearly related to the notion of a minimum acceptable standard.
3 **Attributing responsibility**	A heavily taxed society returns periodically to questions regarding value for money invested in an education system. Those making the greatest personal contribution by way of tax are often the most estranged from the system provided – by virtue of their age, lack of own children etc. How is responsibility for the system exercised and, indeed, by whom?
4 **Planning development**	In reaching decisions about possible expansion, reorganization or general development, adequate information is required about the contribution of the school at present, together with future needs and the potential response of possible types of arrangement or institution. Decisions within a school may relate to developments within the curriculum structure or in the pastoral arrangements.
5 **Understanding the working of an institution**	Concern with immediate teaching and administrative commitments, may result in compartmentalization in the thinking of individuals and groups. From time to time it is necessary to stand back in order to review parts of system. For instance, what is the effect of the present allocation of classrooms to departments? How effective is the

report system for communicating with parents? Is the pastoral care structure satisfactory within the school? (Consideration of information relating to those issues may of course lead to planning change — as in 4. above — usually requiring additional evidence.)

6 **Resolving conflict**   While few in number, the type of situation which gains maximum space in the popular press. An intensive study may be required in order to resolve problems which have affected the well-being of the whole school.

7 **Pupils' decisions**   Pupils are required to make decisions about subjects to be studied, about optional activities, about careers. Also in the future most will become secondary consumers as parents, and become tax-paying citizens. What implications does this have for the content of their curriculum in the senior years of secondary school with respect to thinking about the value and purpose of education?

Table 6.2   Link between decision makers and decision areas

Decision areas	Decision makers			
	Consumers	Professional educators	Administrators	Society in general
Parental choice	✓		✓	
Maintaining standards		✓	✓	
Attributing respon-sibilities			✓	✓
Planning development		✓	✓	
Understanding working of institution		✓	✓	
Resolving conflict		(✓)	✓	(✓)
Pupils' decisions	✓			

approach to any proposed evaluation activity. For example, in their concern to understand the workings of institutions, a local authority may be concerned with the effects of size of school on the curriculum, on the provision of specialist accommodation and on discipline, while the staff of a school may be reorganizing its fourth year curriculum or planning to start an open access sixth form.

If it is agreed that those making decisions in one or more of a variety of decision areas should have the benefit of evaluative evidence, it is necessary to clarify further the way in which such information might be provided and in particular to identify possible evaluation agents. Three classes of agent can be identified:

The school – the staff, working groups, and individuals with research interests or who are involved in courses leading to further qualifications.

The authorities – may be local, within a local education authority or nationally through DES.

The professional researcher – usually based in a tertiary institution or in a research unit, e.g. CERDU (Schools Council), NFER.

But evaluation work has to be instigated and requires time and money to be effected. As a consequence, the distinctions between the three agencies are to some extent blurred when the necessary commissioning and funding are added to the picture. With respect to funding for example, a research unit may carry out a study on behalf of the DES. Groups within a school or schools may be able to obtain a limited grant from the local authority or the Schools Council towards the cost of the evaluation. While cross-group funding does not necessarily jeopardize the independence of the evaluation agency, it is of significance in exhibiting how such studies came about. While it might be thought appropriate for the decision-making groups to be the instigators of studies, it appears that instigation is often closely linked with ability to carry out the work, that is by being one of the evaluation agents. Hence the education authorities locally and nationally, together with educational researchers, have given rise to and carried out the majority of studies. Only fairly recently have professional educators within schools become sponsors and effectors of systematic evaluation work.

Society in general and the consumers (whether parents or pupils) have for the most part to make do with what has been produced at the suggestion of others. It could be that this state of affairs is undergoing a significant change. The activities of the Advisory Centre for Education (ACE) and the ideas discussed in its journal *Where* (Spring, 1974) have developed an awareness among some parents and have encouraged them to raise important questions as consumers. It is to be expected that the small but growing group of professional evaluators will be receiving commissions from parents as well as from the Schools Council and the DES. In a climate of growing concern about accountability, might not a broader range of society seek information and evidence? And is it conceivable that the industrial companies which sponsored much early curriculum development work might be prepared to fund certain types of evaluation study? The Nuffield Foundation has already sponsored studies in higher education. Such activity may well spread to the secondary school, initially on a national scale at a fairly general level; perhaps later at a regional level in response to local interest and demand.

SOME PREVIOUS ATTEMPTS AT SCHOOL EVALUATION

Taking the evaluation agents in the order listed earlier (i.e. schools authorities, professional researchers), they illustrate an increasing capability for sophisticated approaches but almost certainly a decreasing ability to have a direct influence on a particular school. The type of study carried out by Elizabeth Richardson (see p. 123 and Richardson, 1973) at Nailsea School perhaps illustrates an exception to these generalizations in that the researcher's expertise was brought to bear on the growth and development of a particular school. While this approach could hardly become widespread, it seems likely that the interest created by the Nailsea study will spawn other consultative work between individual schools and researchers.

In addition to the dimensions of methodology and effectiveness mentioned already, there is a further dimension on which the position of the evaluation agents may be plotted — that of the degree of accessibility to reports of their activities. The reports of authorities, particularly studies by the inspectorate, appear to be closely guarded and are seldom easy to obtain. Schools may also wish to maintain an aura of privacy over the results of their own evaluation studies. Such confidentiality may be the price paid if individuals within the study were to cooperate. (While the immediate evaluation agent might not be considered a threat, it might be thought that the information in the hands of others could produce a threatening situation.) Further, an individual school may doubt the relevance for others of its work even though the development of ideas gathered from others who are but one step ahead is increasingly recognized as a legitimate way forward.

The studies of researchers are most readily available, and it appears that they have concentrated in the past on the evaluation of: (a) school systems, (b) curriculum programmes, (c) styles of teaching, (d) guidance programmes, and the like. Rarely have they focused on the evaluation of the school as a unit.

Evaluation studies of the school, where they have been attempted, have used one of a variety of models as a framework for the study. Examples of these models are those labelled: *product-centred; sociological-descriptive; pioneer-palliative; inspection*, and *key factor*. It is necessary to elaborate a little on each of these to show the particular emphasis of the work.

The *product-centred* model is designed to measure the product or output of the school. Rowe (1971), in his evaluation of his secondary school in Hull, offers as a measure of the success of his policy both the increase in the public examination successes of his pupils and the increase in the numbers of children who voluntarily stay on in the Sixth Form — also the number of sports and other prizes by the school. This has been a traditional way for parents and outsiders to evaluate a school. For example, during the heyday of the 'eleven plus', primary schools were judged on the number of grammar school passes. At a different level, Manchester Grammar School had the highest number of 'Oxbridge' scholarships and some researchers have actually calculated the financial cost of gaining a GCE A-level subject at Eton compared with other public schools. The advantage of this approach is that the criteria are easily understood and the data are readily available. However, the measures are very crude and give little indication of the affective element in the school.

The *sociological-descriptive* model includes a large number of sub-types. Lambert (1966), for example, looked at the school as a social system and examined the aims of the school, the formal and informal structure, the modes of initiation and compliance and the cultural and value system of the school. Wakeford (1969), in a different study, analysed the school as a series of key concepts such as social initiation, social adaptation and social compliance.

These 'systems' approaches would give a picture of the school as a functioning unit and enable researchers to give some evaluation, however subjective, of the value system and 'tone' of the school as well as an analysis of the school process. The 'anthropological' model of 'illuminative evaluation' approach of Hamilton and Parlett (1976) respresents a more recent variation of this approach.

Ford's work (1969) is an example of the *pioneer-palliative* approach (see also Jackson & Marsden, 1962). It is evident here that the researcher is committed to a certain viewpoint and uses research in order to advance a particular ideology and to bring the school or school system in line with this ideology. Ford sought to evaluate the comprehensive school as a superior distributor of opportunities for pupils when compared with other types of secondary schools. This was done by posing a series of hypotheses and evaluating whether or not the comprehensive school met these requirements. This approach may be adopted by those who seek to advance new teaching techniques or organizational procedures such as team teaching and the integrated day.

The classic method of evaluating the school has been through the general inspection, or the *inspection* approach. This was an administrative and controlling device which has sometimes appeared to have been undertaken for the benefit of the inspectorate rather than the school since the inspectorate had complete control over the information so gathered; this might be communicated (in part or as a whole) to the head, the whole or selected members of the staff in oral or written form. The inspectors might focus particularly on certain criteria, for example, the percentage of possible attendances made by pupils – a factor which accounts for the importance of keeping accurate attendance registers in English schools. On the other hand, the inspectors might be required, as the Norwich School Board was in the 1870s, to answer a series of questions, some of which are given below (Grieves 1962):

3. Is the attendance of pupils regular and punctual?
4. Is the staff complete and efficient? . . .
10. Are the School and Classrooms clean and well warmed and ventilated?

(See Appendix V for complete set of questions.)

By 1888, instructions to inspectors required them to grade schools as bad/ unsatisfactory (and therefore no grant would be forthcoming), fair, good and excellent. An excellent school would have a 'cheerful and yet exact discipline', have premises which were 'clearly and well ordered' and have a timetable which 'provides a proper variety of mental employment and of physical exercise' (see Appendix VI). This approach to school evaluation has gained wide currency in many countries and its comprehensive nature is indicated by a handbook for new inspectors in a developing country in Africa (Dodd 1968). Here the new inspector is provided with a list of some 126 specimen questions to guide his evaluation. These detailed questions range over the curriculum, school organization, buildings, furniture and equipment. The final evaluation report of the inspector is expected to provide an appraisal of the *strengths* and *weaknesses* of the school and of his *overriding impression*.

The last model to be discussed is that of *key factor* approach. In part it has already been subsumed in Rowe's approach (examination passes) and inspections (pupil attendance). Perhaps the most famous example of this technique has been in the work of J. B. Conant, President of Harvard University, which he outlined in 1959 his classic study of *The American High School*. Conant visited a number of schools and drew up a tentative list of criteria which it was considered might be useful to evaluate the school's performance. In addition he noted certain features of school organization which seemed to him to be significant. School administrators helped him draw up the final list which, in brief, is given below. The adequacy of the school in providing a reasonable general education was judged by: the standards of courses in English and American literature and composition; the standard of the courses in social studies; streaming in key subjects; the provision of vocational courses for non-academic boys and girls; supervised works experience programmes;

provision for remedial pupils, especially in reading; provision for gifted pupils; summer vacation programmes for less able pupils; individualized programmes; relatively short lesson periods; the adequacy of the guidance service; a high level of pupil morale; well organized tutorial periods and the attempts made by the staff to help pupils of widely differing abilities and background to mix together well.

The Conant Report was a very influential document in shaping the American high school during the 1960s. Any school staff or LEA advisers could draw up a similar list which would be more appropriate for their school or area. The weakness of the *key factor* approach lies in selecting criteria to measure reasonable standards and in the fact that the list is not comprehensive and that it may miss many important features to be found in a good school. For example, Conant does not mention the provision of adequate mathematics and science programmes, courses in the plastic and visual arts, the morale of the staff or the support forthcoming from parents.

CASE HISTORIES OF TWO EVALUATION STUDIES

It is clear that the evaluation of a school may take place in a variety of ways and at different levels. It is perhaps of value to describe in rather more detail two contrasting styles of evaluation, both carried out in the south west of England. In one case the study was made by a professional researcher, who acted as consultant within a school over several years. In the other the evaluation had developed within the school and involved, in the main, members of the school staff.

Case study A

For a period of three years Elizabeth Richardson, supported by the Schools Council and the School of Education at the University of Bristol, worked closely with the headmaster and staff of Nailsea School in a study of certain aspects of the school (Richardson 1973), in particular in relation to the roles of the staff and the nature of the processes of management. This expanding comprehensive school was undergoing change, having formerly been a grammar school.

In the prologue to the book describing her work, the author discusses a problem central in any such specific evaluation study — the value of the generalized account as against that of the particular account of a school. How far should the research endeavour to talk about schools in general and of what value is a study of a particular institution? While this project was concerned with only one school, the approach and the resulting account will shed

considerable illumination on the working of many other schools. Indeed the
work's value stems in large measure from the exploration of the complexities
of the structure, roles and relationships within an institution.

Following a decision taken fairly early in the work, that the school would
be identified by name in the report, members of staff eventually agreed that
their own names should also be used rather than resorting to initials or con-
trived names. Clearly the former outcome was the author's wish throughout,
since she maintains that, once it is agreed that the institution shall be named,
'everyone who is at any time during the project involved in recorded events
has a responsibility to accept or reject what is being said about the institution'
(Richardson 1973, p. 45).

The three main areas studied were 'Teachers in multiple roles'; 'The task
of headship and the nature of consultation' and 'The staff group as a unit for
in-service education'. The study was to be 'illuminative' and the report derives
from the researcher's observation and participation in well over one hundred
normal meetings of staff (with departments, working parties and the whole
staff), in addition to a large number of meetings with individual staff members.

From the outset it had been made clear that the study could not guarantee
'any solutions to emerging problems', but might be of value in helping staff
to clarify the nature of these problems.

The nature of such an evaluation study has to be understood if one is not
to be disappointed by the absence of a summary of the school's strong and
weak points along the lines of the Consumer Association's magazine, *Which?*
That such a study can give rise to inappropriate expectations is hinted at by
the author when in her epilogue she states that she is not in a position to tell
those who frequently ask her whether Nailsea is a good school; neither is she
in a position to compare it with other schools. While such questions may be
important to residents in the school's catchment area, they clearly have little
relevance to the value of the study for other institutions endeavouring to
understand their workings at a time of change.

Case study B

In a paper prepared for the Organization for Economic Co-operation and
Development (OECD) Seminar in Ulster in 1973 Colin Bayne-Jardine, headmaster of a comprehensive school formed from the amalgamation of two
schools on separated sites, described the development of ideas about evaluation within the school. The account provided is of particular value in that it
indicates the evolution of the school's approach, recording some of the false
trails as well as suggesting paths which appear more productive. Initially a
working party within the school established a plan which owed much to

Bloom and Krathwohl's taxonomies of educational objectives (1956 and 1964). With expertise gained from in-service training courses, members of the party prepared guidelines in order to help departments specify their objectives. In the event, it is reported that only two departments took up the challenge; most departments 'simply shelved the problem and the school year rolled by without teachers discussing the crucial area of objectives within the general aim (of the school)'. Hindsight indicated that the disappointing response was not altogether surprising – the task was perhaps too distant, maybe too theoretical to be obviously relevant in the day-to-day working of departments within the school.

A new line of approach was developed by the school policy committee in which heads of departments were to discuss the 'effectiveness' of their departments with the headmaster at the start of each academic year. The memorandum circulated emphasized that, while examination results would have a place, they were to be only part of the evaluation process. Departments would be encouraged to establish targets for improvement during the next year and consideration would be given to the deployment of resources.

As a starting point in examining its own effectiveness, the school has made use of a simple grid which enables a situational analysis to be made for various aspects of the school. The structure of this grid is shown below in Table 6.3. The grid can be used to classify the stages or levels of progress in the school's development activity. At the planning stage, the objectives are established and, following the circulation of discussion documents and the holding of consultative meetings, detailed plans are made for implementation. Ideally as

Table 6.3   Indications of effective activity in the school

Areas of activity	Indicators of effective activity		
	Planning	Implementation	Evaluation
Curriculum			
Organization			
Welfare of pupils			
Welfare of staff			
Community and school relations			

part of this first stage the evaluation strategy will be formulated so that the implementation may be monitored effectively from the start. After the innovation has been established for some while the evaluation evidence can be examined with a view to improving and adapting the innovation or perhaps rejecting it.

In a more recent paper, Bayne-Jardine (1973) has suggested the increased use of descriptive accounts within the areas of activity identified within the school. Gathered and set out within a recognized framework such accounts can be used as a basis for planning and development. While many such accounts would be contributed by teachers within the school, there is scope for using the expertise of advisers, inspectors and those involved in educational research. The depth of knowledge of the insider and the objectivity of the outsider were interestingly brought together in the commission given to the newly appointed deputy headmaster, to produce a paper on the school's curriculum structure.

The headmaster's view after a period of developing ongoing evaluation activities within the school is expressed as follows — 'The development of simple descriptive accounts of activities set within broad frames as a basis for informed planning should help to reduce anxiety whereas complex management schemes may simply increases stress and could reduce measurement of human beings to a single dimension of examination results' (Bayne-Jardine 1974).

SCHOOL SPONSORED EVALUATION

The education authorities, local and national, are involved in a wide range of studies in response to immediate concerns and to forward planning. Professional researchers will wish to devise their own models in making their studies; the work may spring from their own interests or be in response to commissions from outside their own institution. What is possible for the individual school?

If we assume that the concern is either for a greater understanding of the institution or is towards the planning of development, three approaches are fairly readily identified.

1. Working with an outside consultant

Although the appropriate pool of expertise is inevitably limited, the use of an outside consultant does offer a degree of objectivity without the perceived threat implicit in a study by the local education authority or by HMIs. In offering scope for the negotiation of an appropriate task and role for the consultant, it carries with it uncertainty which may be uncomfortable but which can lead ultimately to a more valid, though not necessarily tension free, working relationship between school and consultant.

The amount of expertise available is perhaps not so discouragingly small if we look beyond the traditional professional researcher. While such a person has particular expertise which can lead to an in-depth study, other qualities of value within a consultancy may be found among teachers from other schools, in particular those who may have worked on research studies as part of their courses for advanced diplomas or higher degrees. While time and knowledge of techniques and instruments of evaluation may be limited, a degree of objectivity together with a professional understanding of the context may lead to a rewarding outcome. Within the advisory service there is potentially another source of consultancy help. However the somewhat vague distinction between inspectorial duties and those of an advisory nature will hamper any threat-free consultancy unless the role of advisers is crystallized in a more independent form.

2. The 'hierarchy' study

In such a case the headteacher and senior staff may carry out a study of particular aspects of the school. They would normally instigate the study, define the objectives, organize the necessary survey work and interpret the results. The approach may well be efficient in the use of time and display clarity of purpose in the development of its activities. It mirrors an approach to evaluation work within industry and, while necessary perhaps for certain aspects of planning and development, it might be considered inappropriate as the standard model within the professionally staffed school.

3. The staff conference/working party

With the increasing degree of involvement of staff in the development of school policy, staff conferences to review various aspects of the school have often been the starting point or have formed part of an evaluation programme. Where local authorities have established a number of in-service days in the school year, time and opportunity is provided for the whole staff to participate in reviewing aspects of the school's work. Initially the unfamiliarity of the opportunity may lead to unreasonable optimism as to what will be achieved quickly, followed by frustration that 'we only talked around the subject'. However some day conferences and other weekend conferences have led on to active working parties reviewing parts of the school's work in depth and leading to reports and proposals for modification in current practice. While the scale of this type of approach may lead to considerable management problems in itself, it has the merit of encouraging the participation of all interested staff.

The first stage in any study will be to clarify questions which are to be answered in relation to the school. Local reorganization or a change of staff may direct attention to particular issues. In contemplating a more general review it may be found helpful to construct a school profile as a means of achieving breadth and in order to reveal areas which require closer study. Essentially this is a checklist of some of the possible services a school should or may perform for its pupils, its staff and its community. First the major activities or aspects of the school life have to be identified; these will then be grouped into major service areas like curriculum activities, pastoral activities and others. Then a number of specific items will be drawn up about these activities. Responses to these items may be factual, for example, 'Does the school allow pupils to have sufficient subject options from which to choose after they have reached the age of 13 years?' would invite a response of YES/NO/SOMETIMES. Alternatively the items may invite qualitative responses, like STRONGLY AGREE/AGREE/SOMETIMES/DISAGREE/ STRONGLY DISAGREE (Oppenheim 1966).

So a table (Table 6.4) may be drawn up as below:

Table 6.4   Profile of school services

Service which may be provided.*	Evaluation	Details of service actually provided	Remedial action proposed
School records are adequate to show details of all individual pupils' progress	Yes/No/Some-times or SA/A/Some-times/D/SA	A school record does exist but this is thought to be inadequate	A staff committee will be set up to recommend changes in the system of records

*For a list of some of these (see sample profile pp. 132–138).

This checklist may be used by head, staff or others in order to contribute to an evaluation of the school. The list given at the end of the chapter is not prescriptive but is offered as a frame from which staff may select or to which they may add items to suit their own particular circumstances. An early version of the lists was circulated and discussed by a group of primary and secondary school heads and teachers. Modifications have been made in the light of their suggestions.

Its strength lies in the comprehensive nature of its coverage of school activities (unlike Conant's work) and in its flexibility — since school staffs may modify it to suit their own particular requirements. Its weaknesses are that it offers no built-in criteria for evaluation and also, by its very nature, a checklist may be regarded as prescriptive, resulting in a degree of fragmentation and of 'tunnel vision' in the execution of the evaluation study. All a checklist of this kind will do is indicate the existence of a function or service rather than evaluate the quality of that function. The evaluation must be provided by the researchers (that is the school staff) themselves and to this extent encourages a professional response to demands for accountability. Further, there is a need to respond to the second in-built weakness by endeavouring to relate the elements of the checklist both to one another and to the whole. Without the inclusion of such a synthesis there exists a real possibility that a set of perfected school components may be developed and exhibited by a school which is by common agreement of participants and observers far from satisfactory.

The discussion in this chapter indicates that thinking about evaluation with respect to the whole school is at an early and formative stage. While researchers develop a variety of models and educational authorities are concerned about accountability in times of economic stringency, teachers have a growing interest in getting to grips with the process of change as well as increased expertise in the study of management and planning. Evaluative activity can therefore be expected to continue on all three fronts and it is to be hoped that the methodology and results will lead to mutually beneficial cross-fertilization. Such a positive state of affairs will demand increased accessibility to the studies made by authorities, more explanation and interpretation by professional researchers and a greater willingness by teachers within schools to recognize the contribution which their very familiarity with a particular institution can make.

SAMPLE OF A SCHOOL PROFILE

The list is divided, for convenience, into seven sections, all of which are inter-related. These are the: (A) communications system, (B) curriculum system, (C) guidance system, (D) assessment system, (E) staff development, (F) pupil-parent involvement and (G) basic considerations.

An evaluation of the school process

Here we are concerned with the functioning of the school, that is, the school in action.

A　　One element of the school process is the school organization, particularly the COMMUNICATION and the 'back-up and support' system. An analysis will be made of this system, especially the consultative and participatory machinery. The methods by which decisions are reached and implemented will be examined, what research is undertaken, how decisions are communicated to the whole staff, the pupil body and the parents.

B   Next the CURRICULUM SYSTEM would be examined in terms of the curriculum content, the teaching methods employed, the use of educational technology, the provision of out-of-school and other extra-curricular activities, examinations and curriculum evaluation and modification procedures.

C   The GUIDANCE or pastoral system in the school would then be analysed in terms of the guidance needs of the pupils, the orientation system, the appraisal and information service, educational guidance, personal guidance, vocational guidance and the provision of counselling services, the relationships with outside school specialized guidance services and the like.

D   THE ASSESSMENT SYSTEM straddles the curriculum and guidance systems. Assessment ideally should involve as many staff as possible and will involve both the study of pupils and the study of their environments. An evaluation of an assessment system might be to consider what is learned about pupils, how much of this is used, how often is the system revised and how much of this is communicated to pupils in order to improve their self-understanding?

E   Another area to be examined is that of STAFF DEVELOPMENT. Here an analysis may be made of the staff's opportunity to participate in decision making in curriculum building, and in examining. Other information which might be sought could include opportunities for the staff to carry out research, the facilities provided for in-service training and development within the school, opportunities for in-service courses outside the school, the help given to staff to follow part-time studies, to visit other schools, etc.

F   One might also look at the opportunities for PARENT-PUPIL OR COMMUNITY INVOLVEMENT in the life of the school. Concerns in this area include the existence, activities and influence of a parent—teacher association, the use of parents as ancillary helpers in the school and for leading extra-curricular and other activities, the opportunities for parents and pupils to take part in the 'school council', the opportunities provided for the 'education' of parents. This is of course an examination of the school-community activities and it is realized that some schools would like to become much more involved with the community than is suggested above. For example, they may invite adults into day classes, or offer special adult courses alongside those classes for pupils, and so on.

G   BASIC CONSIDERATIONS   Essentially this element of the evaluation will concentrate on the input element of the school system. Briefly it will seek to survey first the plant provision, sports facilities, playground, classroom, lighting, heating and ventilation. Second, the pupils will be classified in terms of age composition, social class background, general motivation, delinquency rates, aptitude levels and achievement levels as measured by standardized tests.

Third, the staff will be classified in terms of age composition, qualifications (general and special pupil–teacher ratios), teaching experience, turnover and the like. Another aspect that might be examined is the financial provision for the school. These may be the standard rates offered by the LEAs to all schools, on the other hand the school may recieve special provision as an Educational Priority Area, or the school may have a bequest, aid from parent-teacher associations, etc.

How the profile may be used

Teachers will, of course, be well advised to devise their own ways of using this method of evaluation. They may, however, like to consider this approach:

(a) All members of staff, and possibly a selection of the parents of pupils, will be circulated with a checklist of school activities similar to that on pp. 132–138.

(b) A staff meeting may then be called to decide on the scope of the operation, that is, to decide whether all the school activities should be evaluated or only some of them. Parents may be called in to help.

(c) Staff, and possibly parents, will then be asked to indicate the questions, within the topics chosen, on which they would like to concentrate. They may add other questions if appropriate.

(d) The administration will assess the intensity of feeling about the various topics and sub-topics and add others which they think are appropriate.

(e) On the assumption that a meeting of the whole staff would be too large for detailed discussion, a series of sub-committees might be set up: to sound out the opinion of staff and parents, to evaluate the school's work in the activities under review; and to make recommendations for future action.

(f) The reports of sub-committees will be considered by a meeting of the whole staff and invited parents.

(g) The decisions of the whole staff and parents will then be passed on to another sub-committee which will draw up a concerted plan for future action paying special attention to such areas as existing resources and staffing, other needed resources and staffing, the scheduling and phasing of the new measures, the allocation of responsibilities, the methods of feedback and reporting of progress.

EVALUATION BY MEANS OF A SCHOOL PROFILE: SOME POSSIBLE ITEMS FOR INVESTIGATION

The school process

A–I   ORGANIZATION (COMMUNICATIONS)

(a) All departments have regular meetings to discuss departmental policy.
(b) The whole of the teaching staff meet regularly to discuss school policy.
(c) The staff have adequate opportunities to influence school policy.
(d) All the staff are informed of major policy decisions in writing.
(e) The pupils and parents are all informed in writing of major policy decisions and their reactions are taken into account.
(f) The staff have access to LEA and school regulations such as 'The articles of Government'.
(g) Staff have adequate opportunities to see the head individually if they wish.
(h) Pupils and parents have adequate opportunities to see the head of house or headmaster if needed.
(i) An adequate notice board operates and notices are changed regularly for: (i) staff and (ii) pupils.
(j) Staff have sufficient opportunities to contact officers of the LEA, if necessary.

A–II   ORGANIZATION (BACK-UP AND SUPPORT SERVICES)

(a) The school administrators and the staff have adequate secretarial staff.
(b) The staff have adequate numbers of science, audio-visual and other technicians.
(c) The school is adequately provided with enough school keepers and sports ground attendants.
(d) The infant and primary sections of the school have enough ancillary help.

B   THE CURRICULUM SYSTEM

(a) The aims of the curriculum system are congruent with the aims of the school.
(b) There are adequate programmes offered in: reading, English, maths, science, creative arts, etc.
(c) The curriculum offered satisfies the needs of the pupils and a survey of these needs has recently been made.
(d) Staff are enabled to particpiate in any national curriculum development project if the opportunity presents itself.

(e) The staff may set up the following teaching and organizational strategies
     if they wish:
                        (i)   mixed-ability groups
                        (ii) team teaching
                        (iii) individualized learning
                        (iv) interdisciplinary learning
                        (v)   integrated day.
(f) Provision is made, if needed, for (i) remedial children, and (ii) disturbed
     children.
(g) Provision is made for gifted children.
(h) A curriculum committee on which staff and administrators are represen-
     ted meets periodically to consider modifying the curriculum.
(i) Pupils are given opportunities to choose at the primary level or from
     options after the age of 13/14 years.
(j) Parents and pupils are consulted regularly about the optional subjects
     available, and are asked to make suggestions for additional subjects,
     topics or activities.
(k) The provision of extra-curricular activities is adequate.
(l) Out-of-school activities (visits, outward-bound courses, school journeys,
     etc.) are numerous.
(m) The curriculum system is integrated with those operating in:
                   (i)   contributory or feeder schools
                   (ii) local schools of the same level
                   (iii) middle, secondary schools or colleges which the school feeds.
(n) Linked courses are provided for secondary school pupils at the local
     technical colleges.
(o) The head consults all heads of departments or other staff when allocating
     departmental funds.
(p) Staff have opportunities to consult: (i) LEA advisers, (ii) School Council
     officers, (iii) Curriculum development project teams.

C   THE GUIDANCE OR PASTORAL SYSTEM

(a) The important socio-personal, educational, vocational and other guidance
     needs of the pupils are known by the staff.
(b) The aims of the guidance system are congruent with the aims of the
     school.
(c) The academic staff agree with the pupils on the latter's needs.
(d) The guidance techniques used are adequate for these needs.
(e) The guidance facilities are sufficient to meet these needs.
(f) Appropriate records are kept about individual pupils and these are avail-
     able to sufficient staff so that the pupils may gain maximum benefit.

(g) Sufficient standardized tests and inventories are used and adequate diagnostic methods to identify those children whose achievement levels in reading, writing and numeracy are low.

(h) Sufficient non-testing instruments are used. (Includes rating scales, case studies, etc.).

(i) A sufficiently appropriate induction programme is available for pupils newly arrived in the school.

(j) Adequate information is made available to pupils about the choices in school, and the courses available after they have left school.

(k) Sufficient information is made available for pupils about job opportunities and job requirements.

(l) Enough guidance personnel are available to counsel or discuss problems with individual pupils, small groups of pupils and with academic staff with problems.

(m) The school's guidance system works closely with specialist agencies outside the school (i.e. the child guidance clinic, the educational welfare officer, the school psychological service, the careers officer, the police, etc.) and individual teachers have opportunities to contact these agencies.

(n) Pupils have opportunities of self-referral through the tutorial or the house system, year group or other system.

(o) Pupils receive plenty of encouragement to plan their educational and occupational careers.

(p) The school works closely with the Careers Service in placing the pupils in appropriate jobs.

(q) Adequate educational/occupational visits or experience are arranged.

(r) The school keeps a follow-up record of school leavers in the ecuational and occupational field.

(s) A guidance team exists which regularly reviews guidance policy.

(t) The roles of guidance personnel have been defined.

(u) Adequate resources are made available to guidance personnel to enable them to work efficiently.

D THE ASSESSMENT SYSTEM

(a) The assessment and examination systems are congruent with the aims of the school.

(b) The school records are such that an adequate profile of each pupil is obtained.

(c) The school uses a number of different methods of assessment including:

        (i) written examinations

        (ii) objective tests (such as multiple choice)

        (iii) open-book examinations

        (iv) continuous assessment (projects, essays)

        (v) practical examinations

        (vi) oral examinations, etc.

(d) Written examination and standardized test results are supplemented with non-testing appraisal techniques.

(e) Pupils are acquainted with the assessment procedures and will have knowledge of how the final result is arrived at.

(f) Pupils are encouraged to assess themselves and to keep a permanent record of this.

(g) An extra-school assessment is provided (e.g. the Swindon RPA assessment – see Chapter 2).

(h) The staff have opportunities to serve on or contact: (i) committees or officers of GCE examination boards, (ii) committees or officers of CSE examination boards.

E   THE STAFF DEVELOPMENT SYSTEM

(a) The staff have an opportunity to participate in and influence the policy making bodies concerned with general school organization, the curriculum and assessment systems; the pastoral and other systems.

(b) Staff are allocated time and resources to carry out research.

(c) In-service courses are regularly provided within the school itself.

(d) Staff are given opportunities to participate in a national project if the occasion arises.

(e) Staff are given encouragement to attend: (i) short courses, (ii) one term courses, or (iii) one year courses.

(f) The staff are encouraged to meet and discuss important educational documents (reports, books, etc.) and legislation (e.g. Industrial Training Act of 1964) and important educational developments (e.g. the creation of polytechnics).

(g) Staff are provided with adequate resource centre materials and library facilities.

(h) Staff are encouraged to take extra qualifications such as certificates, diplomas, first and further degrees.

(i) Staff have opportunities to develop and appropriate interests and expertise within the curriculum programmes and extra-curricular activities.

(j) Staff are encouraged and given opportunities to visit: (i) other schools, (ii) local teachers' centres, etc.

(k) The staff is well supported by LEA advisers.

(l) A professional tutor is provided by the school.

(m) Special provision and supervision is made for probationary teachers.

F PUPIL–PARENT OR COMMUNITY INVOLVEMENT

(a) Parents are encouraged to join the parent-teacher association.
(b) Parents, staff and pupils are represented on the school council.
(c) Regular discussion, workshop and experimental groups are laid on for parents.
(d) Parents are encouraged to act as ancillary workers in the classroom, though not to substitute for teachers. In particular, parents could help in the careers education programmes.
(e) Parents are encouraged to take part in extra-curricular activities.
(f) Pupils are encouraged to carry out social activity and participate in programmes for needy people in the community.
(g) Older pupils, of all abilities, are encouraged to help younger pupils with their class work.
(h) The school is used 'after hours' as: (i) a community centre, (ii) youth centre, (iii) adult education centre.
(i) Most parents have positive attitudes towards the school.
(j) Most pupils have positive attitudes towards the school.

G–I BASIC CONSIDERATIONS (PLANT)*

(a) The school is adequately lit, heated, and ventilated.
(b) The school plant is sufficiently homogeneous so as not to impair the efficiency of the school programme.
(c) The school has a sufficiency of ordinary and specialized classrooms to carry out its functions.
(d) The school has enough playground, field sports and swimming facilities, within reasonable distance of the school.
(e) The school has adequate and secure storage space for school equipment.
(f) The school has good facilities for a library and a resource centre.
(g) The school has adequate recreational facilities for staff (staff room) and senior pupils (sixth-form common room).
(h) Sufficient washing and changing facilities are provided for staff and pupils.
(i) Adequate dining facilities are provided for: (i) staff, and (ii) pupils.
(j) The school transport arrangements (e.g. bus and train feeder services) are adequate.
(k) Adequate parking space is provided by the school.
(l) The provision for first aid during emergencies is adequate.

*For an alternative series of items which might be included in the checklist see Society for Education Officers (1972), Management in the Education Services.

G–II   BASIC CONSIDERATIONS (THE PUPIL BODY)*

(Indices of motivation? Prestige of the school? Pupil expectations.)

(a)   More pupils apply for admission to the school than there are places available.

(b)   Absenteeism by pupils from the school is above the national average.

(c)   A considerable number of pupils transfer from this school to another before they reach school leaving age.

(d)   The numbers of pupils staying on after they reach school leaving age is above the national/regional average. (See examples in Rowe 1971.)

(e)   The number of 'official' delinquents in the school is higher than the national average OR is rising.

(f)   The number of pupils who have been suspended from school for bad behaviour is high OR is rising.

(g)   The expectations of pupils can be seen if the proportions of the appropriate age group who enter for public examinations is above the national average:

    – at CSE level
    – at GCE O-level } (see DES statistics)
    – at GCE A-level

(h)   The school has a greater proportion of middle class children (as defined by the Registrar General) than is present in the population at large.

(i)   The school draws from (number here) (infant/junior/primary/middle) feeder schools and all are classified by the (school staff/head/research team) as satisfactory, and regular meetings are held with the staffs of these schools. (It is realized that the LEAs control admissions in many areas and base their choice on such factors as the proximity of the pupil's house to the school and family unity. Further, it is appreciated that some parents transfer their children from one school to another for non-educational reasons (e.g. to save bus fares, to be with friends).

G–III   BASIC CONSIDERATIONS (STAFFING)

(a)   The pupil–teacher ratio is more favourable than the national average.

(b)   The school has an adequate number of teachers with more than three years' experience.

(c)   The school has enough specialist teachers in: reading, maths, English, science, history, geography, creative arts, RE, PE, handicrafts, home economics, remedial teaching, guidance, foreign languages, and other subjects thought necessary.

*For an alternative series of items which might be included in the checklist see Society for Education Officers (1972), Management in the Education Services.

(d) The staff turnover is such that teaching and pastoral duties are not disrupted.

(e) The head fulfils an adequate leadership role.

(f) The staff have adequate opportunities to use ancillary helpers if needed.

G–IV BASIC CONSIDERATIONS (FINANCIAL PROVISION)

(a) The school is receiving the statutory grant from the LEA.

(b) The school is in receipt of special allowances from the LEA.

(c) Funds are available from the PTA, gifts to the school, the proceeds of jumble sales, etc.

(d) There are enough funds to secure enough audio-visual equipment and other extras thought necessary.

References

Bayne-Jardine, C. (1973). 'The new head in the secondary school context', unpublished lead paper for the international seminar at the New University of Ulster sponsored by OECD.

Bayne-Jardine, C. (1974). 'Organizational analysis in secondary schools – a framework for development', *Journal of Applied Educational Studies*, **3**, No. 1, summer, pp. 14–16.

Bloom, B. S. ed. (1956). *A Taxonomy of Educational Objectives: the Classification of Educational Goals*, Handbook 1: *Cognitive Domain*. Longmans.

Conant, J. B. (1959). *The American High School*, pp. 18–19. New York: McGraw-Hill.

Dodd, W. A. (1968). *Primary School Inspection in New Countries*, p. 36 ff. Oxford University Press.

Ford, J. (1969). *Social Class and the Comprehensive School*. Routledge.

Grieves, A. P. (1962). In E. L. Edmonds, *The School Inspectors*, p. 119, Routledge.

Jackson, R. (1973). *Some Aspects of Counselling and Guidance at Higher Education Levels* (adapted from mimeographed publication). Paris: UNESCO.

Jackson, B. and Marsden, D. (1962). *Education in the Working Class*. Routledge.

Krathwohl, D. R. et al. (1964). *A Taxonomy of Educational Objectives: the Classification of Educational Goals*, Handbook 2: *Affective Domain*. Longmans.

Lambert, R. (1966). In G. Kalton, *The Public Schools*. Longmans.

McAlhone, B. (1974). 'Checklist on your child's schooling' I, II & III, in *Where*, Nos. 91–93, April, May & June 1974. Advisory Centre for Education, Cambridge.

Oppenheim, A. N. (1966). *Questionnaire Design and Attitude Measurement*, pp. 133–142. Heinemann Educational.

Parlett, M. & Hamilton, D. (1976). 'Evaluation as illumination', Chapter 5 in *Curriculum Evaluation Today: Trends and Implications*, ed. D. Tawney, Schools Council Research Studies. Macmillan Education.

Richardson, E. (1973). *The Teacher, the School and the Task of Management.* Heinemann Educational.

Rowe, A. (1971). *The School as a Guidance Community.* Hull: Pearson.

Wateford, J. (1969). *The Cloistered Elite.* Macmillan.

7 Summing up the issues raised
Wynne Harlen

Anyone taking up this book thinking that evaluation was all about assessing the performance of pupils, if they read any of the chapters, would find that view challenged and indeed overthrown. The persistent reader who accepts the need for a wider conception of evaluation might, however, have found difficulty in replacing his original view of evaluation by one which is equally neat and tidy. The broadening of the concept of evaluation, to bring the school and all who work in the educational system into its compass, the raising of questions about who is the evaluation for, what is it for and who carries it out, have presented evaluation as a complex process in which many issues are unresolved. The situation cannot be avoided; education is an immensely complex process, how can its evaluation be less so?

In focusing upon teachers' participation in evaluation the authors have tried to extend the idea that there is a role for teachers in evaluation to the claim that evaluation should be a part of a teacher's role. The researcher or outside evaluator has in the past been thought to be best qualified to look at the performance of schools and those within them, the teachers and others inside, lacking the expertise and 'objectivity' required. The emphasis is shifting, however, and the researcher's knowledge of measurement techniques is not such an advantage when it is realized that 'The detail and the pattern of which the insider is aware are unknown to the outsider who relies to a large extent on samples of exterior features and activity' (see Chapter 6, page 114).

Teachers' unique positions give them opportunities for evaluating their work, their pupils, their schools, but is not the same as claiming that they can or should be responsible for evaluation. Whether they can or not depends upon having the resources and time which are required as well as knowledge of approaches and methods which are useful. The examples given in earlier chapters in this book show that the amount of technical knowledge demanded is not great; methods do exist, or can be devised, which are accessible to teachers, but gathering information will inevitably take time. The belief that not only is this time well spent but that teachers ought to be spending some part of their time in evaluating their work is implicit throughout this book. The reasons for this belief rest not only on the claim that the position of teachers gives them access to the information which is needed, but also on the argument that evaluation by teachers themselves is necessary to preserve their autonomy, their control over decisions about their work, which is an essential part of a professional function. Wholly external evaluation, of the 'payment by results' kind leaves teachers little freedom to make decisions about their work; the greater the degree of participation by teachers in evaluation the more freedom they have to decide appropriate goals for their pupils and experiences through which these can be achieved.

Evaluation is a process which cannot be dissociated from a personal stand-point of values and beliefs and the lines of argument pursued by the authors of different chapters reflect their own false judgements. Statements made and conclusions drawn about the nature, purposes and methods of evaluation arise from particular points of view about issues which are involved. The purpose in this chapter is not to review the arguments and evidence but to focus on the issues which teachers will want to consider when discussing evaluation in relation to their work and their part in it.

THE NATURE OF EVALUATION

The authors of each of the chapters in this book have offered descriptions or definitions of evaluation relating to particular areas of concern — the pupil, the teacher, the organization, the curriculum, the whole school. These provide a suitable starting point for weaving together the separately spun threads of this book. Can we find a consensus as to the nature of evaluation? Are there any clear ideas about how evaluation relates to assessment, to research, to policy?

In the early years of curriculum development in this country, the middle and later 1960s, when the focus of activity was the revision of syllabuses and the creation of new teaching material, evaluation was concerned either directly or indirectly with the effect of the changes upon pupils. Where it was seen as 'essentially the process of determining to what extent the educational objec-tives are actually being realized by the program of curriculum and instruction' (Tyler 1949) evaluation was synonymous with assessment, but where the inadequacy of this information was realized the term evaluation took on a much wider meaning than assessment. A discussion of various definitions and of trends and changes in ideas about curriculum evaluation which lie behind them can be found elsewhere (e.g. Cooper 1976, Harlen 1976). But changes were not only taking place in evaluation strategy; as Hamilton and Hickmott point out in Chapter 4, the focus of curriculum activity has moved away from production of teaching materials only, towards consideration of processes and roles at all levels in the class, school and educational system. 'In its turn, curriculum evaluation has responded to these changes and moved away from a reliance on input–output techniques (of pre-tests and post-tests) and, instead, has tried to gain greater understanding of the relationship between organizational forms and the multiplicity of classroom transactions that they generate' (Chapter 4, page 93).

Evaluation in the context of curriculum development has thus come to imply a greater range of activities in relation to a wider field of subjects than conceived, say, ten years ago. We can think of it, as we have done in this book in relation to organizations, to teachers, to systems, as well as to materials and to pupils. The activities it involves are concerned with gathering information, but again the range and forms of information are extremely wide; they are likely to include opinions, impressions, judgements as well as, or perhaps in place of, the kinds of descriptions and assessments which are considered to be more 'objective' and which were once the only kinds of information thought to be acceptable. What determines the information which is gathered and, to some extent, how it is gathered, is the use to which it is to be put. The authors here have all described the purpose of evaluation as being to provide information for decision making in one context or another. This is not as straight-forward as it may at first seem, for there is the problem of relevance; whose ideas about what information is relevant to a decision are to be followed? Here we are reminded of the political aspect of evaluation, a matter to which we will return later.

For the moment there is one further distinction which may help to define the boundaries and limitations of evaluation, the relationship of research and evaluation. A carefully argued account of this relationship has been given by MacDonald (1976) in which he warns against regarding evaluation as an extension of educational research. An important distinction between the two, he says, lies in the selection of the problems which are at the focus of study: 'The researcher is free to select his questions, and to seek answers to them. He will naturally select questions which are susceptible to the problem-solving techniques of this craft. . . . The evaluator, on the other hand, must never fall into the error of answering questions which no-one but he is asking. He must first identify the significant questions, and only then address the technological problems which they raise' (MacDonald 1976, page 131). Thus evaluation must respond to the situation which exists and the decisions which have to be taken. It may mean that crude techniques are more appropriate than sophisti-cated measurement technology; it certainly does mean that new methods of information collection are constantly having to be devised.

The important conclusion emerging from this discussion of the nature of evaluation is that it has moved away from being the preserve of 'experts'. In many cases it uses methods which are accessible to, or can be devised by, teachers. The examples cited throughout this book show that simple techniques, often built upon what teachers already do in some degree, can yield information which should be available when decisions of various kinds are made. But removing the mystique surrounding the techniques of evaluation only goes some of the way towards enabling teachers to take part in evaluating various aspects of their work. To go the rest of the way requires a change in attitude as to how decisions about changes should be made. A tradition has grown up that evaluation should be in the hands of an outsider to the classroom or school, one who decides what information to gather; he may involve teachers in collecting it but rarely in applying it to the problem or area of study. The 'outside' evaluator is in danger of the same pitfall as the educational researcher, of answering questions which he finds fascinating rather than the ones which are immediate to the concerns of those within the school. Moreover, he is unlikely to be sensitive to the changes in the situations affecting problems and indeed to the nature of the problems themselves which are part of the complexity of the school life. On the other hand, those on the 'inside' will be only too aware of the questions they want to answer, of their complex and changing nature; they will be unlikely to gather data for the sake of writing a report; they will want to be sure that what is done is increasing their understanding of their problem. This does not mean that all evaluation can be done by those within the school – this would not be practicable in terms of time demands upon the teacher for one thing – but rather that the balance of roles between insider and outsider should be reconsidered. One way in which the outsider can help the insider, in this case the teacher, to gather information has been given in Chapter 3 (pages 77–85); another approach is described in Chapter 6 (pages 123–124). The general issue here is 'who controls the evaluation'. Many parts of the book contribute to the discussion but the answer in any particular case has to be sought among those concerned.

WHAT USE IS EVALUATION?

It is not easy to find a short answer in general terms, though authors of individual chapters have addressed this question in respect of evaluation in particular contexts. At a general level the question is perhaps best approached by asking first 'For whom is evaluation of use?' It has been claimed that, as well as the teacher, 'the possible initiators and audiences of an evaluative inquiry are extremely diverse. They might include parents anxious to select a school for their children; college lecturers seeking up-to-date material to document current practice; advisers interested in the suitability of specific curriculum materials; headmasters planning to restructure the curriculum within their own schools; students searching for a first appointment to match their aspirations; and teachers seeking promotion through posts that have been advertised' (Chapter 4, page 94). Each of these could find evaluation of use as a source of information for taking action but the particular circumstances of any case will determine whether enough information of the kind required can be obtained. An attempt at gathering information might simply lead to the realization that it cannot be obtained; in such a case the evaluation is not useless but rather of value in showing just how inadequate is the information base of certain decisions or actions. For example, a head planning some reorganization in some part of the school is extremely unlikely to be able to find, if he wants it, information about the differential effect of the changes on the pupils achievement. He must take action on the basis of other information, which he may or may not feel is adequate. As noted in Chapter 6 'it seems important to acknowledge . . . the fact that many decisions are made on the basis of such slim and arguably partisan evidence' (page 113).

The issue of what is adequate information will have to be resolved in particular cases by those involved. Examples of the kind of information which can usefully be sought for particular purposes have been given in the appendices but the authors in this book avoided suggesting lists of items which could be taken as definitive statements of what information is needed for certain decisions. They have instead attempted to stimulate teachers and others into working this out for themselves.

Because it is frequently not possible to obtain information which is sufficient in quantity or quality, when decisions have to be made, hunches, hobby horses and habits take the place of hard facts. But this is only one part of the problem, the other being again bound up with the complex reality of school life. Even if we do have facts which show up that it is better to follow one course than another or to teach in one way than another, the effects of the proposed changes on the rest of the school and on the total experience of the pupils have to be considered. We are never able to anticipate fully the effect of certain changes and so are in difficulty when it comes to considering priorities of one course of action over another. In these situations the final outcomes result from negotiation. This has been illustrated in Chapter 5 'Where priorities have to be decided for a group, it seems that final decisions emerge only after a process of negotiation between the interested parties' (page 109). Inevitably in this negotiation some individuals will give up priorities in favour of the claims of others, provided that they in return can achieve part of their own goals.

Of course all of this could be taken as an argument for saying that the variables are so many and interconnected that evaluation is unlikely to be of use. In this book the opposite conclusion has been drawn, that the complexity of the problems requires more evaluation activity, not less. It has been argued that this should take place within the school so that it can respond to the changes and avoid the situation in which yesterday's data are being used to illuminate today's decisions. The value for those involved will be their greater appreciation of what information is being used in decision making, what information is being ignored or is just not available, and what further information is required to monitor the effect of a decision and build up a knowledge base so that future action can be better informed.

VALUES AND EVALUATION

The kinds of evaluation activity described in this book place the evaluator, or the person who is performing evaluation functions in addition to other roles, right at the centre of the action. Chapter 1 discussed the evaluative parts of the teacher's role with respect to individual pupils, where the teacher decides what information to gather and is responsible for collecting and interpreting it; Chapter 6 cited examples of teachers evaluating the effectiveness of their own school; Chapter 3 has outlined an approach to teacher self-evaluation. In all three cases the evaluation is far from objective; the evaluator a long way from being 'independent'. Evidently the values of the person(s) carrying out evaluation will influence the choices made at all stages. Chapter 5 has attempted to explain the meaning of 'values' in this context and to reveal their influence. It might be thought, however, that to speak of 'values' was not to go far enough and we should follow MacDonald (1976) in acknowledging the political stance which is implied in deciding in the first place to undertake evaluation and then in the way in which it is carried out: 'I have increasingly come to view evaluation itself as a political activity, and to understand its variety of styles and approaches as expressions of differing stances towards the prevailing distribution of educational power' (page 126).

Does this mean that the information a teacher gathers about the pupils and uses in classroom decisions is influenced by a political stance? Is the decision to reorganize the third year in mixed ability groups brought about as a result of a value-laden process? On the surface it seems unlikely. But scratch a little beneath the surface and ask the questions: Why is some information gathered about the children and not others? What is the purpose to which it is put? Who was consulted about extending mixed-ability grouping to the third year? What ends is it expected to achieve in the view of its proponents? It is further suggested in Chapter 3 that values enter into assessing actions as causes (page 48), which underlines the claim that not only is the selection of evidence influenced by subjective judgement of what it is important to consider, but also that the evidence which is included is likely to be interpreted in different ways by those with different viewpoints.

It is possible that some readers will think this political aspect of the process of decision making is being overplayed — we are in danger of seeing the educational equivalent of 'reds-under-the-bed' or sinister motives behind even the introduction of a new reading scheme. It is worth reflecting, however, that many an open-ended discussion among teachers ends up debating 'what education is all about' in an attempt to search for reasons for what we do or for guidelines as to what we might do. There are links to be found between our everyday decisions and our basic beliefs about education. Evaluation often lays these bare; it does not manufacture them. Perhaps one of the main values of evaluation is that it provides a forum for acknowledging and debating values in education.

ACCOUNTABILITY AND EVALUATION

The central issues surrounding the already emotive word 'accountability' relate not to whether teachers should be accountable to others — this is rarely disputed — but rather to whom they should be accountable, and for what; further, what assumptions can be made in evaluating teachers' effectiveness. These are topics which are addressed particularly in Chapter 3 but which underlie any discussion of evaluation with regard to the educational system.

The arguments which have linked decisions about goals with the values of those who make the decisions lead to the realization that the question 'Who determines the goals against which teachers' effectiveness is judged?' really means whose values determine their goals and thus the criteria for judgement of teachers. An issue implicit in what is written in Chapter 3 concerns the question as to whether teachers can be held accountable for failure to achieve goals which they do not themselves perceive to be goals. The point that teachers should be free to define goals and not to accept a limited range of goals imposed on them from outside is connected with their professional responsibility to all groups in society. However, the strength of this argument — that teachers should be able to 'protect a plurality of interests in society including those of their own professional group' (page 57), might also be its weakness — what happens if they neglect this responsibility? A dialogue between teachers, parents and others in the community of the schools is essential for this model of accountability not to end in schools pursuing their own (valued-based) ideas about what is in the interests of society as a whole.

The freedom of teachers in respect of deciding their goals brings with it the obligation upon teachers to evaluate their own performance in relation to these goals. If evaluation is undertaken by the teachers they have the information upon which decisions can be taken about changes in the provision for their pupils. Their autonomy is not restricted by the evaluation process. On the other hand if evaluation is carried out only by outsiders then the information is not in the teachers' hands. Decisions about action to take may then be taken out of teachers' control, their autonomy of action is decreased and with it their freedom to define their goals is likely to be impaired. It follows that if teachers want to protect their freedom to define goals they must accept the responsibility for self-evaluation. Hence the argument for teachers developing a system of professional accountability.

The extent to which teachers can take this responsibility in practice is open to debate. The first reaction of many is likely to be that they have neither the time nor the expertise, but some would argue that what is demanded is a reorganization of priorities. Neither need the help which outsiders could give to teachers be ignored; what should be guarded in the collaboration of teachers with professional evaluators or researchers is the autonomy of the teacher. There is likely to be a lot to gain for teachers, pupils, parents and their groups in society if teachers incorporate into their roles a critical examination of their goals and their effectiveness in achieving them. The question of what may be lost if this critical examination is carried out by people outside the classroom is open to debate. An external monitoring system which imposes its own version of aims of objectives on teachers will ultimately restrict the freedom of action of teachers and thus be seen by them as a threat to their professional autonomy.

The rejection in Chapter 3 of some systems being used in accountability programmes in the US is based upon several criticisms, the main ones which link with central themes in this book concern the techniques being used and the participation of teachers. The narrowness of conventional ways of measuring outcomes of teaching has been emphasized in many contexts, and the importance of using a wide range of techniques for gathering information has been stressed. The issue of accountability has taken this discussion further by declaring that 'tests may assess what pupils have learned or even if they have learned what was intended, but . . . not . . . that what has been learned is a result of what teachers do' (page 53). The point is that the test results, valid or not, still do not evaluate the teaching, for there are numerous other factors which could account for the achievement or non-achievement of the pupils. Elliott concludes that 'A more appropriate way to determine the consequences of teaching may be via case studies of teacher-pupil interactions' (page 53).

The second theme of teachers' involvement in evaluation is also extended by the discussion of accountability beyond the participation in making decisions about their work, its organization and content to making judgements about how they carry out their work. This means that someone else's judgement about what happens in the classroom should not be the only basis for teachers being praised or blamed, for there is the further discussion of moral responsibility to be considered. A teacher's action may be justified by the circumstances (such as by the need to give special treatment to minority groups); alternatively the judgement may be rejected by disclaiming the criterion upon which it was based.

In some states of America, notably Michigan, teachers' rights to determine the criteria by which their work is judged and to answer criticisms have not been recognized. Teachers have complained that the tests used do not reflect the school curriculum and that they have not been consulted adequately about the content of the tests or the way in which they were to be applied. The intention of cutting the funds to schools whose test results fall below a certain level has been successfully thwarted by appeals from teachers, but the intention to do this remains. With movements such as these being reported it is no wonder that the setting up by the DES of the Assessment of Performance Unit (APU) has been seen as threatening by many educators in this country.

According to its terms of reference the APU has been set up outside an accountability framework in order 'to promote the development of methods of assessing and monitoring the achievement of children at school, and to seek to identify the incidence of under-achievement' (White paper, Command 5720). The director of the APU has acknowledged that the fulfilment of these aims in a way which restricts neither the freedom of teachers nor the breadth of experience of pupils requires 'the use of the widest possible range of modes of assessment of which the standardized test may prove to be but one. There will surely be room, too, for the unstructured, if ultimately subjective, assessment of observer, teacher and pupil' (Kay 1975). The APU's work is carefully described in terms of monitoring, an exercise of gathering information, there being as yet no statements as to the kinds of decisions which will be based on this information. It is perhaps the absence of such statements which lead others to speculate and to see the move in a much more sinister light than the work of the unit so far justifies.

COMMUNICATION AND EVALUATION

For information to be of more than immediate value to those who gather it there is need to communicate it to others. The act of recording is not a simple matter of putting information into 'cold storage', it can distort the information, as when qualitative descriptions are turned into a 'score' by checking off the number of items mentioned, or when words are interpreted differently by those who read or write them. Records frequently reduce the utility of information since 'the disagreement which exists about the importance of particular types of information and the validity of the subjective views of colleagues, result in even the most carefully prepared records remaining unused' (Chapter 2, page 30). Evidently in such cases there is no real communication, for information is not conveyed effectively. The likely reasons for the misuse or underuse of records, and therefore the loss of a considerable amount of information helpful for evaluation of various kinds, again seem to involve our main themes — participation of teachers and their professional responsibility.

The inadequacy in the view of teachers of many official LEA record cards has been noted in Chapter 2. Clearly the more successful systems of records are ones devised by those who have to use them, but these seem to be more prevalent within schools than across schools. There is a growing concern at the present time that records do not adequately support a child's transition from one school to another in the same area and when a child moves from one area of the country to another the chances are that his new teachers have to learn everything about him from scratch. This is a slow process and may mean a setback for the child of several months. The solution is not easy, however, for the variation in the design and use of record systems seems to be a way in which teachers' autonomy is manifest; are we not likely to reduce this by a common framework for recording information about children?

The issues surrounding the keeping of records also have political and moral overtones. It has been suggested that those who have information about others thereby have, potentially at least, greater control over them. In this view the communication of information about pupils, teachers or schools provides those who receive the information with a degree of control over those whom the information is about. The question then arises as to whether this control should be given without the knowledge or consent of those who are the subject of the information. The issue here is clearly one of the openness of records to all parties, including the subjects of the information.

One of the most common reasons which teachers give for not using the records made by other teachers — and by the same token not providing records of particular value — is that they do not want to be biased by what others say. Such reactions have been reported on page 30, Chapter 2. They generally prevail in relation to information passed on about pupils. Oddly enough the same teachers would probably be only too eager to gather opinions of colleagues about a new reading aid or some mathematics work cards, or the power structure in a school where they are considering making application for a post. What, then, is the foundation of mistrust of other teachers' observations about children? On the one hand, it might be a mistrust of other teachers' ability to be objective, whilst assuming that their own judgement will necessarily be more trustworthy. On the other hand, it could be the reverse — a fear that they could not prevent their own judgement from being influenced by that of someone else. There are other possibilities, none of which bear close logical examination.

What seems to be lacking in these arguments is acknowledgement that any information, whether gathered by oneself or another, is influenced by the relationship between the observed and the observer. No information is ever wholly accurate or entirely valid, not even so-called objective achievement tests. In several places in this book it has been pointed out that test scores do not convey the kind of information which is required for evaluation; instead it is necessary to use less formal methods of gathering data and accept the subjective element as the price to pay for the greater relevance of the information. If this is so then we have to develop ways of handling these kinds of data, not to dismiss them as too subjective but to work with them in the knowledge that they contain, unavoidably, a large subjective element. An important aspect in this process is to examine information about a subject drawn from as many different points of view as possible (cf. 'triangulation', described in Chapter 3). With this approach every piece of information is useful in building up the picture, none will suffice on its own and each will be interpreted for what it is, a subjective account reflecting one particular view. Were records of pupils to be regarded in this way they could be used to the pupils' benefit more often than is perhaps at present the case.

CONCLUSION

It has been acknowledged in all the foregoing chapters that the kinds of activity described in this book are not new. Teachers do make decisions about the activities of pupils, about class and school organization, about changes in the curriculum; they do make judgements about their own and their colleagues' effectiveness and the potentialities of pupils. These are and always have been integral parts of teachers' roles. But familiar events are often the most difficult to examine critically, which is what has been attempted here in discussing the making of decisions and judgements as evaluation activities.

In looking hard at what we already do the questions to ask are of the kind: are judgements based on relevant evidence, or on general impressions influenced to some degree by prejudice or by non-relevant aspects? We know this happens in relation to judgements about people, or there would be no need for legislation against discrimination; it also happens in relation to judgements about pupils in schools, and in relation to judgements about schools. The same questions should be asked about the basis for decisions about changes in teaching materials and organization at both class and school levels.

It has been argued that teachers are not only in the best position but also have a responsibility to examine how decisions and judgements affecting their pupils and themselves are made at present, and to improve the process where necessary, perhaps by using approaches such as those suggested in this book. Teachers do not have a choice as to whether decision making is part of their role, but they can choose to examine the information base of decisions, that is, to include evaluation within their role.

If they choose to do so, further help will be needed – one of the most valuable sources of such help being the experience of others. Reference has been made in various parts of this book to existing accounts of evaluation by teachers; more are needed. Teachers can help each other by reporting their work so that others have access to it. Perhaps the Schools Council Evaluators' Group also has a part to play in providing a future publication comprising case studies of school-based evaluation activities.

References

Cooper, K. (1976). 'Curriculum evaluation – definitions and boundaries', Chapter 1 in *Curriculum Evaluation Today: Trends and Implications*, ed. D. Tawney, Schools Council Research Studies. Macmillan Education.

Harlen, W. (1976). 'Change and development in evaluation strategy', Chapter 3 in *Curriculum Evaluation Today: Trends and Implications*, ed. D. Tawney, Schools Council Research Studies. Macmillan Education.

Kay, B. W. (1975). 'Monitoring pupils' performance' in *Trends in Education* No. 2, May 1975, pp. 11–18.

MacDonald, B. M. (1976). 'Evaluation and the control of education', Chapter 7 in *Curriculum Evaluation Today: Trends and Implications*, ed. D. Tawney, Schools Council Research Studies. Macmillan Education.

Tyler, R. W. (1949). *Basic Principles of Curriculum and Instruction.* University of Chicago Press (2nd British impression 1973).

Appendices

Illustrative material

I   Primary school records: pages from the New Ash Green County
Primary School (Kent) Record Book (1974)   155

II   Progress in Learning Science record sheet obtained by using the
Checklist for Later Development   159
Examples of checklist items   160

III   Record of Personal Achievement (Swindon) – sample pages   163

IV   A teacher's record of the integated day   167

V   School Board inspection (Norwich, 1870s)   169

VI   Examination and inspection of schools generally (1882)   171

VII Projects mentioned in this text   175

Appendix I
Primary School Records:
from the New Ash Green County
School (Kent) record book (1974)

Record of Individual Experience and Ability in the Basic Skills: Language

		I/1	I/2	J/1	J/2	J/3	J/4
		5−6	6−7	7−8	8−9	9−10	10−11
	Speech						
1	Talks freely to other individual friends						
2	Talks freely to others in his/her group						
3	Talks freely to all children						
4	Talks to teacher when questioned						
5	Talks to teacher quite freely						
6	Talks to adults in school						
7	Talks quite freely to everyone						
8	Takes part in school assembly in a reserved manner						
9	Enjoys taking part in assembly						
10	Enjoys taking assembly with a small number of others						
11	Enjoys reading or talking in front of other individuals						
12	Speaks clearly, but quietly						
13	Speaks clearly and confidently						
	Handwriting						
1	Traces letters in sand or on sandpaper						
2	Makes letters using plasticene/paint						
3	Prints on top of teacher's printing						
4	Prints underneath teacher's printing						
5	Copies printing from blackboard						
6	Does writing patterns						
7	Does letter writing patterns						
8	Copies simple words in joined up handwriting						
9	Copies simple sentences in joined up handwriting						

		I/1	I/2	J/1	J/2	J/3	J/4
		5−6	6−7	7−8	8−9	9−10	10−11
10	Writes short stories/descriptive pieces of writing						
11	Writes neatly in pencil						
12	Writes neatly, fluently in ball pen						
13	Writes neartly, fluently in ink						
14	Presents his/her written work in a legible, neat and attractive way						
15	Writes with reasonable speed						
16	Is developing his/her own individual style						
	Written Language						
1	Writes short simple sentences						
2	Writes short stories/descriptive pieces						
3	Writes long stories/descriptive pieces						
4	Uses capital letters as appropriate						
5	Uses full stops correctly						
6	Uses commas and apostrophes correctly						
7	Understands and uses other punctuation marks, e.g. speech marks, ? and ! marks						
8	Writes in paragraphs						
9	Has an elementary knowledge of various parts of speech						
10	Uses a limited vocabulary						
11	Uses a reasonable vocabulary						
12	Has an extensive vocabulary						
13	Uses own personal word book						
	Pre-reading experiences						
1	Sees simple titles/sentences written by teacher, around the teaching area						
2	Has simple titles/sentences written on his/her work by the teacher						
3	Sees books around the teaching area						
4	Sees teacher/others reading from books						
5	Enjoys listening to stories being read						
6	Takes an interest in picture books						
7	Takes an interest in books						
8	Enjoys pre-reading games in his/her class group						
9	Able to relate objects/pictures and words						
10	Able to relate words to pictures/objects						
11	Able to recognize simple words/names						

	I/1	I/2	J/1	J/2	J/3	J/4
	5–6	6–7				

Mathematics

1   Capacity

11	Sand play	
12	Water play	
13	Conservation of volume	
14	Comparison with arbitary measures	
15	Experience with standard measures, litre, half litre	

3   Area shape symmetry

m1   Play with large bricks, tiles, etc.
m2   Tessellation with apparatus
m3   Covering a flat surface with shapes that 'fit together'
m4   Finding area with arbitary measures – mats, bricks, shapes
m5   Finding area with square as a unit of measure
m6   Recognition of polygons, circles, triangles, square, rectangle, pentagon, hexagon, rhombus
m7   Pattern making with crayon, paint, tracing and with apparatus
m8   Symmetry, folding and cutting, blotting
m9   Polyhedra

– recognition of 'ball' (sphere), cube, cone, rectangular boxes, 'tube boxes', pyramid, etc.

– Junk model building with polyhedra

Play with Dienes Logiblocs – games

4   Graphical representation

n1   Collecting information and making graphs, using objects or symbols
n2   Block graphs
n3   Column graphs
n4   Describing graphs
n5   Making up questions about graphs
n6   Mapping

Appendix II
Progress in Learning
Science Record Sheet

☑ = initial observations   ■ = 1½ terms later

Notes:
1. These headings are only part of those on the Checklist for Later Development; others are concerned with attitudes.
2. Behavioural criteria are suggested at three levels in the checklist, and records are made by blocking in squares from the left up to the level appropriate for the child, using intermediate squares if needed.
3. Behavioural criteria given by the statements in the Checklist for Later Development can be seen on pp. 160–162. (Harlen 1977).
4. For examples of checklist items see pp. 160–162.

PROPOSING ENQUIRIES

Follows up a problem by suggesting possible solutions and ways of testing them which control the variables and enable their separate effects to be investigated.

Suggests problems for enquiry but lacks clear ideas about the possible solutions which could be tested or how to control the variables.

Needs help to express a question or problem in a form which is a basis for enquiry; not able to envisage the kind of enquiry needed or what variables to consider

EXPERIMENTING INVESTIGATING

Has a clear idea of the reason for the various steps in a practical enquiry and can work through them systematically making reasonable decisions with only occasional guidance.

Tries things out somewhat unsystematically unless the various steps in a practical enquiry are planned out for him, in which case he uses materials and collects results satisfactorily.

Is unable to progress from one point to another in a practical investigation or enquiry without help, failing to grasp the overall plan of the enquiry.

COMMUNICATING VERBALLY

Expresses himself clearly, using words appropriately and economically, and at a level which can be understood by whoever receives the message; expands his knowledge through reading.

Seems to have a clear idea himself of what he wants to express but does not always find the words to put it precisely or concisely; prefers to seek information orally than to use books.

What he writes or says is disorganized and difficult to follow; takes time to understand information in books or verbal directions unless these are accompanied by a demonstration of their meaning.

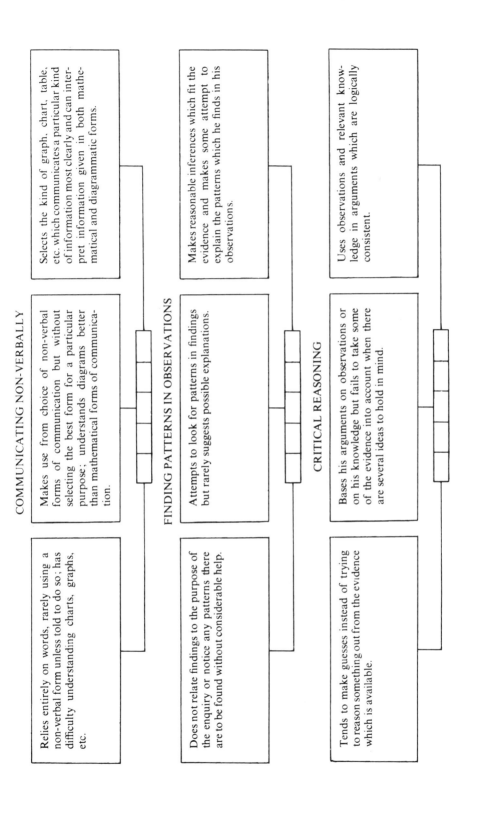

COMMUNICATING NON-VERBALLY

Selects the kind of graph, chart, table, etc. which communicates a particular kind of information most clearly and can interpret information given in both mathematical and diagrammatic forms.

Makes use from choice of non-verbal forms of communication but without selecting the best form for a particular purpose; understands diagrams better than mathematical forms of communication.

Relies entirely on words, rarely using a non-verbal form unless told to do so; has difficulty understanding charts, graphs, etc.

FINDING PATTERNS IN OBSERVATIONS

Makes reasonable inferences which fit the evidence and makes some attempt to explain the patterns which he finds in his observations.

Attempts to look for patterns in findings but rarely suggests possible explanations.

Does not relate findings to the purpose of the enquiry or notice any patterns there are to be found without considerable help.

CRITICAL REASONING

Uses observations and relevant knowledge in arguments which are logically consistent.

Bases his arguments on observations or on his knowledge but fails to take some of the evidence into account when there are several ideas to hold in mind.

Tends to make guesses instead of trying to reason something out from the evidence which is available.

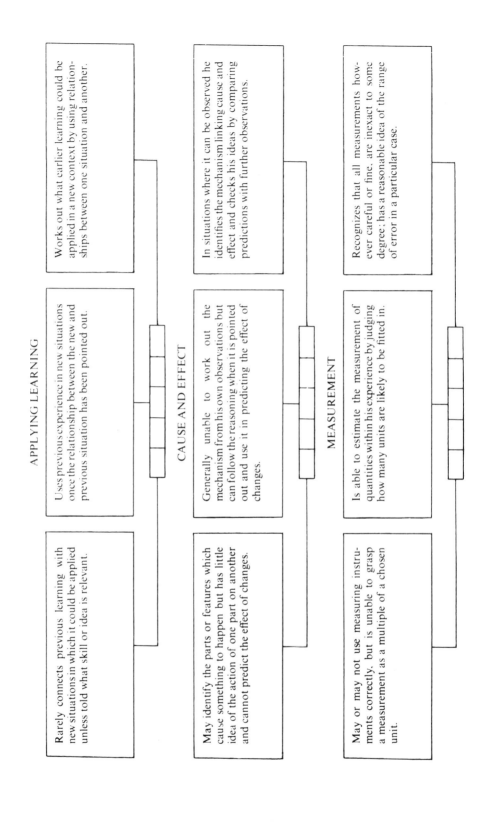

APPLYING LEARNING

Works out what earlier learning could be applied in a new context by using relationships between one situation and another.

Uses previous experience in new situations once the relationship between the new and previous situation has been pointed out.

Rarely connects previous learning with new situations in which it could be applied unless told what skill or idea is relevant.

CAUSE AND EFFECT

In situations where it can be observed he identifies the mechanism linking cause and effect and checks his ideas by comparing predictions with further observations.

Generally unable to work out the mechanism from his own observations but can follow the reasoning when it is pointed out and use it in predicting the effect of changes.

May identify the parts or features which cause something to happen but has little idea of the action of one part on another and cannot predict the effect of changes.

MEASUREMENT

Recognizes that all measurements however careful or fine, are inexact to some degree; has a reasonable idea of the range of error in a particular case.

Is able to estimate the measurement of quantities within his experience by judging how many units are likely to be fitted in.

May or may not use measuring instruments correctly, but is unable to grasp a measurement as a multiple of a chosen unit.

Appendix III
Record of Personal
Achievement (Swindon)

AWAY FROM HOME

DATE FROM	21·10·72	Swindon TO Barnstaple
PLACE	North Dawson	
MEANS OF TRANSPORT		
Coach down Car back		
TYPE OF ACCOMMODATION		
Post office		
ACTIVITY		

We took 6 and a ½ hours to get to Barnstaple when we got
there my brother came to get us in his new car
Sunday Today we went to Westward Ho! Appledor Do the
Washing up Monday Cooked the dinner took Mark and Paul down to
the park Tuesday Went to the pictures to see Neptone and
Samantha and Dumbo Wednesday help do the washing Went
down town and bought some new boots for christmas thursday helped
in the shop Friday did the washing up and did some ironing

SIGNED J Brown.   POSITION Sister in law - brother

AWAY FROM HOME

This card is used when children stay away from home for a minimum
of one night. Events such as 'week-end visits', 'holidays', 'youth hostelling',
'camping' etc., can be recorded here.

Note: These record cards have been reproduced by permission of Chief Education
Officer for Wiltshire. Family names used are fictitious.

RADIO AND TELEVISION PROGRAMMES

DATE	NAME OF PROGRAMME	TOPIC
5-4-73	MAN *BCC 2* ALIVE 9·00	DOCUMENTARY ON A CUSCUS
26-4-73	*MIDLANDS* ARTHER OF THE BRITONS 5·50	IT ABOUT SIXONS AND BRITONS OF action AND IT IS FULL
26-4-73	*BCC 1* OH FATHER Stan 7·50 *MIDLANDS*	Drake Rino is a father in it and it is funny
27-9-73	LOST IN SPACE Stan 4·25 *RADIO 2 8·6*	Billy Mury it about adventure in space
29-9-73	JNR CHOCE STARED STENARD	IT HAS GOOD MUSIC
1-10-73	STAR *BCC 1* TRAK. Stars LENOXD 9·5	NINOY. IT ABOUT SPACE
2-10-73	*MIDLANDS* FATHER DEAR FATHER Stan 8·30	PATHICK CARCLE IT IS VERY FUNNY
2-10-73	*BCC 2* THE STONE TAPE Stars 9·00	JANE ASHER. IT was very good.
3-10-73	*BCC 1* SEARCH CONTROL Stars 7·20	HUGH O'BRIAN IT was full of adventure
3-9-73	*BCC 1* LANCER Stan 2·10	JAMES STACY. I like cowboys
30-9-73	THE MORECAMBE AND WISE SHOW *BCC2* 9·40	It was very funny
4-10-73	TOP *BCC 1* OF THE DOPS 7·00 *MIDLANDS*	It has good music
7-10-73	Black BEAUTY 5·35	It is good and has alot of adventure
7-10-73	*H.T.V* RIPTIDE 2·5	It is very good.
7-10-73	*RADIO 1* SOLID gold SIXTY 1·0	It has good music
SIGNED	N M Green	POSITION Mother

RADIO AND TELEVISION

This is a useful card in the early months of the scheme. As with 'FILMS', children should be encouraged to be selective. Schools broadcasts can also be recorded here.

SERVICE TO OTHERS

DATE	ACTIVITY	SIGNED	POSITION
24·10·72	I Painted mums bedroom. when my dad had finished papering. I painted the window James straining-board door and cupboards in light green.	D. Black	Mother
29·12·72	I helped mum a lot at home I did make the meals and and tidied up and stayed up mone-a-lers all night with uncle frank who is very ill. (I stayed up more than one night)	D Black	Mother.
16·1·7?	Helped mum at home went to the shops for my mum	D. Black	Mother.
16·1·73	Went to the shop for Mrs Broadbent.	D. Broadbent	Friend

SERVICE TO OTHERS

This is usually for voluntary work, which may be undertaken in the home or in the community.

Entries may well range from helping at home to involvement in specific social services.

Frequently a pupil may find with an entry such as 'Helped an old lady across the road' that there is no one to sign the card. On such an occasion a tutor has to sign a card on trust.

Appendix IV
A teacher's record
of the integrated day

Fordbury Primary School:Activity record

Date record started 7.9.71....   Name Peter Holmes....

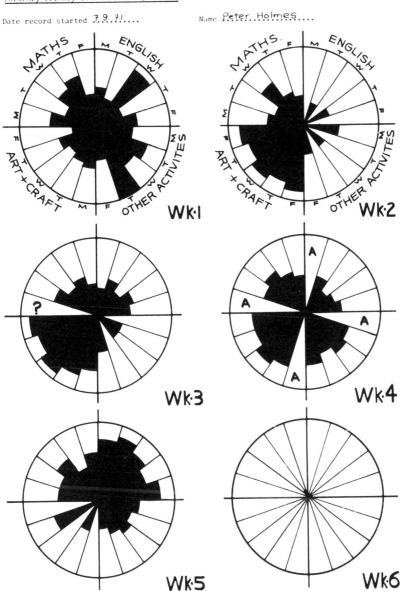

Reproduced, with permission, from *Record Keeping*, by P. Rance, Ward Lock, 1971.

Appendix V
School Board inspection
(Norwich, 1870s)

VISITORS' BOOK

.... School

.... Department

Question

1   Name and Address of Visitor? (i.e. Inspector).
2   Date and hour of Visit.
3   Is the attendance of Teachers regular and punctual?
4   Is the Staff complete and efficient?
5   Are the Pupil Teachers and Monitors regularly instructed and when is instruction given?
6   Is the Time Table duly observed?
7   Do you observe any defect of discipline or organization in the School?
8   Is the average attendance satisfactory, and the attendance of Scholars punctual and regular?
9   Are the Books appointed to be kept by the Teachers in order, and entries duly made therein?
10   Are the School and Class Rooms clean, and well warmed and ventilated?
11   Is the Caretaker attentive to his duties, and careful of the property of the Board?
12   Are the Books, Apparatus, and General Appliances of the School sufficient, and in good order?
13   Is the condition of the Playground, Yards and Offices satisfactory?

.... Signature of Visitor

(E. L. Edmonds, *The School Inspectors*, Routledge, 1962, pp. 18–19)

Appendix VI
Examination and inspection
of schools generally (1882)

Unsatisfactory 30 From bad or unsatisfactory schools it is manifest
schools that the merit grant should be withheld altogether.
The cases which you dealt with under Article 32b
of the former Code, and in which a deduction of
one or more tenths was made for 'faults of instruction or discipline', or in which you have not recom-
mended the grant for 'discipline and organisation'.
would, of course, fall under this head. Other cases
will occur which are not serious enough to justify
actual deduction; but in which you observe that
there is a preponderance of indifferent passes, pre-
ventible disorder, dullness, or irregularity; or that
the teacher is satisfied with a low standard of duty.
To schools of this class no merit grant should be
Fair schools awarded. But a school of humble aims, which
passes only a moderately successful examination,
may properly be designated 'Fair', if its work is
conscientiously done, and is sound as far as it
goes; and if the school is free from any conspicuous
faults.

Good schools 31 Generally, a school may be expected to receive the
mark 'Good', when both the number and the quality
of the passes are satisfactory; when the scholars
pass well in such class subjects as are taken up; and
when the organization, discipline, tone and general
intelligence are such as to deserve commendation.

Excellent 32 It is the intention of their Lordships that the mark
schools 'Excellent' should be reserved for cases of distin-
guished merit. A thoroughly good school in favourable conditions is characterized by cheerful and yet

171

exact discipline, maintained without harshness and without noisy demonstration of authority. Its premises are cleanly and well-ordered; its time-table provides a proper variety of mental employ-ment and of physical exercise; its organisation is such as to distribute the teaching power judiciously, and to secure for every scholar — whether he is likely to bring credit to the school by examination or not — a fair share of instruction and of attention. The teaching is animated and interesting, and yet thorough and accurate. The reading is fluent, care-ful and expressive, and the children are helped by questioning and explanation to follow the meaning of what they read. Arithmetic is so taught as to enable the scholars not only to obtain correct answers to sums, but also to understand the reason of the processes employed. If higher subjects are attempted, the lessons are not confined to memory work and to the learning of technical terms, but are designed to give a clear knowledge of facts, and to train the learner in the practice of thinking and observing. Besides fulfilling these conditions, which are all expressed or implied in the Code, such a school seeks by other means to be of service to the children who attend it. It provides for the upper classes a regular system of home-exercises, and arrangements for correcting them expeditiously and thoroughly. Where circumstances permit, it has also its lending library, its savings bank, and an orderly collection of simple objects and apparatus adapted to illustrate the school lessons, and formed in part by the co-operation of the scholars them-selves. Above all, its teaching and discipline are such as to exert a right influence on the manners, the conduct, and the character of the children, to awaken in them a love of reading, and such an interest in their own mental improvement as may reasonably be expected to last beyond the period of school life. Your attention may be usefully recalled to the following extract from the Code of 1881:—

'The Inspector will bear in mind, in reporting on
the organisation and discipline, the results of any
visits without notice made in the course of the
school year; and will not interfere with any method
of organisation adopted in a training college under
inspection if it is satisfactorily carried out in the
school. To meet the requirements respecting discipline, the managers and teachers will be expected
to satisfy the Inspector that all reasonable care is
taken, in the ordinary management of the school,
to bring up the children in habits of punctuality,
of good manners and language, of cleanliness and
neatness, and also to impress upon the children the
importance of cheerful obedience to duty, of consideration and respect for others, and of honour
and truthfulness in word and act.'

(Edmonds, 1962, pp. 117–119)

Appendix VII
Projects mentioned in this text

SC Change and Innovation in an Expanding Comprehensive School (11—18)
1968–1971
Director: Elizabeth Richardson
Bristol University (see p. 112 Richardson, 1975)

Concepts in Secondary Mathematics and Science (11—16)
Social Science Research Council
1974–1979
Director: Prof Paul Black
Chelsea College for Science Education, London

SC Development of Scientific and Mathematical Concepts in Children (7—11)
1968–1973
Director: Dr J. Rogers
University College, Bangor

SC Education of Severely Educationally Subnormal Children (2—19)
1973–1976
Director: Prof Peter Mittler
Greenbank School, Hartford

SC The Effective Use of Reading (10—14)
1973–1976
Director: Prof E. A. Lunzer and W. K. Gardner
Nottingham University

Ford Teaching Project (7—18)
1973–1975
Director: John Elliott
Classroom Action Research Network
Cambridge Institute of Education, Shaftesbury Road, Cambridge
(SC = Schools Council)

SC Geography for the Young School Leaver (14–16)
1970–1979
Director: T. Higginbottom
Avery Hill College of Education

SC History, Geography and Social Science (8–13)
1971–1975
Director: Prof W. A. L. Blyth
Liverpool University

SC Humanities Curriculum Project (14–16)
1967–1972
Director: Lawrence Stenhouse
East Anglia University

SC Linguistics and English Teaching: Initial Literacy Project (5–7)
1964–1971
Director: Prof M. A. K. Halliday
University College, London (see p. 111, Reid, 1975)

SC Nuffield Mathematics Project (5–13)
1964–1971
Director: Prof Geoffrey Matthews
Nuffield Foundation, London

SC Progress in Learning Science (5–13)
1973–1977
Director: Dr Wynne Harlen
Reading University

SC Record Keeping in Primary Schools (5–11)
1976–1978
Director: P. Clift
National Foundation for Educational Research, Slough

(SC = Schools Council)

SC Science 5/13 (5–13)
1967–1975
Director: L. F. Ennever
Bristol University

Swindon Record of Personal Achievement (now Personal Experience) Scheme
1969–
Director: D. R. Stansbury
Curriculum Study and Development Centre, Swindon

(SC = Schools Council)

Index

Accountability, 51, 52
  criteria of, 55
  democratic, xiv, 56
  democratic-professional, 57, 60, 71,
    75, 77
  evaluation and, 146–148
  professional, 56, 57, 70, 72, 75
  school-sponsored evaluation of, 129
  self-monitoring, 57–90
  self-motivating techniques for, 84–85
  systems, xiv, 51–52, 71, 147
    conformity of teacher to, 47
    development of, 69, 82, 86
    limitations of, 52–54
  utilitarian, 56
ACE *see* Advisory Centre for Education
Achievement, personal
  recording by pupils, 43, 45, 46
  records, planning, 46
  report to employers, 39
  report to parents, 37, 46
  scores, 53
Adelman, C. *and* Elliott, J., 57, 66
Adelman, C. *and* Walker, R., 81, 82, 85,
  86
Advisory Centre for Education, 38, 117
'Agricultural-botany' model
  evaluation of school as a whole, 115
Aims
  in education, 61, 62
  teachers', 62, 63, 72
Analysis
  of curriculum potential, 107
  of education values, 62
  interaction, 59
APU *see* Assessment of Performance Unit

Assessment
  and labelling, 7, 72
  causes of consequences in, 48–49
  checking, 83
  checklists, 20, 21, 26, 38, 128, 129,
    App. II
  criteria for, 3, 4, 5, 11, 43, 60–64, 94
  culpability for consequences in,
    50–51
  cumulative records of, 4–6
  dangers in, 6
  diagnostic, xiii, 13, 25
  effect on teachers' treatment of pupils,
    7
  in geography, history and social
    science, 22
  'halo' effect in, 6, 31
  information gathering for, 7–15
    confidential, 32
    diagnostic, 25
    inadequacy of, 144, 145
    by observers, 85–87
    values in, 100
  instruments for, 15–26
  judgements in, 82, 83
  matching experience and develop-
    ment for, 4, 18, 22
  methods: by observation, 14, 15,
    19–26, 65
    reliability of, 12
    validity of, 12
  norms, 12
  objectives for, 22
  organizational forms for, 94
  overall achievement in, 7
  profiles, 7, 21, 24, 128–138, App. II

Assessment (*cont.*)
  purposes of, 4
  reasons for, 6
  record keeping, 22
    political aspects of, 149
    problems in, 36–40
    purposes of, 40–42
    Schools Council project on, 38, 45
    use of, xiii, 5, 149
  records of, 4, 26–46
    bias and objectivity in, 5, 66, 149
    distortion of information in, 148
    in primary schools, 31–33, App. I
    in secondary schools, 33–36,
      App. III
  relevance of information for, 7–11
  reports of, 7
    to employers, 39
    to parents, 37
  samples of work for, 33
  of school as an entity, 113–139
  of school profile, xvii, 128–138
  self-assessment
    pupil, 42–45, 65
    student, 37
    teacher, 5, 47–90
  self-perception, pupil, 19, 42
  systems, school evaluation of,
    129–131, 133
  teacher achievement scores, 53
  techniques for, 15–26
  test results in, 147
  tests: cloze procedure, 17
    criterion-referenced, 13–18
    diagnostic, 26, 93
    mastery of skills, 13, 32
    reading, 12
    scores, 53
    standardized, 12, 13, 26, 27, 32,
      93
  triangulation, xiv, 66, 67, 150
Assessment of Performance Unit, DES,
  148
Audiences, in evaluation, 71, 82, 84, 94,
  143
Autonomy, teachers', 141, 147

Back-up and support services
  school evaluation of, 132

Baranowski, M., 106
Basic considerations system
  school evaluation of, 129, 130,
    136–138
Basic skills, pupil achievement in, 75
  record of, App. I
Bayne-Jardine, C., 124, 126
Behaviour
  pupil, categories of, 25
    identification of, 41
    patterns of, 32, 64–66
    teacher, patterns of, 58–60, 71–75
Ben-Peretz, M., 107
Bennett Report, 75–77
Bipolar categories
  of teacher actions, 60
Bloom, B. S., 125, 126
Bosworth College, 37, 45
Bowen, B., *et al.*, 78
Braybrooke, D. *and* Lindblom, C. E., 105
Breakthrough to Literacy, 107
Bullock Committee
  report on language, 12, 15, 26

Causal
  influence of teachers' actions, 48–50
  significance of teacher behaviour
    patterns, 60
Central Examinations Research and
  Development Unit, 117
Centre for Applied Research in Educa-
  tion, 56
CERDU *see* Central Examinations
  Research and Development Unit
Checklists, 20, 21, 26
  for parents, 38
  for school-sponsored evaluation, 128,
    129
Choice of schools, parental, 116, 118
Class teaching methods, whole-, 4
Classification
  child's concept of, 16
  of educational goals, 124–126
  methods of teacher behaviour
    patterns, 71–77
Classroom
  Action Research Network, 87
  activities, balance of, 44
  decision-making, xii, 1–27

Classroom (*cont.*)
   observers, xiv, 66–69, 85–87
Clegg, A., 47
Cloze-procedure tests, 17
Communication
   oral, 5
   system, school evaluation of, 129–132
Community, judgements by, 83
Community involvement system,
   school evaluation of, 129–131, 136
Comprehension, oral, 25
Comprehensive school
   evaluation of, 121, 124–126
Conant, J. B., 122, 128
Concepts, key
   evaluation of school in, 121
Conditions, extrinsic enabling, 63
   intrinsic enabling, 63
Confidential information
   accessibility to evaluation agents, 120
   on pupils, 32
Conflict
   promotion of, by changes in
      organizational form, 94
   resolving in whole-school evaluation,
      116, 119
Consensus view, inviting, 68
Constraints
   on curriculum decisions, 107–111
   as decision-making structures, 110
   external, 8, 10, 63
   financial, 108
      in school evaluation, 118
   on material resources, 108
   in organizational form, 95
   time, teacher, 14, 45, 106–108
Consultant role
   in school evaluation, xvi, 126, 127
Control
   evaluation of, 143
   of integrated studies, 96
   teacher as instrument of social, 47
Cooper, K., 22, 23, 141
Coupe, J., 23, 24
Criteria
   of accountability, 55
   for assessing methods of information
      gathering, 11
   for decision making, 105

for designing methods of recording
   by pupils, 4, 43
for evaluating organizational forms,
   94
for judgement of teachers, 146
for objectivity of teachers' accounts,
   66
for pupil assessment, 3, 4
school inspections, 1882, App. VI
for school performance evaluation,
   122–123
for teachers' self-monitoring, 60–64
for teachers' culpability, 70
Criterion-referenced tests, 13, 15–18
CSE Mode III, 97
Culpability
   assessing teacher for, 50–52, 69
   teacher self-monitoring for, 70–75
Curriculum
   decisions, xvi, 102–111
   design, 62
   development, x, xi, xv, 93, 141
   evaluation, 92, 142
   integration, xv, 95
   system, school evaluation of, 129–133

Data collection *see also* Information
   gathering
Deale, R. N., 6, 26
Dean, J., 32
Decision areas
   in school evaluation, 116–120
Decision making
   classroom, 3, 7–11
   curriculum, xvi, 102–111
   diagnostic information for, 25
Decision-making
   evaluation as a tool for, 142
   feedback for, 6, 8, 9, 10
   by groups, 116–120
   inadequate basis for, 144
   levels of, ix, 94
   off-the-cuff, 3
   political aspects of, 146
   priorities in, 144
   records for, 41
   rôle of information in, 105
   structures, formal and informal, 110
   values in, 103–104

Definition
    of evaluation, 1, 100, 115, 141
    of school as an entity, 114
Democratic accountability model, 55–56
Democratic-professional accountability
    model, 56–57, 60
Department of Education and Science,
    45, 117, 148
Design
    curriculum, 62
    record systems, of, 40
        for maintenance by pupils, 43, 45
Development of concepts in children, 2,
    15, 17
Development, planning
    schools, of, 116, 118, 126, 127
Diagnostic
    evaluation of whole school, 115
    information, 25
    tests, 26, 93
    tools, xii, 13
Dialogue, Schools Council newsletter, 106
Differences, evaluator, in values, 49
    individual, 32, 98
Discussion questions, x, 27, 91–101, 111
Displacement effect
    of innovations, 94, 100
Dixon, A., 45
Dodd, W. A., 122
Downie, R. S., *et al.*, 60

Edmonds, E. L., 169, 173
Education
    aims and values in, 61, 62
    authorities, as agents of school
        evaluation, 117
    instrumental value of, 62
    objectives in, 125–126
    political control of, 87
    values in, 103–104, 146
Educational
    aims, 61
    innovation, 92
        displacement effect of, 94
        history of, 97
    process, professional conceptions of,
        62
    values, 60–62, 103–104
Elliott, J. *and* Adelman, C., 57, 66

Elliott, J. *and* MacDonald, B. M., 107
Employers, reports to, 39
Environment, learning, 8, 10, 17
Evaluation,
    agents, of whole school, 120–126
    communication and, 148–150
    control of, 143
    definition of, 1, 100, 115, 141
    experts in, 143
    formative, 1
    human factor in, 95
    illuminative, 121, 123–124
    internal v. external, 141–143
    of people: types of responsibility
        relevant to, 48
    as a political activity, 145, 146
    relationship of research and, 142
    school, as an entity, 113–139
        internal v. external, 114
    by teacher, 124–126
    summative, 1, 9
    teachers' autonomy and, 141, 147
    of teaching, (as distinct from of
        teachers), 48
Evaluators, differing perspectives of,
    49
Examination system, public, 96
External constraints, 8, 10, 63

Feedback, 6, 8, 9, 10, 20
Feinberg, J., 48
Field notes, 77–79
Financial constraints, 108, 118
Flanders, N., 59
Ford, J., 121
Ford Teaching Project, xiv, 54, 57, 58,
    61, 62, 64, 65, 67, 69, 70, 71, 72,
    73, 76, 78, 81, 82, 84
Formative evaluation, 1
Foster, J., 32

General inspections, 115, 121
Geography for the Young School Leaver,
    106
Goals, 8, 9, 10, 11, 26
    inquiry-based, 20
    teachers' freedom to define, 146
Goldhammer, R., 58, 85, 86
Gordon, I. J., 19

Grammar, English
    pupil achievement in, 75
Grieves, A. P., 122
Guidance system
    of school evaluation, 129–131, 133
Guidelines
    for teacher self-monitoring, 58, 59

'Halo' effect, 6, 31
Hamilton, D. *and* Parlett, M., 115, 121
Harré, R. *and* Secord, P. F., 66
Harrison, C., 17
Headships
    and the nature of consultation,
        123–124
Headteachers Association of Scotland,
    24, 25
Hierarchical structure in the teaching
    profession, 97
Hierarchy study
    as a school evaluation, 127
History, Geography and Social Science,
    Evaluation, Assessment and Record
    Keeping in, Schools Council
    project, 22
Home and School Council
    Working Paper on School Reports, 37
House, E. R., 1973, 52, 54, 55
        1972, 54
Humanities Curriculum
    Project, 25, 54, 59, 61, 107, 110
Hypotheses testing, two-way, 84–85

Ideal features of information gathering,
    11, 13
Ideal features of standardized tests, 12
Illuminative evaluation, 121, 123–124
In-service study, 22
    training, xi, 76, 123–126
Independent reasoning, 61–63, 72, 73
Individual pupils
    differences between, 32
    information gathering on, 11–15
    records on, 29–46
    self-perception of, 19
    techniques and instruments for
        evaluation of, 15–26
    See also Pupil performance
Individual reports *see* Records, 29–46

Individualized approaches, 93
    to curriculum, 123
    to teaching methods, xiii, 32
Information
    as base for curriculum decisions, 104
    base for evaluation, 144, 145
    confidential, on pupils, 32
    relative availability for decision-
        making, 105, 106
    relevance to evaluation, 7–11
Information gathering, 11–15, 144
    checking for bias, 83
    confidential, 32
    cumulative, 4
    diagnostic, 25
    inadequacy of, 144, 145
    by observation during normal learning
        activities, 20
    by observers, 85–87
    values in, 100
Innovation, educational, 92
    displacement effect of, 94
    history of, 97
Inquiry-based work, goals of, 20
Insider v. outsider view *see* Outsider v.
    insider
Inspection models
    for whole school evaluation, 120–121
Inspections, school, 115, 121, 122,
        App. V & VI
Inspectorate, xvi, 122, App. V
    of accessibility reports to evaluation
        agents, 120
Institution, understanding working of an,
        116, 118, 119, 123, 124
Instruments for evaluation of individual
        pupils, 15–26
Integrated studies, 95, 96, 97
Interaction, oral, 25
    teacher-pupil, 9–10
Interaction analysis, Flanders, 59
Inter-pupil relationships
    in team teaching, 99
Inter-staff relationships, 95, 98, 99
Intervention by teacher, 23
Interviewing
    as a technique of two-way hypotheses
        testing, 84–85
Iredale, B., 80

Jackson, B. *and* Marden, D., 121
Jacobson, L., 7
Judgemental and diagnostic evaluation
    of whole school, 115
Judgements
    by general community, 83
    overall, of pupil achievement, 7
    by parents, 83
    by pupils, 83
    subjective, 145
    of teacher by teacher, 61, 82
    value, collecting, 71
    influence on curriculum, 103–104

Kay, B. W., 148
Key concepts, 121
Key factor models
    for whole school evaluation, 120, 122
Krathwohl, D. R., *et al.*, 125, 126

Labelling, and assessment, 7, 72
Lambert, R., 121
Language, Bullock Report on, 12, 15, 26
Language development, record of, App. I
LEA *see* Local Education Authority
Leading questions, 67
Learning
    content, preselected, 72, 73
    environment, 8, 10, 17
    opportunities, 5
    organization for, 91–101
    outcomes
        evaluators responsibility for, 49
        maximizing, 75
        teachers' responsibility for, 61, 73,
            75
        with feedback, 9
        without feedback, 10
    self-directed, 61, 72
    situation, teacher influence on, 72, 73
    skills, mastery of, 13
    pupil achievement in, 75
Leeds University, Institute of Education,
    38
Lindblom, C. E. *and* Braybrooke, D., 105
Literacy, Breakthrough to, 107
Local Education Authority
    use of book by advisers, x

MacDonald, B. M., 142, 145
MacDonald, B. M. *and* Elliott, J., 107
Man, a Course of Study, 18, 96
Manchester Grammar School, 121
Marcus, D., 37
Marsden, D. *and* Jackson, B., 121
Mastery of skills, 13, 32, 41
Matching, xii, 4, 18, 22
Materials, teaching, 107
Mathematical Concepts in Children,
    Development of Scientific and, 17
Mathematics,
    record of development, App. I
    pupil achievement in, 75
Mathematics and Science, Concepts in
        Secondary, 18
Mathematics Project, Nuffield, 15
McAlhone, B., 38
Methodology of self-evaluation, 57–77
Methods
    of classification, teacher behaviour
        patterns, 71–77
    of information gathering, 11
    of observation in the classroom,
        85–87
    teaching, formal and informal, 72–77
Miller, G., 25, 26
Mixed-ability grouping, xv, 4, 97–98
    teaching, 4, 93, 104
Mixed teaching styles, 75–77
Mobility, of school population, xiii, 33,
    38
Models
    of accountability, 54–57, 60
    decision-making, 9, 10
    inspection, for whole school evalua-
        tion, 120–121
Modes, learning, 93
Monitoring pupils' progress, 32

Nailsea School, 109, 120, 123–124
National Foundation for Educational
        Research, 38, 45, 117
National Survey Form 6 (NS6) reading
        tests, 12
Negotiation
    of accountability systems, 87
    of priorities, 109, 110, 144
New Ash Green Primary School, 33

NFER *see* National Foundation for
    Educational Research
Non-streaming, 93 *see also* Mixed ability
    teaching
Norms, of observation methods, 14
    of standardized tests, 12
    of teacher behaviour, 59
Norwich School Board
    inspection, 1870's, 122, App. V
Nuffield Combined Science programme, 2
Nuffield Foundation, The, 120
Nuffield Mathematics project, 15
Number, child's concept of, 16
Nuthall, G. *and* Snook, I., 59

Objectives, for assessment, 22
    educational, 125–126
Observation of pupils
    assessment, for general, 14–15
        methods of, 19–26
    classroom, 85–87
Observers, 114
    data collection by, 85–87
    as outsiders, 69
    rôle of, in triangulation, 67
    use of, 66, 68
OECD *see* Organisation for Economic
    Co-operation and Development
Open-plan organization, xv, 93, 94,
    99–100
Oppenheim, A. N., 128
Option system in curriculum, 106
Oral communication, 5
    comprehension, 25
    interaction, 25
    reports to parents, 37
    transmission, 38
Organization
    school evaluation of communications,
        132
    for learning, 91–101
    open-plan, xv, 93, 94, 99–100
Organisation for Economic Co-operation
    and Development, 124
Organizational changes, xv, 92, 93
Outcomes, learning
    evaluators' responsibility for, 49
    maximizing, 75
    teachers' responsibility for, 61, 73, 75

with feedback, 9
without feedback, 10
Outsider
    as consultant, xvi, 127
    as evaluator, 143
    as observer, 69–70
    rôle in two-way interviews, 85
    tape-slide recording by, 81
Outsider v. insider view
    evaluation by, 143
    school as an entity
        development planning in, 126
        evaluation of, 114

Parents
    choice of schools, 116, 118
    cooperation in team teaching, 99
    involvement in school evaluation,
        129–131, 136
    judgement by, 83
    reports to, 37, 46
Parlett, M. *and* Hamilton, D., 115, 121
Pastoral system, of school evaluation,
    129–131, 133
Patterns of behaviour *see* Behaviour
Personal achievement
    planning record, 46
    recording by pupil, design, 43, 45,
        App. III
    report to employers, 39
        to parents, 37, 46
Personal Quality Scales, 39
Personal values
    effect on decision making, 145
    effect on judgement of whole school,
        114, 141
    in information gathering, 100
    teachers', 104
Peters, R. S., 61
Piaget stages, 18, 44
Pioneer-palliative models
    for whole school evaluation, 120–121
Planning development of schools, 116,
    118, 126, 127
Plant, school evaluation of, 136
Polarization
    of traditionalists and progressives, 77
Policy, school, development of, 127

Political activity
    evaluation as a, 145, 146
Population, mobility of school, xiii, 38
Positive reinforcement pattern
    in teacher behaviour, 67
Postman, N., 103
Pre-selected learning, 72, 73
Primary aim categories
    of teacher behaviour patterns, 71–75
Primary school
    open plan design of, xv, 93, 94,
        99–100, App. I
    records, 31–33, App. I
Pring, R. A., 62
Priorities
    decision-making, in, 144
    negotiating, 109, 110, 144
    in using time and resources, 109
Problems
    of curriculum decisions,
        effect on whole school evaluation,
        110
    in record keeping and use, 36–40
Product-centred models
    for whole school evaluation, 120–121
Productivity model of accountability, 54–57
Professional
    accountability, 56–57, 70–75
    conceptions of the educational
        process, 62
    researcher, as evaluation agent, 117
Profiles, xii, 7, 21, 24, App. II
    in criterion-referenced tests, 16
    pupil performance, of, 3
    records, in, 20
    school, xvii, 128–138
    use of in cumulative records, 5
    wider, 3
Progress in Learning Science, 20, 44, 54,
    App. VII
Progress in pupil performance, 42–45
Progressive and traditional teaching,
    polarization of, 77
Provision, school-based, for team
    teaching, 99
Public examination system, 96
Pupil body, the school evaluation of, 137
Pupil behaviour
    categories of, 25

    identification of, 41
    patterns of, 32, 64–66
Pupil-parent involvement system
    of school evaluation, 129–131, 136
Pupil performance
    assessment of
        checking, 83
        checklists, 20, 21, 26, 38, App. II
        criteria for, 4, 5
        dangers in, 6
        designing methods for self-record-
            ing, 43
        diagnostic, xiii, 13
        general, 3–7
        instruments for, 15–26
        objectives for, 22
        by observation, 14, 15, 19–26, 65
        profile, xiii, 7, 16, 21, 24, App. II
        by samples of work, 33
        school evaluation of system,
            129–131, 133
        techniques for, 15–26
    cumulative record of, 4, 5
    factors influencing, 48
    in history, geography and social
        science, 22
    information gathering on, 11–15
        diagnostic, 25
    mastery of skills in, 13, 32, 41
    matching experience and development
        xiii, 4, 18, 22
    norms of, 12
    overall judgement on, 7
    parental involvement system
        of school evaluation, 129–131,
        136
    personal achievement in, 39
    progress in, 42–45, 75
    purposes of evaluation of, 4
    quality scales in, 39
    questionnaires of, 18
    recording, and information distortion,
        148
    records on, 4, 22, 29–46, 66, 67,
        149, 150, App. I, II, III
    reports on, 7, 37–39, 46
    self-assessment on, 37, 42–44,
        App. III
    self-perception in, 19

Pupil performance (*cont.*)
  teacher expectation and, 7
  test range in assessing, 148
  tests of: cloze-procedure, 17
    criterion-referenced, 13–18
    diagnostic, 26, 93
    mastery of skills, 13, 32
    reading, 12
    standardized, 12, 13, 26, 27, 32, 93
Pupil performance
  trends in, 4
Pupils'
  decisions, 116, 119
  differences, individual, 32
  interpretation of teachers' actions, 64
  introspective accounts, 65
  judgements, 83
  opinion survey, 18
  values, 104
Pygmalion in the Classroom, 7

Quality Scales, Personal, report on, 39
Question/answer sequences, 68
Questionnaires, pupil, 18
Questions
  critical, 67
  discussion, x, 27, 91–101, 111
  leading, 67
  for school-sponsored evaluation, 128
  selective, 67

Rance, P., 32, 44, App. IV
Rawls, J., 55, 56
Reading
  Effective Use of, 17
  pupil achievement in, 75
  for remedial pupils, 123
  tests, 12
Reasoning, independent, 61–63, 72, 73
Record-keeping
  innovative systems of, 32, 46
  of personal achievement, 43, 50,
    App. III
  political aspects of, 149
Record keeping
  in primary schools, 31–33, 38, 45,
    App. I, VII
  problems of, 36–40
  purpose of, 40–42

  in secondary schools, 33–36
  teachers' attitudes to, 30
  use of, 40–42
Record Keeping in Primary Schools, 38,
  45, App. VII
Record of Personal Achievement,
  Swindon Education Committee,
  43, 50, App. III
Record systems, 36
  assessment of, 149
  innovative, 32
  purpose and use of, xiii, 40–46
Records, 29–46
  adequacy of, 36
  anecdotal, 32
  bias of, 5, 83
  checklists in, 20, 21, 26, 38, 128,
    129, App. II
  cumulative use of, 4, 5
  distortion of information in, 148
  effectiveness of, 36
  objectivity of, 5, 83
  observation of progress in, 21
  passing on, 5, 149
  political aspects of, 149
  in team teaching, 99
Reid, J., 107
Relationships, staff
  changes in, mixed ability grouping
    influence on, 98
  team teaching and inter-, 99
Relevance of information to context, 8
Reliability
  of methods of information gathering,
    12
  of observations, 14, 26
Reports
  accessibility of, to evaluation
    agents, 120
  school, 37–39
    to employers, 39
    to parents, 37
Research and evaluation
  relationship of, 142
Researcher, professional, as evaluation
  agent, 117, 123–124
Resources
  allocation of records for, 42
  priorities in selecting, 109

Responsibility
    attributing, by evaluative information,
        116, 118
    professional, of teachers, 74–77
    teachers in teaching situation, 60
    to society, 146–148
    types of teacher, 48
Responsibility model of accountability,
    55–57
Results, causes of, and culpability for,
    48–51
Review of record systems by schools, 37,
    40, 45
Richardson, E., 1973 – 109, 120, 123, 124
    1975 – 106
Rogers, T., 106
Rosenthal, R. *and* Jacobson, L., 7
Rowe, A., 121, 122

SAFARI Interim Papers No. 2, 56
Samples, records of pupils' work, 33
School
    -based provision for team teaching,
        99
    inspection, 121–122, App. V, VI
    open plan, 99–100
    policy development, 127
    population, mobility of, xiii, 33, 38
    profile, xvii, 128–138
    services, 128
    as a social system, 121
    -sponsored evaluation, xvii, 126–129
    use of records, 38, 45
    whole, evaluation of, 113–139
Schools Council
    commissions, 119
    Evaluators Group, xi
    Newsletter, *Dialogue*, 106
    projects, xi, xii, App. VII
    Working Papers: No. 33–106
                    No. 53–103, 104
Schwab, J., 54, 66
Science, Concepts in Secondary Mathematics
    and, 18
Science, profile in learning, App. II
Science 5/13, 44, App. VII
Scientific and Mathematical Concepts in
    Children, Development of, 17
Scores, achievement, 53

Secondary school records, 33–36
Secord, P. F. *and* Harré, R., 66
Selective critical questioning pattern
    teacher behaviour, 67
Self-assessment
    student, 37, 42, 65, App. III
    teacher, 5, 47–90
Self-concept scale, 19
Self-directed learning, 61, 72
Self-monitoring
    by teacher, 5, 47–90
    methodology of, 57–77
Self-motivating technique
    interviewing as a, 84–85
Self-paced curriculum, 93
Sequences, question/answer, 68
Services
    back-up and support, evaluation of,
        132
    school, evaluation of, 128
Shayer, M., *et al.*, 18
Shipman, M., 52
Situational categories
    of teacher behaviour patterns, 72–75
Skills
    basic, pupil achievement in, 75
    mastery of, 13
    record of, App. I
Snook, I. *and* Nuthall, G., 59
Social
    control, evaluation of teacher as
        instrument of, 47, 146
    system, school as, 121
Social Science, Evaluation, Assessment
    and Record Keeping in History,
    Geography and, 22
Social Science Research Council, 18,
    App. VII
Society for Education Officers, 136, 137
Sociological-descriptive models
    for whole school evaluation, 120–121
Sockett, H., 56
Staff
    conferences, x, 127
    development systems, school evalua-
        tion of, 129–131, 135
    as evaluation agents, xvii, 117
    hierarchy, 98
    in-service training, xi, 76, 123–126

Staff (*cont.*)
 as in-service unit, 123–124
 inter-, relationships, 95
  influence on mixed ability teaching, 98
  influence on team teaching, 99
  involvement in school policy development, 127
  working party, 127
Staffing, school evaluation of, 137
Stake, R., 53
Standardized tests, 12, 13, 26, 27, 32, 93
Standards, school, maintaining, 116, 118
Stenhouse, L., 1969: 61;
  1975: 80
Structure
 hierarchical, in teaching profession, 97
 need for, in observation, 15, 20
 of observation, 23
Structured observations, 26
 teaching, 60, 72, 73
Studies, integrated, 95, 96, 97
Styles of teaching, 75–77
Subnormal Children, Education of
  Severely Educationally, 23
Subordinate pattern
 of teacher behaviour, 60
Summative evaluation, 1, 9
Super-ordinate pattern
 of teacher behaviour, 60
Survey of record keeping, DES, 45
Swindon Education Committee, 43, 50,
  App. III
Systems
 accountability, 51–52, 71–75, 147
  record, purpose and use of, 40–46
  record-keeping, innovative, 32, 46
  school evaluation, of:
   assessment, 129–131, 134–135,
    136
  basic considerations, 129, 130,
   136–138
  communication, 129–132
  curriculum, 129–133
  guidance, 129–131, 133
  pupil–parent involvement, 129–131,
   136
  staff development, 129–131, 135

Tape recordings, 79–81

Tape-slide recordings, 81–84
Tawney, D., 108
Teacher
 achievement scores, 53
 actions, causal influence of, 48–50
  justification for, 51
  pupils' interpretation of, 64
 aims of, 62–63, 72
 autonomy, preservation of, 141, 147
 behaviour patterns, 58–60, 67, 68
 checklists, 20, 21, 26, 38, 128, 129,
  App. II
 classroom performance, checks on,
  85–87
 constraints on:
  financial, 109
  material resources, 108
  time, 14, 45, 106–108
 curriculum decisions, 102–111
 diagnostic tools for, 13
 evaluation of whole school, 113–139
 expectation of pupil performance, 7
 'halo' effect on assessment by, 6, 31
 hypotheses testing, two-way, 84
 information gathering by, 11–15, 144
  checking for bias, 83
  confidential, xiii, 32
  diagnostic, 25
  during normal activities, 20
  inadequacy of, 144, 145
  relationship between observer and
   observed, 150
  triangulation in, 66, 67, 150
  values in, 100
 inter-staff relationships, 99
  influence of mixed-ability teaching
   on, 98
  team teaching and, 99
 intervention by, 23
 judgements of, by, 82
 in multiple rôles, 123–124, 150
 observation methods, 14–15
  of pupils, 19–26
 as observers, 70
 opinions on records, xii, 30
 -pupil interaction, 9, 10, 53, 54, 147
 record-keeping by
  political aspects of, xiii, 149
 records by, 29–46
  bias in, xiii, 149

Teacher, records by (*cont.*)
    distortion of information in, 148
    integrated day, App. IV
    objectivity of, 5, 66, 149
    passing on, 5, 149
    progress, 21
    use of, xiii, 40–46, 148, 149
reports by, 37–39
responsibility
    for evaluation, 140
    in teaching situation, 60
    to society, 146–148
    school evaluation by, 124–126
    self-monitoring by, ix, xiv, 5, 47–90, 145
    training courses, evaluating, 38
    values, personal, 104
Teaching
    audiences of, 82
    consequences of self-monitoring, 64–70
    decision-making structures in, 110
    individualized methods, xiii, 32
    materials, 107
    methods, formal and informal, 72–77
    mixed ability, 4, 93, 97–98, 104
    patterns of behaviour in, 58–60
    profession, hierarchical structure in, 97
    styles, 75–77
    team, xv, 98–99
    traditional and progressive, polarization of, 77
    typology of, 72–77
    variables, 77
Team teaching, xv, 98–99
Techniques
    for evaluation of individual pupils, 15–26
    self-monitoring, 77–90
    self-motivating, interviewing as a, 84–85
Tests
    achievement scores in, 53
    cloze-procedure, 17
    criterion-referenced, 13–18
    diagnostic, 26, 93
    of mastery of skills, 13
    reading, 12
    standardized, 12, 13, 26, 27, 32, 93
Time constraints on teacher, xvi, 14, 45, 106–108

Timetable, philosophy of, 106
Topic changes by teacher, 58, 60, 67, 68
Traditional and progressive teaching, polarization of, 77
Transcribing tape recordings, 81
Trends in pupil performance, 4
Triangulation, xiv, 66, 67, 150
Two-way hypotheses testing, 84, 85
Tyler, R., 141
Typology of teaching, 72–77

Unstructured teaching, 72, 73
Utilitarian accountability model, 55–56

Validity
    of methods of information gathering, 112
    of observation, 26
Value judgements
    collecting, 71
    influence on curriculum decisions, 103–104
    of teachers by teachers, 82
Values
    in decision-making, xvi, 103–104
    in education, 60–62
    and evaluation, 145–146
    evaluator, perspectives of, 49
    of existing and proposed activities, 108
    personal, effect on decision making, 145
        effect on judgement of whole school, 114
    in information gathering, 100
Video-tape recording, 82

Wakeford, J., 121
Walker, R. *and* Adelman, C., 81, 82, 85, 86
Watts-Vernon reading tests, 12
Where, 38, 117
Which?, 124
Whole-class teaching methods, 4
Whole school, evaluation of, 113–139
Wood, D., 71
Work record on samples of pupils, 33
Working of an institution, understanding, 116, 118, 119